Rough Diamond

The story of my adoption, adventures in the African bush, and spirit guiding me home

THEA KHAMA

Rough Diamond By Thea Khama
Published 2020 by Your Book Angel
Copyright © Thea Khama

This book deals with child abuse, drug abuse and gender-based violence. While the author has taken great lengths to ensure the subject matter is dealt with in a compassionate and respectful manner, it may be troubling for some readers. Reader discretion is advised.

Printed in the United States
About the Author photographer, Shari Kessler
Edited by Keidi Keating and Walter Wasosa
Layout by Rochelle Mensidor

ISBN: 978-1-7356648-0-4

~ Foreword ~

To be asked to write this foreword is a tremendous honor. Dredging my heart for the right words isn't as hard as trying to sift through a lifetime of experiences that I've shared with the author - of love and worry; jumbled feelings of hate, fury, aggravation, and fear – not directed at the author, but shared with the author as she traversed life; magical moments, hysterical moments, memorable moments, and come up with something that is coherent enough for you to appreciate. I've decided to just tell you how I feel and hope that I can give you a glimpse of what I know about Thea Khama. I truly love who she is and I'm hoping you will soon understand why.

I first met Thea many years ago when she was a 20-year old rough diamond. I was old enough to be her mother. A mutual friend thought it would be a good idea for us to meet because she had been adopted as a baby and she was now interested in finding her birth family. I, too, was adopted and had already learned the identities of both my birthmother and birthfather. I'd tracked down and met my birthmother but, I hadn't been as lucky with meeting my birthfather yet, even though I knew who he was.

I had connections to the adoption community I could share with Thea, as well as a deep understanding of the complex feelings one has as an adoptee. Our initial meeting was very exciting for me. Thea's energy and vibrant person impressed me and I knew without a doubt I wanted to help her find her birth family and I wanted to get to know her. I shared all the resources I had about how to conduct a search and put her in touch with the private investigator I'd used to find my birthmother. This is when I realized that it was the beginning of a lifelong friendship.

She spoke with me about the struggles she'd endured in her young life and revealed the brave survivor she had become. We soon discovered that we shared something that transcended age, circumstances, race, and relationship. Our bond was so familiar that there were no words to describe our soulful connection. Anna Grace Taylor writes "I believe certain people come into your life as Angels and that some connections cannot be explained in words alone. You just feel it. You feel it deep down in your soul."

Thea left the United States but stayed in touch. Some time had passed when I got a call from her saying she was returning to the States. Before I knew it, we were shouting with joy because she was coming to live with me and my teenage son! During her stay, we became even closer. Over the years, things haven't changed at all between us except we've grown to a place where there is just a quiet knowing, a peaceful acceptance of something that lies well beyond our grasp. We know on the deepest level that we were brought together as each other's spiritual guide, confidant, and soul support.

Thea has so much to share with others about life. She struggled and fought hard to carve out a niche in a country where she didn't originally belong; she struggled and fought hard to support her family. She struggled and fought hard, digging deep into her own wounds, to create a piece of written work that can be inspirational and uplifting as well as real and relatable to all who read this book.

There came a time when Thea knew she had arrived at a place in her life where she was ready to share her journey with others. She'd had some years to reflect on the events in her life, she had matured in her perspective, and she felt a book was the best way to share her story.

Through these experiences and despite these experiences, she has become an amazing human being who has dedicated her life to guiding and helping youth, supporting the arts, saving wildlife, advocating health and wellness, coaching others and standing up for the underdog. She selflessly goes about life with an inexpressible mission of standing behind the things that she is passionate about. I venture to guess she might be healing some parts of herself through this effort.

Thea's story offers the reader the essence of magic and wonder and fairytale dust which she has woven into this book, despite her having gone through decades of difficulties and hardship that began when she was so young. With an unshakable positive attitude, she proves that one can overcome obstacles with determination and self-driven faith in the outcome, despite the odds. It is that strength, that fortitude, that determination, which drives this woman. Given the same life circumstances, anyone else might have surrendered in defeat to what could have become a very different outcome. But not Thea. Harriet Beecher Stowe said "Never give up, for that is just the place and time that the tide will turn." Thea demonstrates Stowe's wisdom when so many times she was in that dark place we are all familiar with, feeling things would never get better, but she intuitively knew that in the end it would all be okay. She followed her heart and it never failed her.

At her core is a deep well of passion for family and everything she believes in. From the early days of our friendship, and while she was still quite young, Thea would not hesitate to stand up for the things in her life she thought was right. She dug in, holding her ground with eyes ablaze and would not back down even in the face of the most difficult of situations.

Thea had to tell her story – her experiences are rich with life lessons for all of us. I feel there is so much to learn from her. Get ready to tap into your deep wounds and dark places and be reminded of times in your life that were joyful and loving.

The title of this book, Rough Diamond, is the most fitting way to set the stage for Thea's life. The actual origin of the word "diamond" comes from the Greek word, adamas, which means "unbreakable", describing the hardest substance known to man. Diamonds are formed over time and under extreme temperatures and pressure. When Thea was faced with life's hardships and obstacles, she chose to persevere, remain strong, withstand the pressure, harden her character and brace herself throughout these experiences over time - while developing an unbreakable spirit that stood up to the world as it cast its painful arrows upon her. She was unwilling to yield, remaining strong and resilient, chipping off piece by piece one edge at a time from a rough, unpolished, and vulnerable person into an exquisite, multi-faceted one. Our days on this earth will be full of occasions to shine and be brilliant in the face of upheaval and turmoil as long as we believe we can influence the outcome of our circumstances.

Though challenges are always lurking unexpectedly and never quite planned, life is what you make it.

Njambi G Mungai

~ Dedication ~

For my friends and family – You ignite my essence

For T.K., Kaedi, and Tahlia – We are one

For my mother – Your song lives in me

For my father – "I realize that the dawn when we'll meet again will never break, so I give it up little by little, this love. But something in me laughs as I say this, someone shaking his head and chuckling softly, hardly, hardly…" - *Paulo Coelho*

For you – Through my story, know thyself.

~ Acknowledgements ~

This book has taken the better part of seven years to dream about, write, refine and mold into something intimate and meaningful to share. Many great beings have contributed to this project whom I am now at liberty to thank. Of course, there are many more who have encouraged me to forge ahead who I haven't mentioned here, and if you are one of them, let's sit down and toast to your insight and inner knowing!

To the Infinite Creator, my Spirit Guardians and Inner Child: I bow in humble appreciation for the opportunity to share my story with the world upon your stage. Thank you for showing me the linkages between my spirit roots and my biological DNA.

Keidi Keating, my editor and first publisher for your calm, clear-headed approach and inexhaustible patience that has helped me effect the final push of creation…Thank you for finding me and guiding me through my first composition.

Walter Wasosa, my writing colleague, secondary editor and friend, for your critical eye and professional advice when I doubted myself most.

Lisa Tener and Lynda Monk, thank you for being my first book coaches. Lisa, you hold the space for my writing muse and Lynda, my friend, you inspire my creative storyteller.

Peter Monk, thank you for keeping me safe when I found myself plagued by boogie monsters in the Salt Spring cabin in Canada in the wee hours of a writer's "dark night of the soul."

Mustaq Rajan, my soul brother and writing partner, from the moment we met on the Turkish coastline you have been my go-to galaxy, and oh, how well you know me!

Helene Christensen, my long-distance writing partner, you are such a special being. Your words and outlook inspire and mirror my own. I hope to see your book beside mine one of these fine days.

Linda Dobson, my intrepid writing partner, master coach, and mentor! Thank you for your critical eye, unconditional understanding, and heart-warming feedback.

Matheo Galatis, personal coach, true friend, and trainer, you remain a catalyst for deep transformation by being touched and transformed yourself. Thank you for the role you have played in my growth.

Tshekedi Stanford Khama, husband and lifelong partner, my flawless rock, my gateway, my challenger, my lover, and my friend. To be your wife at this momentous time is my singular privilege.

Kaedi Sekgoma Khama, my darling son, you are the one who lights the way. Keep lighting my way, please! Thank you for your constant insistence on me writing this book – it has made me accountable to myself.

Tahlia Naledi Khama, my beloved daughter, you are my twinkling star in the darkest of nights. A drop of heaven to remind me I am home. I wish for your love and happiness every morning as I awake!

Njambi Mungai, my everything. You know how special you are!

Michelle Goushe, Manager at &Beyond… thank you for the bed nights you offered up to me to be with my book and myself in the pristine wilderness of my beloved Botswana.

To Joss Kent and the Sandibe Okavango Safari Lodge Staff in Botswana with special mention to Riaan and O.B. for making sure I was nurtured and had all my needs met on my stay to write, write, write! I am forever grateful.

Karen Lees, Netta Adam, Daryl Hypolite, thanks for being the ones to look after my "other" work and for organizing my life, business, travel, and everything else during the prolonged stages of this labor of love.

Kris Seeman, a matriarch, parental figure, and friend. Thank you for reminiscing with me, sheltering me, and keeping me true.

My sincere thanks to all my own lifelong mentors and daring detractors too – ah yes – you played your chords perfectly.

To all my supporters, mentors, and benefactors: those who believed in me without wavering; you who homed me, encouraged me, and who brought me to the page, in person, or in spirit, time and time again.

Thank you to Janet and George Belding, Thandi Bowe, Raven and Bonnie Raetze, Adam King, Tessa Moronne and Brian Cooke, Candy Androliakos, Michele Trahan, Dr. David and Laurie Brandt, John and Bette Buttny and family, Dr. Robert Harvey, Bill and Nancy Grove, Eland Grove, Patti Sullivan, Carol Martin, Geoff Martin, Dave and Becca Lawler, Ian Britton, Emily Ladner, Rob Matthews, Matt McUne, Sharon Ann McNeil, Donald Maponyane, Joe, Ada, and Pascha Hanson, Johnson and Ishmael Otlaadisa, The Singh Family, Marianne and Joseph Puvimanasinghe, and Dalubuhle A. Malunga. I would also wish to thank the Energym crews, Inner Core crews, Teen Spirit crews, The Pelotshweu Trust, Pula Productions team and all my sponsors and supporters who over the years have encouraged me to write the stories of my life and soar freely.

Introduction

Ever since I can remember, I have held a series of notes in my hand, though I have not always known what to do with them, how to play them, or how to listen to them, but as the writing flowed, these notes came alive. Mysterious musicians plucked them from my hands and played them on invisible strands. As the music described itself, I realized that not only could I hear, but I also could amplify, soften or harmonize with the stroke of my pen.

Working as a love-activator, touch-healer, and life-coach has taught me how we all experience our song, words, art, and indeed life, differently, based on our filters of perception, yet there are common archetypal notes we collectively recognize, such as love, light, darkness, pain, and guidance. These notes of life sustain a similar quality of experience the world over and touch each of us within our core.

Yet within my writing, I noticed a glimmer of something else that yearned to bring beauty to the page: a touch of light where the stage was sometimes too dark. I noticed that many of us have experienced the struggle to exist lovingly and vibrantly upon this Earth 24/7, to be at peace with what I term both the feminine "breath of heaven," and the "creative masculine" –a steady stream, strong and ancient as a monolith of stone. To be purposefully in resonance, with all sentience for all time, is not an easy feat, especially in this dualistic world and linear landscape we endure. My aim while writing this chronological account of my younger years was to remain fresh and kind in the telling, firm and giving, creative and conscious, with myself and with you and to encourage readers to reflect upon their own lives with a fresh lens.

Sometimes, as I wrote, it was painful to re-enter the space of an old emotion, and relive it to bring poignant moments to the page. "How can I shower beauty on moments of despair, sickness, rage, and how shall I do this without changing my truth?" It was a question I asked myself over and over, yet the answer continuously eluded me.

Finally, I let go of any notion of "my truth" and then majestically the stage lit itself.

The most satisfying and miraculous part of the process came as I sat with my story alone in a secluded cabin in the Southern Gulf Islands of Canada. Here, the adult in me gifted the child in me with the language to speak of her pain, her love, her point of view, and experience. My inner child, unfettered by pleasantries, and raw with uncensored emotions, expressed the wish to remain untainted–her wisdom and insight heard. It was not for the adult to put words in her mouth, though I desperately wanted to tend, heal, and celebrate her, yet instead it would be my honor to teach her a language to share her experiences that you might be able to grasp. My encounters with my inner child brought tears and smiles to the tightened muscles of my face and sometimes I had to walk into the woods to breathe again.

People frequently ask me if I believe in destiny or fate. As far as I am aware, much as we are the creators of our own reality and play consciously or unconsciously with how we manifest our living, there is always something that we are called to be and to do while we are here. I refuse to accept the notion that we simply arrive in a place and time for no reason. For example, my energy propels me where I am going, and I include thoughts, emotions, and imaginings in the category of the energy I speak of. In my life I have noticed how I have been shaped for certain happenings and to play certain roles at specific times. Benjamin Franklin once stated that, "There are three things extremely hard: steel, diamond and to know oneself."

Each happening is directly affected by a previous happening. The powerful law of cause and effect operates effortlessly in all places at all times. I am where I need to be, doing what I need to do and being whom I need to be at the time and place I am supposed to be. I sense it is all happening perfectly to bring me to my next moment of awakening on the stage.

The Stage

Earth 1970—Looking down, we see the world from above, peacefully shrouded in an atmosphere of blue. She hangs imperviously meditative, like a crystal ball in our star-studded galaxy. Yet, as we zoom closer and pierce the shell of illusion, life erupts, teeming with all manner of organisms in different stages of becoming. Our Earth is a web of interconnection and inter-relation. In human terms, in this particular year, Earth counts an approximate mass of 3.63 billion human incarnations. She shivers and quakes to shrug 1 million off her shoulders through small and large scale "disasters."

One such incarnation, a spirit made of starlight and other substances unknown to mankind, takes a sudden plunge and finds herself in a raging hot womb. The sensations of turmoil are almost more than one organism can bear. Still, she clings to life with all her might. There is a great purpose for which she has come, and this purpose recruits an army of enlightened guardians to her side. The starlit spirit knows many who are waiting for her arrival on Earth with sinister intent. She lands in their playground and the game is on.

As an organism, she can only survive on pure instinct, having given up a momentous memory in order to walk sincerely with those she is pledged to touch, build the bridges she has promised, and gather a deeper awareness of what will be required of her without assumption, judgment or expectation for that which she must become.

Months pass, and she concentrates only on growth and dreams. Regrettably, every watery breath her new cells draw, pulses thickly in a soup of chemicals and toxic emotions. Her host is a drug addict who has had more than her share of unhappy emotions. These emotions are transmitted vicariously in tides of impurity and sorrow as the spirit's embryonic life form endeavors to grow a body that will stand up to the future trials she knows she must endure.

Her life is rescued from the chaos of her host's womb, on more than one occasion, by great beings that guard her and gently soothe her tiny body with songs of love, showering her infant mind and DNA with images of pretty places where a prayerful existence hangs in the balance. These guardians instruct her in love's universal language: how to heal. They avail themselves 24/7 and stand guard over her contaminated host mother to diminish the chance of further peril to their tiny charge.

"Never underestimate your importance and connection to everything," they croon softly, "Stay connected to the Eternal Light... remain open to your emotion at all costs, dear soul."

Soul Song: Reverberant, Unreasonable Hum

0-1 years–Becoming Human

"How did the rose ever open up its heart and give the world all of its beauty? It felt the encouragement of light against its being..."

— HAFIZ

LIFELINE

Marla, to whose womb my cells cling so tenaciously, is in crisis. Unhindered, she imbibes many powerful substances to deaden the pain she is in mentally, emotionally, and physically. Marla is not prepared for another child. She can barely care for the two she has already conceived with her former husband, and she currently resides unmarried with Jose, who is his own kind of "bad" and worse off than she. Jose is my birth father and he has a sordid history. He has made his way in a new country unlawfully, stealing across the border between Mexico and California, and he is in no position to form the basis of a healthy family leader.

Marla has met Jose through the small-time drug trade she and her sister run underground. Ricardo, Marla's former husband, and father to my half sister and brother (ages two and five), beat Marlene with his fist one too many times, until she rid herself of him, only to fall prey to her current dysfunctional relationship with Jose. Intensely passionate about Marla and her children, a violent jealousy lurks deep inside Jose's anguished ego. He mistrusts Marla terribly. At a young age, and through hard knocks growing up in a home ravaged by poverty, he learned not to trust anyone or anything. Sadly, Jose now uses drugs and alcohol to distract his mind from his frequent bouts of insecurity and instability, yet rather than serving to repel his inner sense of doubt, the drugs amplify his paranoia.

One fateful night, high on drugs and alcohol, Jose trains his shotgun on Marla's head. As she registers the click of the chamber, her inquisitive green eyes open wide. Frightened and angered by such an injustice, she whirls to face him head on, thick brown locks clinging to the sheen of beaded perspiration covering her face. "Jose, what the hell? Please, don't! Don't you do it…"

Time stands still as my powerful angelic guardians move in unison to shield us. I intuit their urgency and feel their anxiety brush my consciousness, which at this moment feels contracted and tight as a pea. As a growing babe, I am only vaguely aware of the warnings coming from far beyond the burning world of amniotic fluids roiling around inside my mother's womb. I may have a life or destiny ahead that must overcome these trials, yet in this moment all I can be is a little fetus in human form with full attention on its evolution.

Jose pulls the trigger.

I register the womb's contraction as Marla and I are hurled sideways, and in the next instant I bounce off spongy surfaces that feel like concrete to my soft newness. I sense a blazing heat rushing through the womb followed by an intense vacuous sensation, like a rocket breaking free of its atmosphere, and then, I am floating in limbo once more. Marla's soul ricochets out of her body and back again as if a huge unseen hand has smacked her irreverent spirit into place. Vibrations rock through her bowels behind the folded space to where my protective light and I have retreated.

From here I perceive alarm bells reverberating inside her cells like the crashing of cymbals in a pit. The light and my regal guardians move as one to embrace me, if only to cover my naked flesh. Then, in a flash, the tidal waves of energy subside. If I had yet a mind of my own, it would be shaking in disbelief and disapproval.

The man who denies he is my father has just blast us backward using the firepower of his shotgun to knock us to the ground. His screams of dismissal pierce the air. Jose's bullet lodges in Marla's arm, and fortunately not her head or belly. The light flows around us, tenderly cocooning me, as it shields my physical form away from the monstrous negation of Jose's wholesome rejection.

Without this protection, the intensity of hormones and shock waves transmitted through Marla's body may have the potential to kill me. Nonetheless, I still feed energetically on my mother's despair. The cross-over of her thought-waves enters the uterus at an unimaginable velocity and blasts tiny holes through the protective shield my unseen protectors have created, conveying certain emotions that vibrate and echo deep in the womb: "Rejected, stupid, good for nothing, undeserving whore, poor, manipulative dumb bitch!" And of course, the hidden meaning beneath all – victim. These are the words Marla imbibes, as she lies alone on the floor shaking, and these are the impressions I receive as an imprint to my newfound awakening consciousness.

The seeds are sown. The lines are drawn from which my life will begin and this story shall be told. I am a little receptor in vitro.

THE POWER OF DENIAL

Some weeks later, as her arm heals, Jose enters our reality once more, only to become combative with Marla over the same topic. She continues to insist I am his progeny, but he stubbornly refuses to believe her. In fact, he has in mind to kill us both. For him, this will be the most convenient way out. A coward's way. His life is tilting on an uneven axis and this reality is far more than he can bear. He offers Marla what she cannot refuse: drugs washed down with alcohol to forget his pain from a seemingly hopeless existence. Narcotics, however, serve only to amplify Jose's personal paranoia and escalate my birth parents' mutual feelings of helplessness. Jose thinks he can get Marla to admit to him that I belong to another man, but she holds to her truth: that I am his seed.

In a maniacal rush of rage at Marla's stubborn insistence that I belong to them both, Jose takes his murderous fist to her body, kicking and grappling with her on another evening well into the pregnancy. Managing to pummel her to the floor, though her fight is strong, he ruptures her spleen, her dignity, and what little happiness she treasures in her miserable life with one near-fatal blow. Marla sprawls on the floor once again as her spirit flees, howling into the dispassionate night. An angelic presence sweeps around us, scanning and cradling my fetus in the tightening womb that faintly pulses with unborn life. The light whispers a song to every cell of my tiny form, commanding each one to live beyond the shock that threatens to close them down. Marla's own unseen spirit-warriors depart the scene in search of her shriveled and fleeing soul as others bow and glance furtively toward my own army of guardians who stand quite still bearing witness as hers take their leave. Marla recovers enough to be taken to hospital where doctors put her to sleep and perform surgery to help save her life and mine.

A month premature, with an Apgar reading of one out of ten, I am born into this world as Julie Marie Gomez, taking my mother's maiden name and not the surname Florez that still belongs to my true birthfather, on a rainy November day in 1970. I have but a few days in Marla's arms, while I bear these names, before she releases me to the world at the insistent coaxing of her own mother of European descent. The two women make a pact that Marla's father Pedro must never find out about me. He is away on business as a sales manager for a large flooring contract company that does work in Central and South America where his native biology serves him well. He is fluent in Spanish, having grown up as a young boy in Mexico, so he communicates easily in these other countries. My Western European grandmother knows how to keep a secret, and she vows to take the secret of my existence to her grave. Throughout the war, she'd imagined she would be with another, who she'd promised to love to her dying day, but my grandfather returned unscathed and refused to let her go: marriage, family, and public image being his highest values. This secret and all the others are her last revenge of a life living as a prisoner of the times and she resolves to drink herself to an early grave.

For two months, while the adoption process takes its time and unknown hands type out the paperwork that will seal my fate, I live in foster care in a blur of sound, sensation, and sleep. It is a time of transition and I have no name. I am simply known as the "baby." I exist to breathe, eat, and feel. The memories of the last eight months rhythmically flush away with the continued cycling of drugs out of my system. Fighting for survival is savage and unpleasant. My foster parents have never seen a baby in such strife.

"So dear person, this is the dawn that never breaks, just as unconditional love never will, and this voice you hear is the music of your soul that contains the power to sing an eternity of beauty, love, and hearts to life. You are a spirit whisperer and a diamond in the making." These are the final words the light murmurs as she disappears discreetly behind the invisible curtain separating this world from the next.

LIFE BEGINS AGAIN

Caucasian-American parents Bard and Lana Witzler adopt me when I am two months old. Both anthropologists have studied Ancient Greek history, culture, art, and language together at the University of Boulder in Colorado and they call me "Thea," which has many meanings and versions in the Greek language depending on its pronunciation. Some translated meanings are: "The Goddess," "panoramic view" or "beautiful perspective," and "Theia" spelled with an 'i' in the center is the name adopted by one of their original mythic Titans; birthmother to the Greek pantheon of gods and goddesses, considered a wise and prophetic bringer of light, whose parentage is none other than Mother Earth (Gaia) and The Eternal Father Sky (Ouranos). The name bears a tremendous amount of responsibility, passion, and purpose, as well as much beauty. It also contains the Mirror of Life deep within its core.

Brought home on a stormy winter's night in January 1971, I hear the wind whip and moan mournfully outside, and I feel the sway and tilt of the car as we climb upward on winding roads high above the sleepy university town of Berkeley, California. Later, snuggled inside the heated shelter of my new abode, I listen to the creaking groans of tree boughs, as they scrape back and forth across the shingled roof upstairs and hear the soft thump of wet pine cones plonking against the spongy needled soil outside. Somehow, I can also smell blue lightning, even though the windows are airtight. Bottles are warmed and ready for my arrival as my new parents busy themselves, settling me into the tidy brick and wood home, tucked away like a magical cottage, in the foggy moss of these ivy-strewn hills. Fluffy toys, pets, and a fancy red crib are all ready to receive me with open arms and paws.

My first attempt at bottle-feeding is something of a fiasco and results in me turning purple as I suck on a nipple cap with all my might! The neighbors next door, an elderly retired doctor and his wife, brave the rain and lightning to show my rookie parents how to remove the nipple cap on the bottle so I can receive nourishment at last, and stop turning darker and darker shades of purple! My wide eyes wink and blink at these caring neighbors who will be like grandparents to me from this moment on.

As a "drug baby," the deadly chemical cocktails take their time to wind their way out of my blood. My new parents are blissfully unaware of the history of my ragged beginnings; public officials at the county office have artfully hidden the secret. My nervous system is integrating physical sensations: reminders of the burning uterus, the gunshot trauma, and the vacuous sensations I felt in the womb. I scream irrepressibly, when brought toward the special plastic baby bath my adoptive parents have proudly purchased at a downtown baby store. My new mother Lana is forced to join me inside the bath herself; to soothe fears that overwhelm my tiny body.

Long and lean, with milky-white freckled skin, silky smooth auburn hair, and a narrow pointy Pennsylvania Dutch nose, my new mom doesn't resemble me at all. I am round and olive skinned, dark eyed and button-nosed with a shock of dark brown hair, and flattened stubby fingers and toes. Lana is a self-proclaimed atheist– a scientist with a heart of gold who believes strongly in nurture over nature, and she swears silently to herself that our disparate looks shall not matter in the years to come. Unaware of any nature versus nurture ideologies happening in my mother's head, I snuggle deep down in the soft baby blankets of the big red crib in the upstairs bedroom next door to my curious new parents. There is quiet and safety in this space that is so different from the stark existence whence I came. Here, as daylight streams into a cozy nook of my bedroom, with its stylish black rocking chair, my adoptive parents lovingly begin to prepare me to live within their world; this new context that has little yet everything to do with who I am and what I will become.

Soon, I become faintly aware of two special pets that are ready to bond, make me laugh, and shelter me in my new surroundings. The two animals work collaboratively to heal me from the trauma of separation from my biological beginnings. Gina, the fluffy long haired orange cat crawls comfortingly into my crib and purrs me to sleep day and night, while Tata a big grey and white Alaskan malamute is ferociously protective, nuzzling me with her big moist nose and rushing to stand guard over my body when strangers show up in our home. In this embrace of love, I experience peace and stability for a short time at home in the foggy California hills.

Soul Song: Sonorous, Epic, and Wild

16 mos-3 years—Into Africa

"We have not inherited the earth from our ancestors; rather we have borrowed it from our children."

— KENYAN PROVERB

NEW DIGS

It is 1971, and my new father, Bard, is busy packing, getting us ready to move halfway around the globe to Ethiopia where he has been invited to assist in archaeological digs as a student of paleontology and a researcher in the paleo ecology field at the University of California at Berkeley. It isn't the first time my parents have lived on the African continent. Previously, both had jobs as Peace Corps volunteers in Nigeria just out of college, and married in the Woodstock era.

Upon our arrival in East Africa, my mother and I nestle into our semi-permanent dwelling – a room in the quaint Ainsworth Hotel at the foot of the Ngong Hills on the borders of Nairobi – the capital of Kenya. The place is peaceful, and the employees are helpful Swahili speakers from surrounding villages. Many other foreigners, research families of roving scientists in the area, take out long-stay rental agreements inside the hotel's bungalows or rows of hotel rooms with outdoor verandahs. Bountiful bougainvillea bushes climb overhead in a smattering of orange, fuchsia, and magenta blush almost as high as the contiguous thorn trees that dot the fence line, while verdant fever trees, red flowering flame trees, and indigenous shrubs cast suede shadows upon sumptuous lawns.

There is a daycare nursery school within walking distance, and our little room becomes my mother's office and home base while looking after me and working for the San Francisco-based Friends of the Earth organization in a bid to extend her experience in environmental protection and human resources while she dreams of future careers in these fields. Together, my parents share the duties of rearing me. It is not an easy arrangement for them to be miles apart, in foreign lands, keeping divergent interests stimulated and questioning their marriage vows; that when tested, seem mostly impotent. However, they manage to keep my best interests at heart while striving to be happy.

Bard comes and goes as he travels regularly to Addis Ababa and the Ethiopian archeological dig sites northeast of the capital, working closely with the American anthropologist Donald Johanson* (Discovered Lucy Australopithecus afarensis linked to the possible bi-pedal ancient human evolution 3.5 million years ago) and traveling to the remote rugged terrain of the Olduvai Gorge in Tanzania where he and another team of experts are overseen by the famed white Kenyan-born Louis Leakey a fellow paleo anthropologist and his London-born wife Mary, who have also set up various scientific research camps looking for traces of humanity's evolution. Bard spends his days carefully scraping the earth around the bones of ancient rodents, and other long-extinct creatures and artifacts, looking for clues to life from another time.

THE HYENA'S FOOTPRINTS

One starry desert night in the beginning of my second year of life, Lana and I visit Bard's camp with its throng of anthropologists, paleontologists, and archaeologists. I drift to sleep in my new mother's arms as she places me down carefully in Bard's sturdy canvas tent situated a few hundred meters from the campfire. Here I nestle comfortably, away from the raucous scientists and their enthusiastic chatter. Lana and Bard return to the fire to enjoy a nightcap with the group when the panting coughs of a pride of territorial lion begin to reverberate off every angle of the gorge. As the roaring lions close in, Bard and Lana arise and walk determinedly toward the tent, torches lowered, scanning the dry grasslands for snakes, and more importantly, the gleaming eyes of other pertinent nocturnal predators, wishing to bring me closer to the firelight.

Upon arrival, the pair is aghast to discover that there are claw marks scored in the sand outside the tent, where it appears some large animal has scratched and scraped the earth just beyond the entrance. With hearts hammering they dash through the flaps and shine their torches toward my palette, fearing the worst. There I am, sleeping peacefully, whilst the soap on the makeshift stand outside the door lies shredded in strips on the dusty ground.

I am unharmed; though lions are on everyone's mind. They pick me up and cuddle me cheek-to-cheek, while their adept African colleagues identify the animal tracks as those of a pack of hyena. Hyenas are the great scavengers of the bush, and they are craftily proficient at tracking lion and stealing scraps from their kills. They are also incredible opportunists with a keen sense of smell, so it seems remarkable that I was left alone.

It is interesting that these great dogs with jaws of steel, notoriously repugnant survivalists, happened to inspect the area around me. After all, I am born under the sign of the Dog in Chinese astrology and I am learning loyalty to my new pack every day! Indigenous peoples believe in tales and portents of nature and use them as reflective compasses or markers for their lives on earth and such storytelling has worked exceptionally well for my ancestors, so why not for me? This is not my last exposure to hyena, as time will tell. The wild will continuously leave its paw prints on my life from this day on.

ELEPHANT EARS

Recollections reaching as far back as twenty years are known in African circles as one possessing an elephant's memory. These amazing giants of our time have been known to store imagery, wisdom, and emotional attachments in their large prefrontal cortex for many years. Three months after birth, an early happening is stored in my own accessible memory banks...

I curl deep into Lana's arms as she dances, swirling me gaily around the living room. She reaches overhead and takes the huge black earphones off her head and fits them over mine and my eyes open wide with shock! Booming waves of sound seamlessly snake their way past my eardrums and reverberate sonically off my bones. Magnetized by the thrumming wall of sound, unable to tell her of the sweet agony rushing to greet my senses, I am at a loss: language-less.

This memory is impressed and real and I will make sense of it when I am older, however right now I don't understand. Today, the presence of an African elephant will loom in my awareness as it makes its own indelible mark on my memory.

The hired game ranger chats with us amiably in the front seat as he drives over a graded dirt track and points out a grassy plain dotted with small clusters of giraffe, antelope, zebra, and warthog foraging off in the distance to our right. I am with my maternal grandparents who are enraptured by the sound of the game guide talking and the sight of the wide golden savannah and graceful wildlife on display.

Perched comfortably on my grandfather's lap, bored of seeing what everyone else sees, I stare up at the dun-colored cliff looming above us to the left. I notice sprigs of green life growing out of the rocky soil. This part of the road is heavily corrugated and our driver slows to negotiate the bumpy terrain, still pointing out animals on the right. We are crammed into a little 4x4 U.S. Postal jeep that has been converted into a game drive vehicle and is painted in zebra-fashion. It sways from side to side as we move along the track. I am more fascinated by the lizards, birds, and small dragonflies clinging to the rock face as we trundle along than the grazing herbivores to the right that intrigue my grandparents.

I spy him first as we round a bend where he is gathering leaves to feed from the new trees peeping out of the cliff. His great grey wrinkled form and powerful trunk mesmerize me. Tiny eyes narrow into beady black bullets as he trumpets in shock and indignation at our sudden appearance. Large grey ears lift and flare impressively wider than the little jeep and with a determined thwack he pins them against his giant skull, bows his head, tucks in his trunk, preparing to charge and impale us with his enormous set of ivory tusks. Our quick-witted ranger reads all the signs and throws the old vehicle in reverse, so we careen backwards on the dirt track going as fast as the little van can.

The whining engine squeals plaintively above the roar of the enraged jumbo, now intently focused on his target, as the zebra-striped boxcar backs hastily away. Next, the bull elephant commits himself to a fully-fledged charge. Most likely in mating season, he trumpets with fury, all his hormones gone wild. It is also quite possible he has been hunted by men at some juncture and does not appreciate the sudden exposure during his previously peaceful snack of vines against the side of the cliff.

Time slows, as it tends to do in life and death circumstances, and I become aware of a large carnelian bug two inches long crawling along the window beside me. I am suddenly more consumed with fear of this scary slimy bug than the raging bull elephant charging full force down upon us! Our guide shares my trepidation as he finds a way out of the elephant predicament. His dexterous hand reaches down to grope for a box of tissues under the seat and once found, flings it to my grandfather who heroically grabs the bug and hurls it out the window minus the white tissue. The ranger expertly maneuvers us out of harm's way, spinning the vehicle around like a seasoned rally driver in a small clearing of trees and we are on our way. Whew, we only just made it through!

The experience leaves me wide-eyed and excited as our party of four erupts in mad cheers of glee and sighs of relief. As my grandparents squeeze me tight, I feel the great bull elephant reach out to touch me from afar with his powerful mind. He is the first physical being to show me my size as a human. How small am I against his fabulous fury?

The glorious raw power of this experience, delivered up from the dust of the land, shall not be forgotten. My grandparents wisely shelter me from any possible perspective of fear. They choose instead to celebrate this experience with joy. The elephant encounter blesses my mind with memory – a very long one!

THOSE "BAD BOONS"

During my third year of life, my mother, her parents and I settle down for a peaceful picnic at an idyllic roadside clearing in a canopy of trees overlooking Lake Manyara, in the East African Rift Valley of Tanzania. The adults have spread out an array of goodies: sumptuous sandwiches, fresh fruits, tasty juices, and tempting teas spread our on a lightweight Kenyan "kanga" cloth over the rustic wooden picnic table. We sit comfortably on felled logs munching our lunch and chatting merrily in the ambiance of the secret arboreal retreat, when all at once, a plucky male baboon drops to the earth before us, reaches up one large hairy hand, whips a piece of bread from our table, and dashes back to the trees above calling to his mates in triumph.

Our heads jerk up, and to our horror, we see an entire troop erupt from the foliage overhead. My mother leaps to action, instructing my gran and I to take cover in the vehicle and bellows at her father to help her shoo away the menacing beasts away. The primates swing into view splitting the air with guttural barks and show their enormous canines as they roar around the picnic spot, surrounding us on every side. My family moves swiftly to throw anything inedible, including me, into the van, while my mother and grandfather hoist the sitting logs that demarcate our picnic area to their shoulders, and hurl them over the edge of the picnic ledge toward the advancing troop. All this action is enough to confuse and scatter ill-disposed clan for just an instant so we can gather our things and beat a hasty retreat. We scream our own panicked retorts at the advancing primates as we leave, angry too, that our delicious picnic lunch has been spoiled.

My psyche absorbs this intense demonstration of nature's ability to claim its rightful territory. There seems to be little fear in the congress of baboons that now brawls amongst themselves in the canopy overhead for a few human-made sandwiches. "Those bad boons!" I exclaim, wide-eyed. The adults laugh and this becomes our new label for the primates.

Our adventure continues as we camp on the edge of the Ngorogoro reserve. Whilst falling asleep in a canvas-paneled tent for six, we feel our accommodation begin to sway and buck all around us. There is no movement from the ground so the adults concur that it isn't an earthquake. The rocking of the tent increases and the poles threaten to collapse. We jump to our feet in alarm but we are informed in a terse whisper from my father to keep as quiet as possible.

A male Cape buffalo is scratching his back on the tent poles outside. Cape buffaloes are some of the most unpredictable and dangerous animals of the African bush. A fully-grown male can weigh a massive eight hundred kilograms and has a mean set of horns fused to his skull forming a protective shield sometimes a meter wide from tip-to-tip. We are lucky to have some knowledge of the power of the beast, and to be in a tent full of humans who respect that power. Later, I hear the adults imagining what would have happened if we had tried to shoo our midnight visitor away as we had to the "bad-boons."

In East Africa time yawns lethargically as hours melt into days, days blend into weeks, and weeks coagulate into months. I begin to manifest an allergy to milk proteins, and become lactose intolerant so Lana puts me on a strict diet that makes me feel hungry all the time. I am learning about all the colors of the rainbow, the names of the resident bad-boons nicknamed for their naughty behavior, the "Elfie-nuts" – my childish name for elephants that live in giant herds a few kilometers up the road, and I register the sheer size of their "bowmie" my childhood term for the enormous bowel movements composed of seeds and fibrous grassy material dotted across the now familiar African savannah.

I celebrate my second and third birthdays still living in Kenya. My parents tour with me everywhere, carrying me on their backs in a bright orange backpack carrier. Lana calls me a "brown nutberry" as my assumed Hispanic-American genes produce a compact body, tanned a rich golden brown. My dark hair and eyes have lightened to the color of honey exposed to the scorching African sun. I inhale a myriad of aromas as we pass through the African markets that Lana spends hours exploring. She seems energized by the culture and language of the local tradesmen and women in the marketplace. I coo and chortle happily from the safety of her pack, grinning and reflecting the laughter of the amiable Swahili speaking tribes-people. The infectious way they express their love of children enchants me. Their salt-of-the-earth approach, open smiles and curiosity glow mischievously in dark inquisitive eyes, and their brawny ebony arms are almost always at the ready; willing and eager to embrace me.

Bard, Lana, and I explore the rows of open markets and the camel-colored beaches of Kenya and Tanzania together, where I showcase my squat castles built of sea sand against the backdrop of the bottle green ocean choked full of the seaweed seeds that I love to pop noisily under my feet. I play fearlessly here, swimming between my parents, with bright orange armbands bouncing gaily off my arms washed gently by the warm waves of the Indian Ocean. These experiences cause my soul to pause and connect me to this mother continent and her rhythms. People say Africa "gets into your blood" and I believe this is true. The raw cacao of the earth, the sweeping skies, and historic heritage are celebrated and enjoyed. Spices from Asia have made their way down the balmy coastline of the Indian Ocean and seeped into the richly seasoned Swahili-style dishes that match the vibrancy of the culture here.

I view the world from my perch on Bard and Lana's backs as they hike the dun-colored trails of the dry Ngong Hills outside the capital Nairobi, and observe the little settlements sprinkled upon vast tracks of tribal land far below on the faded savannah, awash with their scorched-gold grasslands contrasted against an alluring azure sky. Listening to cicadas singing amongst the thick yellow grasses we watch "Shirley's baboons"* grooming each other on the rocks at Gilgil.

Once, on safari, we get bogged down in quicksand in an expedition Land Rover while my father bravely sets out on foot with no weapons save his wit and a Braveheart approach through the predator-infested game park. I find myself standing atop the vehicle with my mother, a little olive-skinned girl clutching a black African baby-doll and a soft suede nappy blanket dubbed Jinky to my chest. Sticking my tummy out, mimicking the African village children, I suck my thumb for comfort in this big wide world. I am oblivious to the life and death decisions being made by the adults around me.

At two and a half years, differences in skin coloration begin to pique my interest and I ask Lana if my ayah** Deborah, is brown. Lana catches me wondering out loud if my new Japanese friend is the same as Tay our Korean friend. I learn that I am special because I am adopted and regularly announce this fact to everyone. "Hi! I'm Thea! I'm special. I'm 'dopted!'" As much as my mother tries to be politically correct, my eyes and ears begin to catalog and categorize different appearances, languages and customs and I point them out innocently without a formal understanding that these differences are sometimes considered "better" or "worse" than each other in this world I inhabit. My parents insist I call them by their first names,

---

*   Shirley Strum is the author of Almost Human
** a nursemaid or nanny employed by Europeans in former British territories)

not "Mommy" or "Daddy," and I'm only dimly aware of this as a difference or oddity in itself, and the strain they are both under in their marriage as compared with other family friends.

Lana reads me beautifully illustrated children's books at nighttime and the stories take us out of my African reality and into the realm of imaginary worlds that look nothing like my current African experience. Instead, the tales tie me to the imaginative culture of my own European and Native American* lineage. Bunny rabbits, wolves, bears, fishes, coyotes and raccoons take on human characteristics and light up the scenes in the magical tales. I am enchanted, as the whippoorwill calls out in the trees of a raccoon's night and a little dog laughs while a dish runs away with a spoon. My imagination is drawn to the fanciful pictures and words, and Cinderella's fairy godmother is a possibility that lights up something mystical at the back of my brain.

Lana, ever concerned with cultural integration, and an almost fanatical determination to mold me into her version of what a new generation of "evolved human" should be, shops to find me books that are appropriate to where we live and before long a few African fairy tales appear on the library shelf in our room as well. Some of the stories include adapted versions of Cinderella. One in particular contains a story about genital mutilation, which is a real issue for young women where we are living. My dollies are brown and black-skinned beauties and I never own a "white" baby doll while living in Africa. I love my dollies and stuffed animals with a fierce protective energy. It is how I come to love people and animals much later on. Skin color is of no consequence; respect for existence is of key importance.

When I first learn to walk and swim on holiday at my grandparents' home in Hawaii, I have a dream of a leviathan that later becomes a reality. The whale appears as a huge shadow, flowing silently beneath our sailboat outside Kealakekua Bay on the big island of Hawaii where my grandparents have retired, surging gracefully and powerfully upward – a humpback whale who leaps right up beside us to rock our boat in a giant wave of exultation.

---

* later in life my DNA heritage reveals my roots extend further than we ever realized as I am sure is true for most people. I am predominately Spanish and Portuguese, 35% Native American from all the Americas (North and South except Alaska), 7% Middle Eastern, 6% Irish, some Greek, Moroccan, Algerian and 1% Asian.

I am a conscious witness, paying close and curious attention to the world around me, always aware of sensation that is my true guide. I am fortunate to live in a primal environment while exploring this bold new world in the first three years of my adopted life. Memories of my birth and adoption into the world have now faded behind the veil of my subconscious mind. I have no idea how I am being shaped by the hands of creation even now.

Soul Song: Muted, Ambient, Opaque

3 years–Bougainvillea Scars

"We cannot grow when we are in shame, and we can't use shame to change ourselves or others."

— BRENE BROWN

NAIROBI

Every morning, I wake up and learn a bit of the local language, Ki-Swahili, as our teacher begins counting, "Mojo, Mbili, Tatu," around the low green table in the center of the small Gujarati pre-school I attend just down the road from the hotel, opposite the National Museum.

On one of these sunny East African mornings, my father Bard is home and is taking me to school. I am eager to impress him, so I take little heed of his loud whistle of warning as I race ahead. Anxious to show him I now know the way, I skip straight into the thorny embrace of a low-hanging vine of a wild bougainvillea bush dipping over the path. The vine, with its plethora of magenta flowers, hangs at eye level and I accidentally impale myself on one of its thorns. The thorn hooks my lid, and bloody tears streak down my cheeks as I cry out in pain, piercing the tranquil daybreak. Lana bursts out of our hotel room, heart pounding, and races along the path to the scene with gardeners and hotel ground staff in hot pursuit.

Once he has ascertained I am not badly wounded, Bard shakes his head at me in disapproval and shames me, deciding to make an example of the incident so I obey him in future. He wants to impress on me that my stubborn, free, strong-willed, and independent childlike behavior needs to be checked. He refuses to see past the mistake nor will he take me in his arms to reassure me.

The Kenyan ground staffs speak gently to soothe me. They do not believe in shaming a child, only in showing her. "Please Bwana," they plead with my father, "It's our fault! We shouldn't have allowed the tree to grow so low over the walkway! Anyone could have been hurt, eh? Don't be angry with your child." A gardener with a machete is brought straight-away to trim the offending vine as my mother takes me back to the hotel to wash my tear-stained, bloody face. Although the cut above my eyelid heals in no time, the internal scarring felt by my father's visceral reaction and shame does remain.

THE WESTERN WORLD

In my third year of life I begin to form a more cohesive bond with my adopted father. We travel to Switzerland where I am thrilled to snowplow on little red skis, all bundled up in a cuddly red-hooded snowsuit on the lower slopes of the famous San Maritz ski resort. It is here that Bard and I get to play more and spend precious moments bonding in the powdery snow while Lana cuts a lonely figure against the backdrop of the alpine slopes. She perches high above on the bright snow-filled decks of the expensive ski slope chalet rented by Bard, occasionally glancing up and snapping pictures of us in the late afternoon sun. It is not my first experience of the powdery whiteness falling from the sky, but this is my first conscious exploration of it, and vastly different from the red-hot savannah sands I am accustomed to in Kenya, Ethiopia or Tanzania. I love the soft white flakes that tickle my nose and cheeks..

Then in Belgium, in a park in Brussels, I learn to swing. My newfound capacity for experiencing flight as a direct result of my own leg-pumping action has me smiling and squealing with wonderment. The idea that I can pump my legs and rock my body to become "airborne" keeps me highly amused and occupied, and I revel in the whooping cheers of my mother. "Look at you go!" she shouts over and over as she claps excitedly from the sidelines. As the sun wanes in the Northern sky, Bard returns and Lana shares the day's excitement with him. Although he seems distracted and detached, she pulls him to the park to watch me.

In London, Lana continues to read to me. Whispering songs of the whippoorwill dance through my vision as together we weave and wander worlds within worlds. Stories of the popular French speaking elephant Babar, and his side-kick Lyle, the Friendly Crocodile, come alive as we huddle under blankets atop starched white sheets, sipping scalding hot cocoa in cozy hotel rooms while sleet and rain pelt the lamp-lined streets below.

Subtle though they may be, my mother's frantic nesting movements tell me that we are homeless and adrift again, living between homes, in tents, and hotel rooms. In Western Europe, my father drifts further away, preferring to be dry, warm, and inaccessible somewhere alone with a distant past only he can see in the bowels of magnificent museums, whilst up above it seems dreary and empty on the spinning earth with only my mother and me. Not one to waste time moping, Lana takes me out with her to pound the pavements. Together we visit shops, nature parks, historic sites, and Lana people watches and absorbs as much as she can of the local culture, with me in tow.

Our next stop is Great Britain, where I find myself worlds away from the warm African savannah and the friendly Kenyans who love children. Here in the streets, I observe mothers bustling their crying children along the hard concrete sidewalks, flanked by tall buildings that block out a grey brooding sky. Men shoulder past wearing long navy, black or tweed capes sprinkled with recent rain. Red double decker buses plow through the traffic on Oxford Street, catching my eye, and all the noise of honking horns is exhaustive.

Nobody makes eye contact here; smiles are hurried, glances shrewd, with half-veiled appraisals directed our way come from the corners of squinty eyes. I miss the animated, friendly Kenyans with their wide ivory smiles strikingly contrasted against rounded ebony features who warmly encourage us to buy handmade wares and humorously haggle or share culture and food. That being said, it is a true comfort to have my mother's undivided attention, if only for this moment.

It is 1974 and my mother enrolls me in an afternoon dance school, Temple Beth El. The dance school is established in an impressive Greco mansion set into the hillside, across the San Francisco Bay and almost hidden by trees. I dance here with children my age, both boys and girls bound in colorful frocks and shorts across a smooth polished floor where a circle has been outlined in the center of the domed airy practice hall to depict the moon. An elderly Caucasian teacher with cinder grey curls pinned up all over her head with tiny flowers, gracefully waves her long arms overhead and mouths, "Reach high for the sky!" She is dressed in the most elegant flowing garments styled after Isadora Duncan, a famous dancer of the early 1900s. She directs our practice with heaps of praise, grace, and aplomb. We learn how to leap "high over the moon" without making a sound when we land.

At the dance school, I am paired with Reina, another adoptee. She has a feisty sense of humor beneath a sober exterior that causes me to titter gleefully, hoping to turn her attention towards me. Reina's face is crowned by an Afro-halo of soft curls that enhances darkly etched brows and jet-black curled lashes framing bright flashing eyes. She is the first dark-skinned person I have come into contact with since leaving African soil, but she has a distinct American accent and knows nothing of the Africa where I have been living. Sylphlike, she takes my hand in hers and I squeeze it firmly, knowing at once we are to be bosom buddies for life.

Reina is under the love and care of two well-to-do Caucasian-American parents who have one biological son and several other children hailing from as far afield as India and Vietnam. The family embraces disabilities and works tirelessly around the clock to bring out the best in each little person no matter what physical or mental challenges they face. Rescued from poverty and unknown trials, they now lead a privileged life in a triple story mansion that I love to visit and explore. Reina and I laugh at our funny faces in the floor-to-ceiling mirrors installed in her perfectly pink "princess room," and we tiptoe past her siblings and disappear into the bushes under the shady trees of the mansion's garden to investigate the lives of bugs and earthworms we find in the soil there.

Soul Song: Syncopated, Diminished, and Grave

4 years–Divergence

"Every beginning is a consequence.
Every beginning brings an end."

— ANONYMOUS

GRIZZLY PEAK, BERKELEY

R ed is my mother's favorite color for me. She likes to dress me up in a red sweater, red corduroy trousers, and a red poncho. The fire color corresponds with the lava of resentment that bubbles ominously in her core. Her anger and frustration are palpable, and passionate blood reds seep into my toys, my bed, my rugs, and wall hangings. At home in Berkeley, my room is decorated in wine reds, contrasting strongly against black and white geometrics that adorn the floor and tasteful pieces of abstract rainbow-embroidered wall art. Lana takes great care and pride in her eclectic décor, always daring and striving to be unconventional. These are not the usual colors for a child's bedroom. Then again, nothing about Bard, Lana or the life we have been living is usual.

It is now the fall of 1974, and I am enrolled in kindergarten full-time in a small schoolhouse around the corner from our home in the hills. Just as I have become accustomed to an earthly existence, the fragile emotional state of my adopted home is coming to an end. My parent's relationship unravels in front of me as we walk with our female malamute Tata in the hills above our hometown. The acorn and pine-strewn trails are filled with the heady scent of eucalyptus trees. We hike together in the warm Northern California wilderness, while emotionally and spiritually our hearts roam far apart. At home, our cozy little house strains to incorporate and contain all the upset generated from the parental split ongoing within its wooded mossy walls.

Two Vivian's happen into our lives at this time. They are each hired separately to babysit me when my parents go out. One of the two is available 24/7 like a true au pair. Together, she and I create castles from blocks in my toy box, lying side-by-side on our tummies for extended periods of time as she sings cheerfully at me, imitating the voices of the Disney mice characters from the Cinderella classic that plays on my real working plastic toy record player. I giggle and clap as she mimics the tiny voices so perfectly. I am enchanted by her sunny smile and long blonde hair. My parents dub her "V" to differentiate between her and the other dark-haired au pair. "V" is my immediate friend, and we share childhood secrets and happiness together playfully.

I quickly learn the difference between "minder" and "friend." The other babysitter, dark-haired Vivian is strict, mature, and almost indifferent toward me. One dark winter's night, as raindrops leave silver tears on the windowpanes, I find myself in a battle of wills with this Vivian. I am feverous with a bad cough and sore throat and I need her care and attention. I moan and continuously wander out from my room demanding her attention. Frustrated and exasperated from the constant distraction and interruption to her reading, her face twitches, until suddenly she pops up from the couch in genuine anger.

"Thea, go to bed! How many times must I tell you? If you don't rest you won't get well!" I turn away, feeling wounded by the cutting edge of her voice. What can I do to get her to help me? I have a sudden brainwave, and sneak off to the kitchen, grabbing the medicine bottle Bard and Lana left behind for me on the counter. I hold it out to her as she sits back reading her book in the lamplight of the darkened lounge.

"Here, Vivian, see what Lana left for me!" I thrust the medicine toward her. She glances up over her study books and her eyes narrow on the glass bottle of purple syrup.

"It is not time yet, Thea," she declares acidly. "I'll give you some when you have gotten yourself ready for bed. Now leave." She points toward the stairs.

A final whimper escapes my fevered lips and I fall in a mournful heap at her feet. I am so sick, and I want to be comforted. Why won't she show me some love? I fear she will hit me but I persist, seeking her attention anyway. Why doesn't she look up from the page? I want her to see that I have dressed myself in pajamas. Vivian smiles to herself and does her best to ignore the large brown eyes that keep boring through the back of her book.

Unshed tears glisten in my eyes and threaten to spill down my hot swollen cheeks. Then finally, without looking directly at me, something causes her to lean forward and touch my burning forehead with a cool white hand. "Oh, my goodness, you are flushed!" she exclaims, shock and horror laces her tone as if the fever is a secret evil that had been kept from her all along. "Where's that medicine you told me about? Go and get it and bring it here!"

I point to the African stool-table by her side.

She snatches the bottle of grape flavored medicine out of my stubby hand, reads the instructions, and quickly pours me a measure of the purple liquid, which I gulp down straight-away. The stuff is strong and tastes foul, but I manage.

"Right, young lady, let's get you to bed."

As she moves to take me, I can't keep the medicine down and heave helplessly at her feet.

"Oh God! Sit over there and don't move!" She leaps over with a curse and handles the necessary clean up, then takes me firmly by the hand and tucks me into bed. As I lie there staring at the animal mobile hanging overhead, I long for my friend "V" to come and sing me to sleep, but "V" never comes to our home again and Vivian is the only one left to look after me when my parents go out.

Vivian, or Viv as my father now affectionately refers to her, shows up frequently when Lana is away on business and Bard is on his own with me. She raps at the door at odd hours, always with stories that focus Bard's attention entirely on her, making a dubious impression on my young mind. Vivian's exotic features, slanted almond eyes, and long ebony tresses, give her an Asian appearance, but she claims she is of Dutch descent. She is a belted karate apprentice and accomplished tap dancer who likes to practice her moves between studying books. A born Aries, she is inquisitive, determined, and the self-created master of everything she puts her attention to. Her sights are now firmly on Bard.

Unlike the critical worldly disenchantment Bard suffers in conversations with Lana, he is overwhelmed by Viv's svelte body, witty mind, sense of adventure, fun and humor, and the way she pulsates subtly to ensnare his fancy. Bard is from a family of innovative inventors, a product of a broken home, a rich cosseted mother, and a father who has had little to do with the upbringing of his children. His parents sent him off in his primary years to boarding school and he was raised into high society largely by nannies and teachers.

Bard's father, a distant yet magnanimous man, rarely spent time with his sons. He was an intellectual who inherited most of his fortunes from a long family dynasty of Germanic lords and American investors and inventors. Bard's mother's family line were inventors too and she inherited millions. She divorced his father and sought out spiritualists to heal her pain. She was prone to fits of glamour and sullen rage. Bard fled from this fiefdom as soon as he had the courage. College life, and meeting Lana was provided him a window out of his cage.

Now, finding himself in conflict with feelings about his own marriage he offers the enigmatic Vivian his protection, his shelter, riches, and adventure; and he inspires her with fascinating stories, dreams and fantasy, reeling her into his world of dreams as far as he can get from the reality he experiences in everyday life. Bard and Viv fall hard for one another before my unknowing eyes, and though he tries to show restraint, for my sake and the sake of his tattered vows to Lana, he easily caves into the tug of desire he feels as Viv presses her feminine wiles warmly against the backdrop of the internal gloom that threatens to overwhelm his fragile conscience.

Disagreements begin to erupt between Lana and Bard that shatter the cradle of love I have briefly been cocooned in. Lana pulls her silky auburn hair over one shoulder and pinches her pale face into a paragon of pain. Bard sits long nights resisting her acrid remarks with a goblet in hand and a bottle of Bordeaux on the glass coffee table between them. Even as anxiety etches my mother's features, I see her as unendingly beautiful. I keep my head and eyes cast down, playing quietly with my toys while their aggravated, unhappy voices spit venomously like two African cobras, dangerously mesmerized by their dance. I pretend to busy myself on the floor nearby, building forts with my wooden blocks or playing games with my red fire fighter's truck, lest either parent notices me eavesdropping. From time to time, I cannot help myself and stop what I am doing to glance up, open-mouthed, as I witness noxious energy spilling out of their mouths.

They stop abruptly once they notice my silence, and glance over at my plaintive wide-eyed gaze. Then, suddenly they each turn and mock me. They stare at me, jutting their chins forward in a parody of my surprise and horror. It only lasts a few seconds but it feels like years and I turn away, ashamed and embarrassed. I close my lips and fix my eyes firmly upon my tiny tanned fingers that involuntarily clutch and tug at the scratchy woolen carpet beneath my knees, trying my best not to cry. What I have seen and heard coming from their mouths is revolting. They remind me of the "bad-boons" of Kenya, out of control and instinctual.

My inner eye sees danger, hatred, blame, and pain erupting in twisted coils of dark energy from their bodies. It is so ugly and crude that when I first see it, I want to hide, but I freeze and stare at it anyway. In these moments, I re-live the blasted heat of Marla's womb all over again, now in a different set of circumstances that I can see from the outside. My parent's conflict sparks an ember of despair that burns deep inside of me, which is almost more than I can bear.

NATURALLY ZEN

I have come to this life as a bridge between dualities: dark and light, rich and poor, male and female, Heaven and Earth. Therefore, it is no surprise that I experience both chaos and stability in equal measure. Lana and Bard take an active interest in Zen Buddhism and we often drive together, several miles across the San Francisco Bay, to sit quietly in a private zendo sanctuary called Green Gulch near the sea. I am always happy to come along to see them together, privately hoping this will be what unites them once more. Many times, we arrive while the zendo chanting is already underway.

While my parents sit with other adults inside in the zazen meditation practice, I sit outside under towering eucalyptus trees on an open-air timber deck, drenched in sunlight to wait. The natural world and I sit side-by-side as I sip herbal tea and chat with the friendly staff that come and go. My drawing journal and box of pens is always with me and most conversations arise from it. I am determined to be on my best behavior so I can continue to enjoy the space and not be moved elsewhere.

The monks, both male and female, with their shaved heads open to the elements, fascinate me as they wander the sand-swept paths in billowing brown or black robes. I follow their mindful movements. They seem to be shrouded in peace, raw emotions contained, having less impact on the environment than others as they walk about. Some are studious and intensely purposeful, while others have mastered just being radiantly alive and smile affectionately in my direction.

In the summertime, we transition to a sister retreat center in the mountainous valleys of Big Sur called "Tassajara" where professionals and laymen from all levels of society come to get away from the modern world and its rapid pace. Doctors, lawyers, and carpenters break bread together, meditate, study, write, work in the gardens or kitchens, while interning monks sweep the rock-strewn paths, and bathe daily in the communal dipping pools built into the rocks above natural hot springs.

Here in the Santa Cruz mountains, we cool off in icy streams born from the snowy peaks above; soak in the rock-hewn steam baths that arise from the sulfurous soil and the visitors and community rest upon smooth pale boulders marbled with streaks and strands of dark grey and pearly white. All around us, the history of man reveals its stories in the ancient arrowheads and artifacts strewn along the sandy walking trails, pointed out eagerly by my father, who whisks me back to a time before white people came to claim this territory from the First Peoples. I feel so connected here, as if I am one with this place and its history.

Bard trains me to walk softly upon the earthen trails, one foot in front of the other, as quiet as "a Native American princess." I solemnly follow without making a sound, until not even a leaf dares to crackle under my toes, and he claims I am a natural. The scientist in him models the observer in me. It is here I begin my lifelong training in focused listening and observation that in years to come will be my emotional and spiritual strength.

As the two of us walk calmly between the shoulders of this narrow valley retreat, miniature reptilian creatures dart across our path and he teaches me not to be afraid. He lectures me about horned lizards, garter snakes, and dragonflies that we find on the path. Squirrels scamper in the trees overhead, sometimes chattering loudly over the gurgling stream. I learn to listen for the warning sound of rattlesnakes and move away from their fat scaled bodies, keeping a respectful distance. Bard occasionally reaches down with a makeshift walking stick to move them into the leaves far off the path, keeping us safe from their venomous bites.

Minnows, turtles, and crawdads reveal themselves in the freshwater streams that make their way from these inland mountains to the sea. I take long moments to convince myself to touch them as Bard waits patiently nearby, and sometimes I fear the crawdad pincers will cling too hard to my toes! This is a child-perfect outdoor classroom, drenched in tranquil serenity. A love of the natural world is born in me; an appreciation for history, the magic of the earth, and new possibilities occur as Bard draws pictures of woodland fairies in my drawing journal, awakening my ripe imagination to portals of other dimensions of reality.

Now that I am almost five years of age, Bard teaches me to ride my child-size red Schwinn bike on the meandering quiet streets of our neighborhood and at the playground of the private school I attend at Grizzly Peak on the weekends when it is deserted. I balance in terror, on my saddle, peddling down the steep playground slope, punching my little thighs frantically to maintain my perch and finally make it up the other side of the concrete slope without falling. Then one day, Bard removes the training wheels and lets me go by myself. I scream in terror, then chirrup with amazement as I keep my balance and learn to ride. He applauds and hugs me close to his chest. I crave these fatherly affections. It seems it can never be enough.

✷✷✷✷✷✷✷

A RENDING OF HEARTS

Most mornings I visit my parents in their spacious sunny bedroom, climb in between the patterned sheets beneath their big geometrically designed blue, white and green quilt, and snuggle down inside feeling their mutual love for me. Tata joins us in bed and kisses me awake with her big wet nose and ticklish tongue. We always play games together before making breakfast in the newly fitted 70's retro kitchen that is painted orange downstairs.

One morning, I bounce into the room for my routine cuddle to find Lana all by herself under the big bedspread and ask her, "Where is Bard?"

She tells me he is sleeping on the couch in his study.

Curious, and unable to stay still and wonder, I jump out of her arms to go find him. As I push open the study door, he invites me into the tiny oak-paneled room and beckons me undercover with him on the narrow suede couch in his tiny pitched roof office under the eaves. There is sadness in his tone and I notice it also in his bleary brown eyes. I decide I don't like finding my parents apart. After a short time stroking my hair, my father sends me back to my mother. They take turns each morning to cuddle me, and help me to the toilet, making sure I stand on my booster stool to brush my baby teeth.

One day, I hide under the round breakfast nook table by the front door, unseen, as I listen to their raised voices coming from deep within the house. These unwelcome sounds break into my play beneath the table, causing my body to stiffen and turn toward the sound. Moments later, I witness my father's tan brown corduroys and shoes storm past, his worn brown leather briefcase in hand. The door opens and slams and I jump, belatedly hitting my head on the round underside of the tabletop above.

Lana does not follow. I worry what this could mean. After sitting on my haunches for a while I decide to crawl out from under the table to investigate. I find her busying herself with the vacuum cleaner, lips pursed in a thin crooked line. I dare to ask her if Bard is going to come home? She shrugs nonchalantly and assures me he will, however, he stays away longer and longer each time they argue. He spends long important moments with me at the park near our house, then one day, without explanation, he leaves our comfy home in the pine trees for good. Bard takes refuge in Vivian's bed, staying at her apartment for weeks on end until he finds a place to rent.

It seems forever for me until he reappears and comes to fetch me for a father-daughter date at our favorite ice cream parlor. I am excited to spend time with him, as I am about to turn six and have a list of Birthday wishes and exciting things to tell him about my classmates and teachers at kindergarten. After our date, we sit in the front of his van, and as we both clip on our seat belts, I notice that he doesn't put the car in gear to drive out of the lot. Instead, he tunes the radio to a classical music station. This is the same station we usually play to imagine and tell stories of faerie gardens, but today, instead of asking me to play the game, he slowly turns to face me in the passenger seat.

I concentrate on the outline of his soft brown curls and dare not look into his sad chestnut colored eyes as he takes his time to begin the hard conversation he has been putting off for weeks. He looks away and back again before he starts. I wait and watch his every move, somehow understanding something important is about to be conveyed and that he is unsure how I will take it. Bard has my full attention as he explains he has made an adult decision to move away from home and will never be returning to life with Lana. He says the two of them cannot get along anymore and they have agreed that he and I will visit each other, but it will be best for me to stay in her care full time. He tells me this is not my fault, and he is committed to being my father forever.

"You understand, Wart?" He uses this slightly insulting yet, oddly fond nickname, and reaches over to ruffle my thick shock of shiny brown hair. The look on his face is half worry and half relief as if he needs my encouragement somehow.

Understand? How can I be okay to "understand" something that will affect me the rest of my life, but that I have no say about? It is no different to how I felt as a babe in utero or upon arrival in this world being given away by my mother, taken from my sister and brother, grandparents and culture simply because the family were unable to cope or give up narcotic abuse.

I am inwardly devastated, but I try to put up a front to impress him, nodding solemnly with big doe eyes, wide and tearless, not knowing now that it is his promise he will never be able to keep, either emotionally or physically. I feel the happiness of our date wilt like a rose that hasn't yet had a chance to bloom into its most beautiful expression.

My young heart is breaking and I don't know how I can keep it intact. I wrap myself in silence. Bard sees my reluctance to talk more and revs the engine, reversing out of the carpark wrapped tightly in his own thoughts.

At home, in anger and pain, Lana brazenly lets me know her world is falling to pieces. Sometimes sleepless, she shakes with an all-consuming rage, and bundles me out of my bed late in the evening to accompany her to Bard's new abode. Bard, who clearly abhors confrontation, refuses to pick up her calls, so she rouses him outside his residence and all the neighbors as well. Lana hurls stones at his windowpane to attract his attention, and when he ignores the racket, she bangs repeatedly on his door, screaming and demanding to be heard.

Inwardly, I deplore Lana for becoming a tree with two sides I don't understand: both a screaming banshee and a weeping willow. I begin to have recurring nightmares about Lana turning into a hag and chasing me throughout the grey twilit streets of a dim concrete jungle across the bay in San Francisco. In the dream, both Lana and Bard's lover Vivian appear interchangeably as the two formidable female figures in my world; witches with ill intentions whom I follow down perpetually darkening streets, and lose sight of, until they pop out from around corners of buildings taunting me menacingly. I force myself to follow them, afraid and intrigued at the same time. I wake up with a start when their frightening faces get way too close for comfort.

Bard's sudden departure causes me to search for answers I have no way of finding at present. I have just begun to build loving bonds with my adoptive father. Time lost with him is a wound that cuts deep and slow. It doesn't help when I hear Lana sob in her bed in the early hours of morning and late at night as she beats her pillows in outrage at her failed love, family-life, and marriage a reality she feels has been thrust upon her. Bitterness sinks in that only faith and renewed hope can prevent, yet she vehemently slams shut all doors to this possibility as well.

As if this isn't enough, Lana's father, the only grandfather I know, suddenly endures a fatal heart attack and dies unexpectedly in Hawaii. In one year, Lana loses both husband and father. I lose a father and grandfather. During this time, I am the only outlet for Lana's love and her greatest burden when all she wants is to do is bury her head. Once, when I give her trouble, she takes a belt to my behind, standing me in front of a mirror as she does the whipping to double impress upon me her control and authority. I am unable to forget this moment and I don't think she does either, for she tells me she is sorry.

I match the intensity of the energy in my environment by biting one or two children in the playground, passing on the fierce emotions of rage inside me. My fury at the injustice of losing my loving home bubbles to the surface as I test the strength of my will upon my peers and my mother with equal passion. Not knowing what to do with the force of my energy, Lana moves me to my bedroom and locks the door. The intensity of the emotions that drench my little body turn me as red as my clothes and the toy fire engine I have become so attached to in the darkest corner of our living room. When people ask what I want to be when I grow up, I tell them I will be a fire fighter. I cannot bear the tortuous isolation and separation that burns like a wildfire in my fevered heart.

I scream and kick at the locked door with all my might. Stomping angrily up and down on the carpet, I know my mother can hear me below. I hold onto the bars of my antique brass bed and pound the floor rhythmically with my feet. It takes me three quarters of an hour to stop fighting and snarling, and at last I crumple helplessly against the door, my cries of anguish deliberately ignored as I lie in a heap on the carpet. Exhausted, I resort to sucking my thumb and clenching my softest baby blanket, "Jinky" to my heart.

On more subdued days, I walk into Lana's room and am startled to find her slamming down the telephone handset in tears. "What's wrong?" I ask in a small voice, standing at the entrance of her bedroom, my big almond eyes searching hers.

"Just hold me, Thea. Come here and give me a hu-u-gg," She clutches me to her heart, sobbing endlessly. I take her into my tiny child's arms and squeeze her tight. I try my best to soothe her. After a time, she releases me and tells me I am a big help to her.

Life feels like a whirlpool. We are isolated and alone. Friends take sides. They identify with the plight of one parent, or disengage both. People begin to come and go in our lives. The foundation of any formal family life departs with the rise and fall of emotions as we all float outwards into a vast sea of uncertainty. The tearing of my heart is excruciating, tugging like a craven animal continuously dragging me to its den. At night, I am scared to breathe in case I shatter the crystal of hope that continues to shimmer faintly inside my heart.

Soul Song: Lyrical, Poignant, and Magical

4-5 years–Reaching for the Light

"Every child has known God,
Not the God of Names,
Not the God of Don'ts,
Not the God who never does anything weird,
but the God who knows only four words
and keeps repeating them, saying:
Come dance with me, come dance."

— HAFIZ

SHINE, ANGELIC SAVIOR

D uring the dramatic dissolution of my adoptive parent's marriage, a time that seems to stretch into forever, an angel visits my room. I do not think to question such a visit from the unseen realms of spirit. I simply accept with gratitude what comes and I invite her in.

She first appears as I play by myself in a wide band of sunlight and dust motes streaming in from outside as I simultaneously hum and chirrup softly to myself. The angel appears a little older than me; perhaps 8 or 10 years of age and shimmers brightly in a pool of light all her own. She beams down at me joyfully from the windowpane and encourages me to join her in a game. I am more than happy to have her company, and through her I receive a diversion from the dark, worried, un-childlike thoughts that have begun to plague my playtimes.

"What's your name?" I blink shyly, appraising her ethereal beauty.

"My name is that which you would call me!"

She chimes back and spins away again, begging me to catch hold of her prances about the room.

Okay, so what will I call her?

"Shine is your name!"

I cry with a burst of child-like inspiration.

That settles the matter. We talk and play for hours on end, which gives my mother a much-needed break from my questioning and incessant chitter-chatter. I am content and enchanted by Shine's presence and the golden halo of light that sparkles and dazzles all around her. She keeps me entertained for hours on end.

One day, curious about what keeps me so occupied, Lana hovers in the doorway of my room and asks with whom I am speaking.

I tell her, "It's Shine! Come and meet Shine. She comes from Hawaii."

And after a while of long introductions and listening, Lana dubs her, "Thea's imaginary friend." I am disappointed my mother cannot see my sparkly friend the way I do. Lana says only I can see her, but Shine tells me it's all right, and speaks to Lana through me. My mother continues to indulge me, happy for the positive diversion.

As it turns out, Shine is all about gifts.

One day, Shine takes my hand in hers and offers to trade places with me. Her home is on a beautiful island with birds of paradise, hibiscus and poinsettia flowers, palm, mango and banana groves growing ubiquitously throughout the hilly property, and colorful creatures twittering happily in the indelibly balmy breeze. Standing on her multi-leveled wooden decking, I am treated to a sumptuous view from the edge of a crystal-clear infinity pool that blends into the teal and turquoise sea beyond.

The big bay windows face outward framing a spacious modern lounge unlike like anything I have ever seen before. I accept Shine's invitation to swap places readily; it feels like the times I have traveled for Christmas and holidays to see Lana's parents, my maternal grandparents, who live on the Kona coastline of the Big Island of Hawaii, and before I know what is happening, I feel a tingle up my spine as Shine seamlessly enters a space in my physical body.

I, in turn, 'check out,' switching places to be in her realm, as I linger for what seems like hours there, playing in her infinite pool of blue and Lana plays along. She and Shine bustle about the house having long conversations with one another. "Shine" relays everything to me when I return. My mother loves it when Shine takes my place as She always displays pure goodness, cleans my room, picks up after herself, and washes the dishes without being asked. Lana thankfully doesn't ask too many questions. Shine will not divulge where I happen to be, hiding me away where I may remain protected, and she laughs with my mother easily, helping her with the household chores.

Shine helps me to understand that I am my own link for miracles and magic. She whispers to me that I am *blessed, loved, and protected*, and she puts a dressing over the emotional wounds of fear and uncertainty that tug incessantly at my heart and soul.

Soul Song: Reedy, Forlorn, and Forsaken

5-6 years–Reinvention

"To be infinitely patient is not to wait in time or forever, with the idea of some future moment when everything will dissolve. It is to rest right now with whatever is there."

— SCOTT KILOBY

LANA

The seasons have turned, and the warm arms of summer reach out to embrace us once more. Lana moves me and our dog Tata snuggly into a timber-built summerhouse near the windswept shores of Bolinas on the westernmost point of a narrow peninsula that juts out from the Pacific waters of the San Francisco Bay. We move into co-habitation here with a male friend of my mother's, who is also going through a divorce and has brought his only son along with him: a boy my age, named Jesse. Jack, and my mother spend long mornings and evenings together writing, walking, and talking politics while Jesse and I spend time playing in the tall blended beach grasses, intent on building the best-ever driftwood forts in coves of the wind-combed beaches and dunes nearby. We all take hikes together in the lavender and heather-filled hills of Stinson or the cool shadows of the National Redwood Forest Park.

I love creating art: drawing, coloring, painting, making shell and drift-wood collages, and riding horses at a little school down the road. Jesse and I are propelled out of our melancholy existence alone together at the small house in the hills. Bard has recently taken me to see gymnasts perform on the backs of dazzling white Lipizzaner horses at a big circus in the city and I can't stop thinking of their tall white-feathered plumes bouncing above their fancy bridles. I imagine this is going to be me one day... a graceful sequined acrobat, dancing on horseback.

Lana soon realizes, of course, with the gentle prodding of Jack, that she must create some sort of safety raft for herself and for me to protect us as we seem to be tossed casually about by this sea called Life. She takes his advice and reaches out to those with whom she can immediately identify: whales – the leviathans of the deep who appear helpless against the Great Human Shadow, which takes the form of Japanese whalers with their bloodied harpoons and Danish Faroe Islanders with their century-old tradition of massacre slaughtering hundreds of pilot whales and dolphins every year for nothing other than a show of manhood. Lana enthusiastically channels all her energy and passion on mobilizing her resources for a Save the Whales campaign and begins fervently sourcing non-profit work through her ties to environmental organizations. Before long she manages to join whale saving NGOs, Green Peace, Sierra Club, and the Save-the-Whales campaigns to create one giant tidal wave of gradual change in policy and perception that will sweep the nation.

Being a realist, she is undeterred by the volume of research and the statistics of brutal whale deaths worldwide. Lana's personal campaign is a grassroots movement that teaches primary school children how to love these giants of the deep just as much as she does. Then, through the use of media, both audio and visual, poetry, art, story and sound, she uses giant self-created whale puppets and other edutainment models and edutools to deliver her message to schools across California. Lana is proud to be at the helm of creating statewide awareness about the torture these innocent mammals are experiencing and what could happen to our precious seas, and us, come to think of it – if we annihilate them all.

She enlists whole classrooms of students to write letters to their con-gressmen and send their artwork and related poems to the highest offices in the land. She even tackles the distracted adult population, by launching her cause in public awareness campaigns at a myriad of fundraising events and fairs that begin to pop up all across the California coastline. Lana becomes known as "The Whale Lady" and drives "The Whale Bus" – a fancy white VW van painted with blue and green waves and whales.

As soon as Lana is back into the golden vein of life, she revisits a love-affair kindled in her heart long ago. Love comes in the form of a lean golden-haired Aussie named Damian several years her junior who completely backs her cause. Damian takes the long and expensive journey across the Pacific Ocean to visit us in Bolinas. He embraces me lovingly as a part of the package that is Lana, and we form a fast friendship. Damian reads to me, plays with me, and showers me with gifts from his far-flung homeland of Australia: a tiny golden Kookaburra* pin decorated with seed pearls, and sends me book sets full of stories of Australia's legendary silver brumbies.** Lana finally gives in to his pleas to meet him in his country, and plans a working trip, all expenses paid, so she can to visit him there.

When Lana leaves, I am left in the care of Bard, and separated from the female malamute Tata that has been my constant companion and motherly protector throughout my parent's separation. As communication is now stunted and strained between Lana and Bard, the grey and white female malamute is left in the care of Lana's friends, who do not have a very tall fence. During this unsettled time, our beloved Tata disappears mysteriously out of their yard. Bard and I search the streets calling her name and we visit dog pounds and shelter but we can't seem to find her. We don't know if she jumped out, ran away, or was stolen and sold off to the highest bidder.

Something breaks inside me as the days pass by under Bard's care, and I feel hope of finding our doggie seeping out of every pore. For the first time in my life, hatred and blame flare up deep within. This causes a determined hardening of the rough and raw substance I am made of. Both parents push aside and accept this new loss of our doggie, as adults may, but for me it is a trauma I am forced to compress and try to contain. I try to be a big girl as I swallow my grief whole. The excitement I feel living with my father has

---

* A member of the kingfisher bird family native to New Guinea and Australia, known for its distinctive laughing sounds

** Wild horses indigenous to Southern Australia and descendants of lost horses from early settlers

been marred by this unfortunate event. He is sad too, and he doesn't hide his emotion or his anger at my mother for not leaving the dog with him.

"At least your mother didn't take the cat," he grumbles, only adding to my grief.

He tries his best to distract me with trips to Golden Gate Park and the museums across the bay in San Francisco, or he lets me help care for his bonsai collection in the backyard. We spend time visiting our old neighbors whom he has maintained a friendship with up in the Berkeley hills so I can feel close to my old home hidden by a fence and locked gate. When the adults are conversing, I sneak out their kitchen door and peer through the holes in the fence, staring into our old yard and longing for my old life and better days.

Shine, my imaginary friend and savior, is mute and doesn't come to play with me anymore, so I self-soothe, and dive deep into a space of no sound, preferring my own company playing make-believe and drawing pictures quietly in a corner or playing with the Star Wars figurines my father has collected on the shelf in my bedroom at his home. I don't have an auntie or an uncle or any other family member to help me figure out my grief, so I press pause on the pain and live each day as it comes. Wherever I am, I promise my Tata I will always search for her. I can feel her answering howl on the edge of my consciousness. She longs for me too.

Soul Song: Symbolic, Symphonic, and Crescendo

6 years–Unchartered Territory

"In the face of pain there are no heroes."

— GEORGE ORWELL

SEPARATE LIVES

After Bard and Lana's divorce is finalized, my mother sells our quaint suburban home in the hills and moves us into a large three-story Victorian urban-farmhouse in a low-cost, low-income area of Berkeley, California. Lana's relationship with her Aussie lover has come to an end, and she has met a new man; a self-styled hippie-drifter of Moorish Irish extraction and the son of a large extended family. Not an academic, he has spent time in the Navy and then lived in various of the grid arrangements and lives and works in an urban-farm communal living set up where he teaches compost management to the public. Searle shows up at our house from time to time with his conga drums or guitar in hand, flashing his perfect set of pearly whites, and running his big fingers through a shock of thick wavy hair he sports like a long-curled lion's mane. The man is a giant and has the wide, muscular form of a 6 foot 7-inch tall gladiator and an olive completion somewhat like my own. His voice booms through the quiet of our home adding color and a great deal of energy.

It is the mid-70s, just before kidnapping and rape reach a peak in America. I am saddened to be separated from my English-Peruvian neighbor Pascale whose house is nestled two doors down from our former home in the Berkeley Hills, however, Lana is eager to cut all ties with our past lives, and quickly eliminates any people she feels may judge her unfairly – including many of the parents and kids from my old playgroups at school and the playground parks we used to frequent. I am removed from the Grizzly Peak primary school and secured a place in a new private school called Black Pine Circle. My adopted friend Reina also comes to attend this school, which is just a couple of miles from our new home in the flats.

The schoolhouse sits on a quiet tree-lined street just a few blocks away from a newly emerging warehouse neighborhood along the railway on Fourth Street. As a stoutly built six-year-old with sun-streaked bob pinned away from my face and striped blue, red and white tights, peeking out from my short jean skirt, I make my daily trek to school. I carry a little red rucksack on my shoulders as I hike unaccompanied to and from my lessons each day. On two occasions, a greasy man in a brown trench coat shadows me in his low-rider car on my way to school. I report him to Lana immediately. She takes time off work to follow me surreptitiously in her own car several days in a row. I decide that walking to school is not fun. I am not happy to be independent even though Lana tries her best to encourage me by telling me I'm such a big girl now.

After a few months getting used to the hike, I run into trouble. One early morning, I am surprised and jumped by twin twelve-year-old boys that race out of a slum apartment complex on a busy street corner. They sandwich me between their lanky brown bodies and begin to gyrate their hips against my helpless form, pinning me between them so I am unable to move. My backpack is the only thing keeping them from squashing me completely! I can hardly breathe. Cars pass adjacent to us on the wet tarmac, but it is the early morning rush hour and nobody stops. When I arrive at school, I am reprimanded for being tardy in front of the entire class and sent to the Principal's office for an hour. I don't know what to say to my classmates or the teachers and feel the rising embarrassment set my cheeks on fire.

As Lana cannot afford to take time off work to take me to school every day, Bard is cajoled into buying me a new bike, which on one of my visitation dates with him, he takes me to pick out at the Schwinn bicycle outlet downtown. As I skip excitedly along the rows of bikes hanging from the ceiling and parked on the floor, my father smiles. He benevolently allows me to pick the girliest bike in the shop with plastic rainbow tassels dangling from the handlebars, and a white basket on the front for carrying things, knowing full well my mother will disapprove of such frivolity. She wanted a son, and he is letting me be a girly-girl with all my choices. He chuckles inwardly having his way.

The bike makes getting to school faster and creates more route options, but the fear of perpetrators still rides with me wherever I go. I have become hyper-vigilant and street-wise to every possible danger: loose dogs, homeless crazies, perverts, and thugs. Goose bumps appear on my thighs when I calculate my chances, always imagining I have seen something suspicious. I find myself ducking, pedaling, and diving down shaded streets and alleyways, never taking a direct route home through the hoods as my nerves get the better of me. I cry inwardly for protection and imagine a host of unseen angels who ride the wind by my side as I pedal up and down to school each day.

Sometimes I speak to these angels, or sing to faithful unseen guardians that I come to realize are always at my side... I privately share personal stories with them, but when I mention them to adults or peers I draw strange looks and rolling eyes, so I begin to fold them back into to the wishful thinking department of my brain and learn to keep encounters with them to myself.

I soon realize that I am different and this seems to separate me from people even more. Even Lana doesn't have the time to know me as I come to know myself. I quickly learn that to fit in I must model the more normal behaviors of other kids my age, while at home I privately hold conversations out loud with my collection of unicorns, stuffed toys, and sometimes Shine drops in for a quick cup of tea. My imagination and empathic nature flourishes while I pretend I am one with the faeries of nature. I dance and hum to myself in our big back yard, climb high in the boughs of an apple tree or dance below the plum tree bowing low to ask the nature sprites if I may sip the early morning dew from their green leaves in the tangerine and blood orange nasturtium beds planted along the edges of our home.

SEARLE

Searle moves into our lives cautiously, and it is Lana's idea to ease him gradually into my presence. At first, he agrees to stay in our backyard barn, sleeping on a mattress outside with Lana all night and having her sneak home to her bed before I am awake. I play along pretending I don't know what he and Lana are up to as he finally moves into the third floor bedroom with Lana and makes himself useful, hammering away at the chicken coop, fixing my backyard swing set, and mowing our small patch of lawn while singing sea shanties and making pancakes for us on the weekends. He continues to shape and work our yard enthusiastically, using his in-depth knowledge of urban horticulture and propagation to create us a flourishing organic vegetable patch. He croons and whistles an array of folksongs as he works on our property, happy to have a place in the world, and his voice rises and falls on the breeze outside as I go about my chores and hang the washing on the line from our backdoor patio.

I learn he is here to stay the day when he totes his prized conga drums through the door as easily as Bard decidedly walked out of the front door of our home in the hills. Lana and her friends are treated to alternative evenings of song, dance, and political discourse as his practiced gifts of humor, song, and charm fire up our otherwise morosely quiet lifestyle. As an only child, I am included in most of these adult get-togethers and learn about things far beyond my years. It is the mid-seventies in California, and marijuana makes the rounds at the dinner table.

Lana asserts firmly that in her house this is an adult thing. If she and Searle partake, I never see them do it nor am I to speak of seeing it happen as I am told it is none of my business what the adults get up to. I watch Searle carefully, judging his right to be by my mother's side. The men in her life do not usually stay. He seems decidedly comfortable in his bid for her attention. At this point, Lana is shakily regaining control, minus Bard, who I still yearn for with all my might. Her primary concern is to re-build a social life and a carve out a career. She is also determined to modify and define her home, her rules, and her way. There is very little space for building anything cooperatively with this man five years her junior, and he, a bigger than life kind of guy, is not taking kindly to being "molded." Nevertheless, she tries and he rebels.

Searle's close extended Irish family carries with it a sordid history of alcohol abuse, domestic violence, and practiced denial. Not all of them have escaped unscathed, and he least of all. As the eldest, of five children he tells of how he had to witness drunken arguments between his parents at a young age and had to be the protector of his mother from his father's entoxicated rages as he was growing up in the family home. He joined the Navy and bought a motorcycle to be free after graduating high school, and after a bad accident where he injured his leg, he now limps slightly and uses a built-up shoe.

When disagreements erupt between Lana and Searle, he easily forgets his past and takes the upper hand in the moment, being louder, taller, and much stronger. He doesn't fight using wits and intellect like Bard, nor does he fight fair if there is any such thing, he is the biggest bully on the block. Lana innocently instigates most of their disagreements, starting with a declaration of her boundaries that he rejects outright or stubbornly refuses to stick to. The whole combination backfires each time with horrible repercussions. Over and over there is war in our home. I make myself scarce or hide in my bedroom, but many times I am caught in the crossfire right there.

I quietly observe this man, who carries me gently in his arms, clasp his big hand around Lana's throat and lift her high over his head to shake her like a ragdoll, forgetting I am in the room. I watch as he howls at her in a fury, slam her against her prized antique furniture, or break her ceramic-wares. In fearful tantrums I witness him hurl household items from three stories up standing on top of our pitched roof bellowing obscenities for all to see, while she bustles me out of the door and into the car telling me not to look. I watch him break up not only ours, but his own property, as he screams maniacally for the entire neighborhood to hear. Most times he will bare his teeth, spit, and blast his breath in close quarters at my mother's frightened face. His language is palpably foul, and the verbal abuse is beyond anything my young ears have ever heard.

Now almost halfway through the third decade of her life, Lana trembles, cringes, pleads and cries real tears for Searle to stop. He bellows for her to listen to him, crushes his hands over her pale face and quivering lips, and slams her forcibly against the hollow walls, while punching holes in doors terrifying me. Our timber house absorbs every blow like a mute witness and soon it becomes a very fearful place to be. I stop seeing energies emerge from the adults in my life, and begin to feel them in my body instead. They resonate with the long forgotten cellular memories that reside in me from birth, and just beneath my awareness they reawaken.

Before long, I become hypersensitive to any loud noises or bangs. My heart pulsates wildly in my chest, my mouth goes dry, and I always look for an exit or a place to hide, yet most times I find myself rooted to the floor unable to move. In private moments alone, I stop to wonder why my mother continues to allow him a place at her side. She has told me how people should treat people. She lobbies for the whales' right to live free lives and for women and children of the world to have equal rights, so why not us? I can tell when Lana and Searle are building up to an explosion. Subtle energies move in me, sliding down to congeal in a tight blob in my tummy. I conceal myself then, shrinking down behind walls or curtains of our home, petrified, watching and listening.

The terror happens anywhere, either out in the backyard or inside the house. When I hear them make love passionately, I assume they are fighting and my senses go into overdrive, and my mind scrambles about how to interrupt them. Sometimes, I wander upstairs, surprising them in the act, hoping to save my mother from imminent disaster. But most times, I tremble in my bed alone at night listening for the final blow that I am sure will come. My legs quiver and soul cringes, while at the same time I lean in, curious about what will happen next. I simultaneously admire and hate this man and refuse to accept him as a father figure. I worry helplessly for Lana, and at the same time I begin to inwardly reject her too. Who will protect me?

Bard has forbidden me to speak of life with my mother, thinking to protect me from being a messenger between old friends who now hate each other. I take this agreement seriously. I will not jeopardize the sacred relationship and precious time I have with my father, so I remain mute about what is really happening in my other life. Bard's home is my secret sanctuary. I stuff down the words I want to say and give him my best of smiles. Sometimes he picks up or notices my melancholic moods, yet he rarely pries, deciding I must be over-tired and he leaves me to my own thoughts never asking.

Soul Song: Benevolent, Kinetic, and Improvisatory

6-7 years–The Girl Next Door

"Tender words we spoke to one another are sealed in the secret vaults of heaven. One day like rain, they will fall to earth and grow green all over the world."

— RUMI

KINDRED SPIRITS

The first day we move onto our street, I am introduced to the neighbors. On one side of our double lot is the comfortable home of two proud, hard-working lesbians who own a hot tub and invite us to bathe in their backyard grotto anytime we like. On the other side, in the corner house, lives Lacy, a single mother and recent divorcee like Lana. Lacy has two children hanging off her apron strings. Lacy is an eclectic type, once a well-to-do housewife like my mother, she is reinventing herself as a modern dance teacher and pre-school owner still struggling to make ends meet. She has a little girl one year younger than me called Raven. Lana tells me that before she adopted me, she and my father had requested for a Native American boy and she had planned to name him Raven, but when they unexpectedly received a call that there was a little Hispanic girl in need they acquiesced and took me.

This Raven is nothing like the scary images of raven birds in fairy tales. Far from being a harbinger of death, she is chirrupy, exploratory, and fun. Raven is more than happy to have a playmate on her block. She looks a lot like my mother, with light chestnut hair, milky skin, and a pointy freckled nose. She has a younger brother called Zane, who is into little boy stuff and rarely bothers us. Raven quickly becomes my bosom buddy and kindred spirit and we see one another almost every day – on weekends and after school.

Raven and I cheerfully hang out on the corner across the street selling our parents' organic homegrown squashes, zucchinis, and pumpkins on the weekends to any passersby. We also travel side-by-side in the backseat of Lana's Volkswagen van that is headed down the coast to pick the tangy in-season olallie berries with Lana and Searle for my Lana's yummy baked olallie berry crumble, and we churn out homemade olallie berry ice cream on the back porch using an antique wooden ice cream maker.

Sometimes, we keep other neighborhood kids amused with our hula-hoops, play hopscotch with multi-colored chalk on the sidewalk, and Chinese jump rope in my driveway. However, our favorite activity by far is to bike or roller-skate around and around our block and up and down to the corner store for milk where we can't resist using some of Lana's change on the old-fashioned gumball machine. In the spring and summer, we cycle to swimming lessons at the public pool and buy bagels with lox and cream cheese from a boutique bagel shop for our parents and ourselves on the way home. In the winter, we help to decorate one another's Christmas trees, and go on trick-or-treating adventures together in the fall. In our backyard world, our parents install a secret gate between our homes. We dig a hole in the soil next to the secret gate and inside the hole we place a secret message canister for the "underground" placement of trinkets and messages. Searle creates us a grassy lid that forms the top-secret trap door where we have fun posting hidden messages for one another to find at all hours of the day and night.

Raven is the first and only one of my friends to ever witness the horror of Searle's acts of violence and physical abuse toward Lana. She sits beside me squeezing my hand, as tears shimmer in our eyes and our hearts pound in unison. My mouth turns dry as we peer out the window of my second-floor bedroom watching his hand clasp around Lana's throat as he pins her high onto the driveway fence. He screams obscenities in her face and uses his other clenched fist to smash the boards next to her head, causing splinters to fly into the air. "Searle, stop, please, I'll do whatever you want!" she cries, eyes wide with fear.

Scared to see more, Raven and I huddle together under my bed trying not to breathe. After a while, when all is quiet, Raven creeps out and whispers to me that she needs to go home now. She sneaks out of our house and runs home through the secret gate. I don't know where my mother is or if Searle has left the property. I stay in my room, forgotten until I am called out hours later for supper. Lana's eyes appear distant and sad and Searle is trying to be over-friendly to me at the table. I keep my head low and sip on my soup, secretly furious at him and worried for Lana.

Soul Song: Heraldic, Adventuresome, and Strong

7 years–Nature's Dancer

"Beauty is eternity gazing at itself in a mirror.
But you are eternity and you are the mirror."

— KHALIL GIBRAN

IN THE SIERRAS

Lana is an avid outdoor hiker and a member of the Sierra Club, a non-profit environmental organization that focuses on conservation and protection of ecosystems, that includes education, publishing, and eco-outings. She and I have the rare opportunity in the spring to holiday alone together. We are booked for our adventure soon after Lana learns that children are allowed on the trip. It is a daunting five-day trek with mules into the mountains and about twenty other outdoor enthusiasts join our journey to hike a wide loop in the Sierras near Yosemite National Park.

On the first day of the trek we are each issued a mule and instructed to look after his feeding and grooming regime. We are also taught the special rope knot to tether him to a tree. My mule's name is Jack. I love him to bits, complete with his coarse layer of hair, wiry mane, heavyset body, and a somewhat indifferent attitude!

The organizers are safety conscious and detail-oriented. We are given a list of items to carry on our backs and items the mules will carry. We are also set kitchen duty detail for the sleeping stops along the way. None of this is new to me. Lana and Searle have taken me to many communal events or camping trips where organization and volunteer service is critical. We have been to logging camps where every person is vital to the team. I am used to mucking in with the chores and camping outdoors in the cold and rain. Notably the youngest person on this particular journey, I am delighted to see a freckled boy of ten is also joining our group!

The first day is only a half-day trek as we get used to walking in our boots and pulling the mules. We hike through fields of blue, yellow, and purple wildflowers, up and down a few craggy ravines, and then into forested glades of green and gold. Crickets sing symphonies in the grass as the sun threads its way lazily through the trees and birds and squirrels squeak and chitter in the branches above as we pass. In the morning, as we break our fast, my mule Jack knocks into a hive of bees and has everyone running for cover except the heroic beekeeper, Lana, who bravely rushes to free the kicking mule from its tether with our swarthy trek leader, Andy, who runs for the rope hot on her heels. After they move the mule, we smoke the bees, to keep them calm and move the rest of the camp and campers quickly.

The second day is grueling, and the 10-year-old "Freckles" is in full swing with his routine of complaints. We only lead the mules for a short while, and then, so as not to slow down the pace, we are allowed to depart ahead with the deputy guide. On the trail, we begin to sing songs to while the hours away while the seasoned walkers, Lana included, silently bring up the rear hauling the pack mules. The elderly, the oversized, and us two kids are laughingly given the group name "Turtles" as we skip ahead on the path with lightweight backpacks on our shoulders and no mules to lead. Us Turtles are led by a Chinese-American guide named Gan who cleverly points out interesting flora and fauna along the way.

We head higher each day and stop to rest on the sides of mountains to admire the view, play and wash clothes in a deep blue lake, and pause to skip rocks against the dark mirror-like surface before hiking further into the interior. At one campsite, we wander the hills nearby to bathe in natural hot spring pools hidden high up in the rocky hills and gratefully ease our aching muscles. Nature comes alive in the North American wilderness peppering the warm breeze and winking at me from the boulders that sparkle with silver and gold mica. Mule dandruff mingles with the more delicate perfume of purple, yellow and amber wildflowers. The pine trees shade our path and occasionally drop pine cones onto our rucksacks as we move through the wilderness quietly in single file. Fields of Monarch butterflies lift their wings and flicker like celebratory carroty confetti all around us, taking advantage of the gentle afternoon breeze. We all cook and gobble down warm hearty camp-made meals and huddle around the evening fire, telling tales under the night sky as we lean against our camping packs in the dark nooks of the sheltering woods. We are meticulous about stringing up our food in well-sealed bags overhead so the California brown bears don't come by looking for easy pickings.

I make it my duty to massage all the weary adults' shoulders, including one giant Russian lady, Olga, who waxes lyrical about her life's adventures in her home country and expresses her opinions on everything in a large preponderant voice. She always requests a second massage. "Dig deeper, my girl, dig deep!" she commands as I dig my elbows and knees on her enormous shoulders. A reluctant "Freckles" performs the second round when some of the others protest that I have done enough and must rest up for the morrow. My mother and I have hardly spent a moment alone during the trek, and only connect briefly at night in our two-person pop tent after caring for Jack and finishing our chores. Freckles and I cough rhythmically at each other in code, from tent to tent, giggling to ourselves as we drive our parents insane.

The day before we are due to finalize the expedition, we prepare with our two leaders to hike over the toughest mountain pass. The way is full of switchbacks and it is a path our group leader Gan has not traveled before. The expedition separates, with Lana in the rear group with the mules, and my group "The Turtles" in the lead, in the hopes that the seasoned backpackers with the mules will catch us up at the top. Storms are frequent at this time of the year in the high Sierras. We arrive at a fork in the road just as it begins to drizzle and we don our thin-layer rain ponchos over summer t-shirts to keep out the biting breeze. No one is prepared for this sudden change of weather.

Gan leaves us huddled together against a lone juniper tree and doubles back, looking for the mule group carrying our warmer garments that was supposed to meet us at the base of the mountain. Olga places herself bullishly at the center of our seven-person huddle while Freckles and I are left shivering mercilessly on the outer edges of the group with no jackets. We mutter miserably in whispers to each other that we should be in the center since we are still children. It seems like hours before Gan returns. Everyone looks up hopefully as he jogs toward us.

"Bad news first guys," he reports once he has caught his breath.

"I couldn't get the radio to work and I traced the tracks of the others… unfortunately, rain washed their tracks away over a riverbed and I had to turn back. If we don't get over the pass before nightfall we'll have to hike back down the mountain and make a plan to camp without tents."

After scouting up the road again with one of the men in our group he returns and hauls each of us to our feet.

"I've found a way I think we can link up with the road at the base, but we'll need to move out immediately." He pauses to look at us. "You kids ready? Have you rested enough?" We nod and share some trail mix from his pack before setting out in the driving rain. We turn off the main path and stumble across wastelands of scrub and shale and after what seems an age, we finally hit the base of the mountain. Here we are able with binoculars to spot the others disappearing into the cold mists shrouding the top of the long climb. We cup our hands around our mouths and shout and wave, but they are too high to hear us as they clamber up the mountain switchbacks heading over the pass. The wind and rain whips away our desperate calls.

We are happy at least to know that we are moving in the right direction and we scramble as best we can on two legs up along the shale-strewn path, keeping a rhythmic pace set by the optimistic Gan. Halfway up, he takes off his lightweight long-sleeved shirt and puts it over my thin t-shirt under my poncho. My teeth are clacking loudly, but I don't complain. I am too busy concentrating! The extra layer doesn't do much to warm me and my lips remain blue. Gan leads us at a break-neck pace up the switchback pass. Eventually, our little Turtles team is worn out and must stop. We "Turtles" are not cut out for this pace. Several of the adults are wheezing and puffing uncontrollably. Olga complains she is going to have a heart attack. As strong as I am, the pace is fast and Freckles and I are tired.

I fidget nervously at the back of the group. I need to relieve myself and I am too embarrassed to squat out on the open shale, so I sit on a rock in an icy pool of rainwater and release my bladder. Ashamed, I hide my urine and water-soaked trousers under the long poncho and hope the rainwater washes the scent away. This soon becomes the least of my concerns, as my pants don't dry but freeze instead! Now, I shudder hopelessly as the last of the sun's rays fold into lurking lightening that licks the darkening horizon far in the distance. We hike faster to beat the twilight.

At last, in near darkness, we arrive at the summit of the narrow pass in a whining blizzard of icy wind and sleeting snow. The trek's leader Andy has hiked back to wait for us at the top and he advises us to jump one-by-one over a large slippery crevice that has broken the trail in two. The drop below is more daunting than the distance to the other side and I am wet, cold, and full of fear. Gan ties one end of a rope between us and insists on me jumping across to Andy. They shout at me to make a move, as the time is tight before it is too late for all crossings and the storm punches the mountain pass in the face. The others hold him from behind securing him as I make the leap.

We finally arrive at a base camp covered in snow and Lana rushes forward to bundle me up in dry towels in our pop tent and sleeping bags. My lips have turned indigo and I can't stop shaking, so she makes me strip out of my wet clothes, throws on some dry ones, and zips me up in my sleeping bag. Then she dives inside with me and clasps me tight to her bosom sharing her body heat. She only goes out to bring me food an hour later when I have thawed enough to stop shivering. I am not allowed out of the tent that night while she pours boiling water in a plastic camping bottle and shoves it deep into the sleeping bag to keep my toes warm.

This little lesson and adventure in survival has taught me about will-power, strength and fortitude and it has developed my trust in Lana. Even though she is a tough mom, she comes through in the end to offer warmth, adventure, and unconditional love. Searle is there to meet us at the final bend of the trail in the Sierras and takes us home.

DOLPHIN ANGELS

On a bright breezy day in Kealakekua Bay, home to the Captain Cook Monument off the Kona coast of the Big Island in Hawaii, Lana and I sail on a yacht with a crew of environmentalists looking for humpback whales along the coastline. I am aware of the strangers surrounding us on deck, and keep close to my mother, not fully trusting these odd-looking characters. Lana tows me along the same way she continues to carry emotions that weigh heavy like a solid pine cross upon her shoulders, and on this particular day she is busy losing her inhibitions through inebriation and laughter with this group of strangers.

Being the only child on the boat, I am bored.

"Laaaa-na," I plead, snatching at her hand. "Come and swim with me!"

"In a while, Sweetie," she promises while she turns her face to the sun, waving her hand gently toward the starboard ladder. "Why don't you go in alone? You know how to swim."

"But I don't want to go alone. You come with me."

"I'll come later. Right now, I'm busy." She sighs.

"No! I want you to come with me." I stamp my legs impatiently on the deck.

Finally, she excuses herself, and grabs my hand firmly, pulling me to the ladder leading down to the tempting waters below. It looks like a long way down, although in reality it is only about four or five rungs down. Ropes line the side of the boat and dip in and out of the glistening waves with the gentle rocking of the sailboat.

"Look at the pretty fish." She points at the glassy waters below. "Hurry up, I'm watching you."

"But I want you to come in with me," I whine, holding onto the top of the step ladder, fidgeting, and begging her to go in ahead of me.

"If you don't get in the water now, I'll leave you!" Lana throws up her hands in exasperation.

Disgruntled that she will not acquiesce to my demands, I venture timidly down the steps. As I enter the tourmaline waters below, I look down to see the rainbow shadows of tropical fish darting back and forth around my bare legs.

"Watch me, watch me!" I holler up at her, coughing through mouthfuls of seawater as I twirl vigorously; at the same time keeping a watchful eye on my mother, frightened she will walk off.

"Mmmhmm, I see you," she murmurs absently as she stares toward the party getting underway without her on deck. They are smoking the green stuff and opening bottles of beer, as they lounge in the hot sun listening to Bob Marley and Bob Dylan crooning over the speakers.

"Look at me Lana, I'm *doing* it!"

Then, as I begin to relax and have fun, the sea reaches up unexpectedly to pull me away from Lana and the boat. I feel cold streams flow past my legs, and storm clouds gather ominously overhead blocking out the sun. I panic while gulping down the salty seawater. "Heeeelp, I can't... get... ba-a-ack!" I gag.

The current sucks and tugs at my flesh as it bears me further away from the safety of the yacht. In less than a minute I am unable to return. Thrashing and sputtering, I glance down, as the sea becomes a living giant trying to pull me under.

Realizing I am beginning to panic, Lana clambers down the ladder and instructs me to kick and grab the rope on the side of the boat. Nevertheless, the closer I come to the rope, the swelling current seems to want to pull me under the boat. I try, but my little arms can't reach, and I soon give up letting the ocean take me where it will. Soon I am drifting a good ten yards from the side of the anchored vessel.

Lana dives into the cooling waters, but now struggles to see me over waves, which seem suddenly as large as mini mountains. She shouts over her shoulder for help as she watches me disappear into the darkening swell.

Something bumps against my leg, turning me cold with dread. I don't have any idea what it might be, but the fear of the unknown is worse than any fear I may have of what I can see. My eyes pop wide, and all I can feel is my heart racing and the salt water choking me as I fight the current that is pulling me away from safety. I wail loudly for my mother, who I catch glimpses of as she swims frantically toward me through mountainous waves, and I squeal in distress wondering if I will ever be safe again.

Lana is bobbing up and down in the waves to see where I am and she hears me let out one last terrified shriek as she sees a silver dolphin emerge by my side and turn its head into the wave. With one nudge of its beak it lifts and propels me toward her and the boat.

All the crew and passengers on the boat suddenly become aware there are dolphins swimming in the waves around us and one overzealous drunk takes a dive into the water and heads straight for me. He makes a bid to rescue me, but as he reaches me, he seems to have difficulty breathing and begins to flounder and pull me under instead. His swollen belly bumps against my legs and I fight him off me as best I can, but he is pulling me down not up! Abruptly, the waters erupt with dolphin everywhere! Dolphins swim pointedly between us, pushing him away from me and swimming right up underneath my belly to nudge me to the surface.

Soon after, a golden-haired Adonis leaps off the boat and brings me to safety. Standing in a row along the edge of the sailboat, the rest of the party dives into the undertow in desperation to be close to the wild cetaceans, but the instant they know I'm safe, the pod melts deep into the shelter of the whispering waves and disappear. Shivering uncontrollably, I am bundled onto the deck in heaps of towels and thrust into Lana's waiting arms. I do not get the chance to thank my saviors of the sea. I close my eyes in the fading sun and a vision comes forth.

Still waters run deep – in these parts at least. Turquoise sea mirrors azure sky. In a flash of sunlight and water silver dancers spin upward. Leaping, dancing, swishing, swaying, rocking, and resting in the waves... They blow, breathe, and exhale, communicating with me in steamy plumes of salty sea air. These spectacular species kiss-awake compassion, love, intuition, and humanity; gifts I receive in innocence as I fall asleep, rocked by the sailboat on our way to harbor.

Soul Song: Ragged Cacophony

7 years–In the Lion's Den

"We love because we can lose.
If there was no threat of separation,
no death to shake us to our core,
we probably wouldn't love much at all."

— DONNA LYNN HOPE

ANCESTRAL RESISTANCE

Lately, I seem to be rubbing Lana the wrong way. She has little patience to indulge my friends or me and expects us to model adult behaviors in her presence.

"What are you looking at?"

"Sometimes I wonder who you think you are?"

"The world isn't fair. Get used to it."

"Pretty is as pretty does. If you want to be treated well, then act well."

"Raven, what's that rat's nest on your head? Go home and brush your hair before coming over here."

"Be quiet, kids, this isn't a playground."

"Thea, if you want to argue with me, I'll send your friends home."

"Just get out of here. Hurry up!"

The adages, warnings, and life lessons are frequent and they are becoming more severe everyday. Before long, I rebel against my own suppression and snap

73

at my well-meaning bossy mother. All my emotions and fury for losing my father, for being in this fearful life with Searle, and living according to her strict rules and decisions for me to be more than a child bubble hotly to the surface.

I snap back at her when she challenges me or sullenly refuse to move when she tells me to. Shocked at these new reactions, Lana regularly runs to collect an antique silver hairbrush lying on the dresser in my bedroom, or the hard wooden spoon next to the stove in the kitchen. Either one cracks down like a hurricane as she smacks my backside with blazing hot strokes that sting my flesh for hours. Her hands grope determinedly as I hurl myself beneath my single brass bed in order to hide from her clawing grasp. I find myself locked in my room and stay under the bed for ages, playing with toys I have horded below, to keep myself amused, frightened that she will return. She always does, telling me to come out and eat supper, but sometimes I am too stubborn for that. I fantasize daily about resisting the adults in my life, but I know I'm still too little.

At last the day comes that I am able to stand up for myself. I dream about it the night before, when ancient Native American men hold council around a familiar campfire. One points to an image in a clearing nearby. I look over and see my small self and Lana quarrelling. As Lana moves to strike, the smaller me reaches up to grab her wrist and holds it tight. I am fierce and strong, a product of my gymnastics training and tomboy antics. Lana pushes back, but can't overpower me physically. Her eyes dilate in surprise at my sudden temerity and the image fades slowly from view.

To my surprise the exact same thing happens the following day. I play out my dream effortlessly. It is a small victory that moistens the parched seed of survival that lies dormant in my DNA. *"Rough diamond of the earth, you are your own warrior. You have your own power. You can turn dreams into reality; be polished, strong, and brave,"* the seed of survival sings as it snuggles closer to the surface ready to crack open.

BARD AND VIVIAN

My wistful expectation for my parents to come back together only begins to fade in my seventh year of life. Time shared separately with Lana and Bard is having an effect on my person hood. I am stronger now and learning to cope with separation and loneliness. At night my panic attacks subside, although I still have a fear of the world ending. Lately, Bard spends most of his time renovating and selling the homes he has bought and shares with Viv. This woman and her quirkiness are beginning to captivate us, along with her quick wit and humorous nature. Cautiously, my father invites her to join me and him on weekends when he shares time with me at his home. She is now far from the stern babysitter of my younger years. I see Viv as an archetypal geisha like one of the folkloric courtesans of ancient Japanese couture whose mesmerising kimonos knocked some men flat out. Men of our era are charmed by her lean elegant legs, alabaster skin and the waterfall of crows hair that cascades just above her waist. She is neatly styled in clogs and beautiful flowing clothes – a kimono could have easily complemented her Japanese veneer.

Her hearty laugh rings throughout Bard's home as she bakes me fun themed birthday cakes, listens avidly to my stories, or tells elaborate stories of her own. We share a bath in my father's deep blue mosaic tub and throw bath suds at one another, giggling mirthlessly as we paint ourselves with beards and mustaches. Despite her efforts to be my friend, she blows hot and cold with the weather. The hag of my nightmares and the serious unreachable babysitter I once knew can return at will.

One night, I creep down the hall in my father's home and overhear the pair arguing quietly in his living room. I listen intently, barely breathing, as Bard requests Viv to leave and return to her apartment across town. From what I can tell he is explaining to her that it is too soon for her to stay with us while I am visiting his home. She is not charmed. We have just spent a very successful and enjoyable evening together, cooking, playing games, and laughing in the bath. She demands to know what she has done to cause any harm? She wants to share fully in his life. He re-iterates as tenderly as he can that he has certain boundaries she must not jeopardize.

"If Thea tells Lana about our time together, Lana might cause trouble," he sighs worriedly. "Viv, there are legal agreements in place. Let's just wait, please, my love."

There is a stony silence and I wonder if I should rush back to bed and pretend to be asleep. Then I hear distant sobbing as she tries her best to win him over. He begs her to stop, think, and understand his position. She shoots him down with a hasty harsh ultimatum. He has pushed her too far, so she unleashes an inner avatar, akin to a lioness berating the male lion for his reluctance to share in the hunt.

"Don't you understand what I just told you?" She lashes out.

I feel the sharp warning in her voice and audibly hear the swish of her skirts as she rises to her feet down the hall. I quickly step back toward my bedroom door. "I will leave you, Bard!" she hisses at my father. "You must decide, dammit." I hear her foot stamp the floor to make her point.

Bard's heart is conflicted. I can tell from the way he desperately tries to soothe her. "Please Viv, don't do this, it isn't like that." His voice is tinged with surprise and a little fear at her outburst and ultimatum. I hastily retreat into the dark shadowed bedroom feeling awkward and conflicted myself.

In the morning, I awake to find Viv making breakfast and though the sun streams brightly into the kitchen and sparkles happily through Gina the fluffy cat's orange tail, the mood is subdued. Her eyes are downcast as she asks me what I would like to eat, and I notice Bard's eyes are almost as red-rimmed as the doves that frequent my gran's rooftop in Hawaii cooing plaintively at the dawn.

I wonder to myself if Vivian really cares for me or not.

"Avocado on English Muffin, please," I say brightly, trying to cheer up the mood.

"Okay, you know how to make the toast yourself. I'll cut the avo."

Suddenly, it seems as if she is artfully playing a pretend role. All I want is a safe haven to love and be loved in return, but now, in my father's home, I am aware of an unspoken animosity between us all that I do not fully comprehend. I wish I had not overheard their conversation.

My father does not withstand her demands for long. Vivian's passion moves swiftly to overpower him and I must learn to embrace her presence or risk losing someone dear to me. Skillfully and powerfully, the more experienced lioness takes the upper hand. She outlines her new set of house rules that we shall all abide by, and as long as we 'toe the line' there is harmony in my father's home. Now it is my turn to accept her unconditionally, treading carefully where once I felt secure as I walked barefoot and free upon the earth.

Vivian symbolically cuts and perms her hair into a wild Afro and together the pair moves to a smaller home, preparing their finances for bigger and better things.

Soul Song: Tortured, and Achingly Bright

7-8 years–Raven's Gift

"One who knows how to show and to accept kindness will be a better friend than any possession."

— SOPHOCLES

TORMENTORS

I tell myself I am Raven's great protector, valiant and strong. She is the little sister I don't have. I am with her when she is harassed by a pair of elderly African American women on the other side of our block, sitting in bathrobes on their front porch sharing a six-pack of beer. As we pass, they call out to us, screwing up their wrinkled faces to sneer at my friend, calling her "white trash" when she pauses to greet them with an innocent, "Hello."

The old woman gestures her to come closer.

"What did you say, lil' girl?" They slur and cackle at each other to some private joke.

"I said, hello Mrs." Raven calls out sweetly.

She obeys their requests to come up to their seating area by the front door of the rundown box house, despite my tug on her sleeve. I don't like the glint in their eyes; it reminds me of Searle right before he pounces on my mother.

"Say whaaat, lil' white girl?" they gaff nastily.

"Ha! You don't get to talk back to us, you hear? You little presumptive bitch!"

Without warning they both reach out and stamp their cigarette butts on one of her bare freckled shoulders, searing the flesh, hysterical and wild-eyed at their own temerity as she cries out in pain and runs away.

I shout angrily at them from the sidewalk and tell them to leave her alone. Raven dumps me with her bike and flees to her house. Our mothers are impelled later that afternoon to walk over to warn the old crones, women to women. The two of them tone down their behavior after threats of police charges, but they continue to growl obscenities at us whenever we pass.

I get so annoyed that I stick my tongue out and stand challenging them from the sidewalk while Raven begs me to come away. She has a softer nature and tells me we should just leave them be. She says they must be sad to behave this way. She is right, of course, but I can't help but taunt them from a safe distance.

On another side of our block, we are racing each other on roller-skates with Raven in the lead when, out of the blue, two young African American boys lift and throw a pair of hefty rusted chains at her head. Splitting her skull open, they see me coming and run, knowing what they have done is very wrong.

Fury rises as my belly burns with the injustice to my innocent friend. It is now becoming very dangerous for us to play outside. I bellow at them and chase them, pigtails flying behind me. They are smaller than me and lighter so they manage to split up and run away. Raven is screaming in agony on the sidewalk and manages to get up and run home with blood pouring down her face. My Latin DNA boils hotly in my veins. Why her? She is loving to all peoples. Instead of chasing them further, I pick up my friend and the evidence and we hurry to her front gate. Shocked to the core, her mother Lacy sends me straight home and bundles her daughter into a blanket in the car to take her to an emergency room for stitches. I am scared their family will decide to move away.

A SHADOW OF SHAME

Despite viewing her incredible resilience and willingness to remain open to all people despite the attacks on her fair-skinned physique, something in Raven's palpable vulnerability unravels a shadow in my own psyche.

While I am away visiting my grandmother in Hawaii, Raven gets to know another girl staying on our block. Though Raven and I attend different schools and socialize with different friends, neither of us seems to tire of the convenient companionship at home. Raven is truly my "Shine" reborn into physical reality. Whenever other friends come over to play, they end up sharing time with one of us as well, whether they like it or not.

Eventually, concerned at this circular socialization pattern, Raven's mother puts a strict ban on my attendance at her home when Raven has other friends over for play dates, but Tara is a neighbor friend so the rule doesn't apply to her. Tara lives in a small dark house where she and her sister watch cartoons all day long. Television in our home is restricted to specific channels as Lana keeps the only television in our house under lock and key in a cupboard in her bedroom. Raven's mom is much the same, preferring we play outside and do other things to keep amused. Tara and I are age-mates but she and Raven make good friends quickly.

When I realize I may be left out of this threesome, I insert myself deliberately into Raven and Tara's cartoon-watching haze, and strong arm them to join me on roller-skates or hopscotch on the sidewalk, and to march with me around the block on the circus stilts Searle has fashioned for us out of heavy pinewood planks. Raven is enraptured with the fast food TV culture indoors but Tara readily breaks the mold to play with me outside.

I can tell Raven is unhappy with me for butting into her Tara-time and something subtly shifts in the shadows, just below the surface of my awareness, and then awakens abruptly one summer morning as we begin a new play day. It stretches languidly and pulls me to my feet, whispering for me to follow its lead. I have no experience to stop it, nor do I recognize this feeling in my own being. Could it be envy? It feels as if I am losing my bosom buddy to another girl and her TV lifestyle. I head to Tara's home with a resolve to somehow end these ridiculous playdates.

I suggest a new game outdoors and give Raven the choice to play or go home. She is outnumbered and chooses not to fight so she puts on her skates to leave us. This was not a part of my plan. I don't really want to be left alone with Tara who I find tiresome and boring. Anger flares up inside me and a dark fire glints mischievously in my eyes. Upon seeing the glow in my eye, Tara's inner bully eagerly rears up to join forces with mine. Raven takes one look at us and realizes she must race away or possibly forfeit her life. She has no time to waste in shock at two friends whom she would least expect to bully her, so she hightails it out of the gate.

Of course, we cannot let her go unharmed. It is like two cats chasing down a tiny mouse. We fly after her like eagles, gathering momentum as we race down the pavement. Risking one last glance behind, Raven becomes airborne, somehow scaling her mother's six-foot high wooden fence still wearing her white and pink roller-skates. I connect just as she is about to go over and rake my claws down the soft flesh of an open shoulder that her plaid summer halter-top does not cover. When my nails connect, I hear a roaring sound as a guttural cry of triumph escapes my lips. She screams and tumbles to safety on the other side, falling with a thump into the safety of her backyard.

RAVEN'S GIFT

After realizing I also have a tormentor in me and seeing the consequence of allowing it to hurt my innocent friend, I am shocked to the core. I do not see my best friend for three long weeks. I do not dare set foot in her mother's home. My mother has, of course, been contacted, and I have been grounded from playing with others while I reflect on my actions and what I should do about them.

"What in the world were you thinking? I don't know how you think you'll make up for your terrible behavior?" Lana demands to know and sticks to the rules of not letting me play with anyone else for the time. I have no answer to her question, because the point is, I wasn't thinking! Lacy won't allow me over to even apologize and I dare not face her anyway. I decide to leave some notes in the secret canister, but the can remains untouched: unopened and unchecked.

I now know what it feels like to be a bully and I quickly decide I want no part of it. As I sit on the double-sized swing in my backyard I am overcome with feelings of remorse, boredom, and loneliness. How could I do this to my best friend? Will I ever see her again?

Then, lost in thought, I look up to see her standing therein my yard, having slipped in unnoticed through the private gate. I slow down the swing with a mixture of wonder and disbelief. She rocks back and forth on her heels showing no signs of fear, as she stands before me, a little human angel with a secret smile playing over her lips and a heartbreaking empathy in her squinty eyes. She peers up at me quizzically, observing me from under her straight-cut bangs with her little freckled nose all scrunched up, and I realize she is waiting for me to make a move. "I'm so sorry, Raven," I offer meekly. I feel so inadequate to be in her presence, as if I will crumble. My legs wobble like jeely as she beckons me into her arms and heavenly embrace.

"I know you are sorry. I know." She lifts up on her toes to whisper words of solace in my ear as tears stick to the back of my throat and I hear myself sob upon her shoulder. Comforted in her scrawny arms, I feel as if the whole world has forgiven me for some terrible sin. Here I am, her wrongdoer, and she is comforting me, while deep down I feel as if it should be the other way around!

I am not sure, but I think I hear the light whisper of a song long forgotten. The power of compassion and forgiveness are a lesson I receive humbly adding to my own life melody as "Raven's gift."

Soul Song: Measured, Clear, and Essential

8 years–A Kaleidoscope of Hope

"Logic will get you from A to Z;
imagination will get you everywhere."

— ALBERT EINSTEIN

A NEW LIFE

Black Pine Circle is a self-styled Berkeley progressive school designed to be accepting of all children no matter what their background as long as their parents are willing to afford the exorbitant fees. Here is where I find out how much I love reading. The teacher likes to bring me up in front of the class to read to everyone. Storytelling is my favorite activity. Math is my most confusing. What is the point and why is one sheep always left behind when all the other ten sheep are on the other side of the wall? Maybe, if I tell the teacher that Owen is busy pulling Amy's hair, she will forget about these sheep problems. I spend a lot of time in the hall or the principal's office, but that doesn't stop me from making the other kids laugh in their seats when I show them the trick I have learned of pushing all the blood to my head and turning purple. Though it is unusual for a child to repeat Kindergarten, it is recommended that I retake my first year of school to catch up.

The following year, I am more self-assured. I am one of the only kids at school who can cross the schoolyard and socialize with either the popular or unpopular. A growth spurt has made me one of the tallest girls in the class. I flex fluidly into a friendly athletic rivalry running against the most popular girl in the class, Zinnia. There is no track and field so we use the concrete city block to run around. Oh, how I wish I could be Zinnia! Her life seems ideal to me, like the flawless honey-gold strands of hair that fall long and straight down her back. Her hair is never out of place, while I have to braid mine or else it will be a tangled mess. She has perfectly formed bronze Wonder Girl legs and a Colgate smile that beams big and bright, with genuine happiness. She even looks pretty when she is sad. Come to think of it, I have never seen her cry.

Zinnia lives right at the top of Marin, the steepest street in Berkeley. She has a tall gorgeous older brother who all the girls in the class adore. Her conservative, older, stay-at home mom is always around to supervise our playdates and make us sandwiches on white bread for lunch. My mother is obsessed with recycling, eating what we grow, and dreams up chores for my friends and me as her idea of fun. I am so tired of it.

Playdates at Zinnia's are like a fantasy come to life! Her mother's modern home style centers on contemporary furniture and décor in muted tones of light grey, beige, cream, and white, and is spotlessly clean. On playdates, we are instructed to take off our shoes and wear white socks so the wall-to-wall white carpets don't pick up stains. The only white thing in my home is the lace curtain that hangs above our kitchen sink! Zinnia apologizes shyly for her mother's obsession, but I am enthralled and more than happy to oblige.

Shortly after my friendship with Zinnia blossoms, I begin to see auras in the big mirror in the girls' washroom. I point excitedly at the mirror and ask others if they can see the same silver outline as I? They look at me curiously then back at the mirror. Each in turn shakes their heads and give me dubious looks. After a while, Zinnia distances herself and chooses another best friend in our class who is outspoken and isn't shy around boys, and I decide to keep my "seeing things" to myself. Out on the playground, my focus turns to two girls who are labeled as "oddballs" by some of the other students. I decide to ask them if I may join them for lunch one day. Caitlin and Celina appear pleased to add a friend to their twosome and both reveal their magical qualities and robust imaginations.

The three of us form a kind of unspoken pact not to hold onto any adult-imposed doubts about the magical creatures and places that exist for us. Though they can't see the auras in the mirror, they believe I can and that is good enough. We practice telling each other stories to bring magic to life. Out of the unseen, new worlds are created. We form our tales from real-life adventures and observations in nature.

Still wary of criticism, even from these two, I decide to keep my personal relationship with my light beings a secret, and instead, I conjure up newly imagined stories out of the grass and trees, and dream up a great lioness as my totem, which Caitlin and Celina get to know as Cassiopeia. Cassiopeia becomes as real to me as my long haired pet cat, Befir. Outside the playground, extramural activities include piano playing at home and gymnastics at a warehouse down the road. I form a lifetime bond of friendship with my Italian–American home piano teacher Tess, and through her belief in my abilities and personhood, my life lights up colorfully despite the challenges at home where Lana is still under physical and verbal attack by an unapologetic Searle.

DENIZEN OF THE WOODS

One balmy spring day our classroom teachers decide to hold an end of term family picnic in Tilden a beautifully preserved wilderness park nestled in the hills above our town. It is Bard's turn to take me to the school function as Lana is working full time. The world is alive with a sense of possibility as my friends and I run through fields of wildflowers and gasp in amazement at the beauty of our surroundings. The scents of silt, soil, and wet bark from the recent rains waft redolently on the cool morning breeze.

I enjoy exploring a dry creek bed, together with Caitlin and Celina, under the dense woodland trees in the park that cast sun-dappled shadows everywhere. As we play, we imagine ourselves as our radiant self-created alter egos, the mythic self-imagined creatures: Cassiopeia, Windchester, and Samsara. Magic is under every rock and in every tree. I find myself meandering alone around puddles of rainwater feeling mysterious and otherworldly, suddenly separated from my classmates as they play games further in the woods.

As I wander past a small muddy puddle full of rainwater and leaves, I allow my senses to expand. The boys' voices ring out loudly further down the stream bed. I stare skyward toward the branches that form intricate bowers above me and oh how I wish for silence! Then, slowly, completely in the moment, I cast my gaze downward again to inspect the rain puddle, which clearly reflects the wispy clouds and sylvan trees above. As I stare, my attention is drawn to one wispy branch hanging low above the pond, and what I see resting upon it causes me to take a step forward in utter surprise, nearly getting my feet wet in the mud.

I notice a spindly little creature, black as bark, sitting on the tree branch blinking at me. Losing my balance causes me to lose control of my voice and I cry out awkwardly. Stunned that I have seen it, the miniature being is now shocked into a standing position. Its hair appears like a tangled mess of Rastafarian twigs standing up in a kind of afro-do, as its arms open up involuntarily wide under an oilskin rag of a shirt. Its enlarged eyes open in surprise and fear. At the same time, the creature's tiny mouth forms an "o" shape and it lets out a high-pitched shriek that nearly pierces my eardrums, and dives headfirst into the pond below with a visible splash and swims away beneath the yellow and brown leaves that float in the rainwater puddle. What the heck was that?

I rush to find my mates and call some of the boys who race over with sticks to slap and dig at the mud beneath the yellowed leaves, stabbing them viciously into the pond, hungry to discover what I have seen. I feel terribly responsible for this rough behavior and beg them to be more careful, but they won't; so unable to watch, I turn away in shame. Caitlin and Celina hurry to follow me as I flee the scene.

"What did you see? What did it look like?" they demand breathlessly. As we run, we all hear the sound of horses' hooves galloping high above us… where there is no trail. We stop briefly and ask each other if we all can hear the same thing and Caitlin claims it is her alter ego, Windchester, who is half-leopard half-horse.

"That creature looked like a tiny part of the tree," I exclaim breathlessly, finally filling them in once we are out of earshot of the others. "It was a tiny black twiggy thing with big round eyes and twig-like hair sticking up like this!" I gesture to my head and fan my fingers out like antlers. "It had a tattered piece of dirty cloth on its body and it was angry and frightened at being seen." Caitlin looks disappointed, as she wasn't the one to see it.

Celina gives us both a bemused sigh, "Well, maybe you just saw a frog. Are you sure it wasn't a frog?" I can see that I will not be able to convince even my best bosom buddies of what I have seen. "Maybe it was only a frog," I shrug finally. "Let's go get something to eat. Those boys are making a racket."

Inwardly, I hear myself say, *magic does exist in trees. I promise to make good. I will never forget you little one! I have seen what I have seen, but why me?*

Soul Song: Hollow, Eerie, and Grave

8 years–Supernatural Misgivings

"To him who is in fear everything rustles."

— SOPHOCLES

GHOSTLY ADVENTURES

One blustery grey morning, I struggle to find things to entertain myself indoors. I begin to pester Lana who is home for the weekend and washing dishes in the kitchen. Bored with myself, I complain loudly until Lana is moved to distraction and tells me to go play with Raven next door, forgetting there is a rule in place and Raven has a guest over. Maybe, I think to myself, Raven's mom Lacy won't be home to shoo me away. I creep up the old wooden stairs of her back porch determinedly, avoiding glancing down at the dirty old cobwebbed windowpane below that leads to the darkened basement nestled halfway beneath the earth and home. Raven and I are terrified of this place and never venture too close in our play. The kitchen door is ajar and with trepidation I call out, "Hello! Is anybody home?"

The house remains eerily silent as a feeling of impending danger creeps across my skin. I tiptoe inside Raven's house; a house I know so well, yet which suddenly seems a menacing and ominous place to be. A strong sense of foreboding lurks beside me as I tiptoe halfway up Lacy's new set of modern pinewood floating stairs at the center of the home and move quietly toward the upstairs bedrooms on the second floor to call out again. "Hello! Is anyone home?" No one answers. The air seems dank and heavy and now I am unable to contain the feeling of dread that is pulsing through every nerve ending in my body.

Get out, and get out now! Voices in my head scream at me to move. I leap into action and my body obeys. Lithe and agile, I peal down the stairs, taking two at a time, and burst out the kitchen door, and then I bound down more stairs to land unceremoniously in the backyard grass next to the basement window. Now, too worried to run all the way home, I pause and gulp mouthfuls of the cool California air and dare myself to move along the exterior basement wall to see if Raven is playing around at the front of the house. I reason dryly that going home to be bored is no option!

I steal my courage and turn alongside the house where I intend to lope down the towering three-story wall where there is another dark window staring out of a different part of the forbidden basement. However, I am startled as Raven and her friend Coral burst around the first corner of the house and knock into me so we all lose our footing and become a screaming tangle of arms and legs sprawled upon on the ground. I can see my own dread mirrored in their wide-eyed freckled faces.

"There's a ghost in the house!" Raven announces as soon as we are all on our feet, and her friend Coral nods in agreement, blonde braids bobbing on her shoulders and round grey eyes blinking wide with fear.

"Aw, come on, where's your mom? That can't be true," I scoff, stepping into my big sister role and trying my best to be the voice of reason.

I am certainly unnerved by their heavy pronouncement, but I want to appear heroic as I begin to believe myself secure now that there are three of us. More forces equal more protection, right? I think this inwardly as eternal guardians of light shift uncomfortably at my side.

"It's true. Don't go up there to the house," Raven pleads shakily. I notice she is holding Coral's hand tightly. I pout inwardly. Who is this Coral-girl anyway, to hold my best friend's hand like that? I want to hold someone's hand, too. Nonetheless, not wanting to miss out, I ignore my sudden pangs of jealousy and concentrate on Raven's nerve-wracking report...

"We heard lots of things shaking in there..." Raven's lip quivers, and she looks with trepidation toward the open back door and kitchen stairs that only moments earlier I had practically tumbled out of, trying to run from the insane icy panic that had gripped my own senses.

"But, Raven, I was just inside and nothing was moving at all. In fact, it was very silent. Maybe you felt an earthqua…" I don't have time to finish my sentence. The windows of the house are buckling and banging. We are aware that pots and pans are clanging wildly together in the kitchen above as if there is an earthquake underway, but when we look down the ground beneath our feet is not shaking.

With hearts hammering wildly, our bodies move in unison with one goal: we need to get far away from here.

"I told you!" Raven screams at me as we hightail it to her front gate. I run flatfooted behind Coral in hot pursuit of my two young friends, trying not to glance at what might be following us from behind… The wind whips and whines in my ears as we let ourselves out of Raven's front gate and run barefoot around the corner along the grey sidewalk corner and up to mine.

"Where's your mother?" I manage to gasp at Raven as we arrive and open my front gate. My house is fenced off with an aging timber fence two meters high.

"She went to the shops and left us home alone." Raven stares at me, and I notice all the color has drained from her face.

"My parents are home." I offer, and reach out a hand to steady us both. "Searle will know what to do; he's gardening in the back." I try to infuse confidence in my tone.

A sudden blast of cold air swishes above our heads as we come face-to-face with the Victorian railings that climb their way up the steep steps my mother has recently painted in varying shades of purple and blue all the way to our front door.

Our eyes are drawn upward as we hear a baleful wailing moan, deeply masculine in tone, escape from beneath Lana's unopened front door. In stunned silence, we look at each other in horror to see if everyone has heard the same thing. One glance confirms it is true and we all leap to slam the front gate behind us. Our hearts pound in time with the sounds of our bare feet slapping the sidewalk- out of time.

Gusts of warm and cold wind sigh sibilantly like a pack of banshees in my ears. We continue to pound the pavement and argue about the best route to take. The world as we know it has turned upside down, and fear nips at us with slavering jaws. We seem to run endlessly onward until I remember something Bard once taught me.

He had warned me about such situations over a lunchtime conversation we were having about spirits and ghosts while sitting in The Pirates of the Caribbean restaurant in Disneyland, on one of those intimate father-daughter trips to Southern California. He was sharing a story from when he was a young boy, where he had learned that fear could be tamed and spectral energies could be told to leave a person alone. I decide to take his advice in this moment and calm myself inwardly, commanding the shrieking banshees to disappear. "What happens to people if they can't do it?" I remember asking him. "I mean, what if you're too scared in that moment?"

"Then, it's possible for someone to go crazy," he had replied.

"What happens when someone goes crazy?"

"They lose their mind and are at the mercy of these evil spirits."

If I don't get a grip here, I may go mad!

This one thought seems scarier to me than what is happening right now. I stop for an instant and inwardly command an end to the howling. The wind dies down, almost immediately, and the screaming is silenced. Raven and Coral are still running and crying hysterically ahead of me. I reach for them and grab their blouses, excited to share my revelation, but they are gripped in a panic and pull away, running all the way to the corner store where they refuse to hear me out.

Once we arrive at the convenience store, Coral and Raven are at ease being closer to humankind. We glance back from whence we came, all of us shaken. We often come to this corner shop to buy milk or other small household supplies for our families. The African American shopkeepers know us by sight. Raven and Coral hatch a plan outside the open screen door before we go inside.

"We're going to ask to call my mom and she'll come fetch us," Raven decides.

I roll my eyes at her. "And what are you going to tell her? I bet these men here won't believe a word you say. Do you still hear the wind?"

"*Yessss!*" they cry, eyes rolling in unison. "Don't you?"

"Not anymore. It's gone because I banished it," I assert confidently. "Do you want to know how? I think you can too."

"Okay. You can go home alone then since you're so brave," Raven sniffs unhappily. "You aren't even supposed to have been with us, and I'm going to ask these men to help us." She boldly stretches out her small wiry frame, trying to match me in height.

I consider walking home by myself, but I'm not sure I am ready to face whatever awaits. The worst of it for me was at my house! What we have all heard and seen still scares me, so I hover nervously in the aisles of the convenience store while Raven and Coral march up to the sales counter and announce loudly to the stunned shopkeeper, "There's a ghost in our house and we want to use your phone to call our mum."

The two men look at one another and immediately try to hide their mirth to appear serious. The younger of the two has to bend over low to cover his mouth. Once they have recovered their composure the older of the two leans across the linoleum counter to speak.

"Say what, little one? Is there someone in your house? Where is your house?"

Uh oh. They're nodding and pointing at to me.

"Is that little girl over there with you?"

The younger man comes around the counter and grabs my arm. He leads me outside and tries to get me to point out my home, but I have been versed not to tell strangers everything about myself or where I reside.

"It's up there," I respond vaguely, pointing in the general direction.

"Well, if there's somebody in your house, I'll come and get them out if they aren't supposed to be there."

"Nooo, Sir, there's no one really there," I mumble miserably. "My friends are just scared."

After speaking to Raven and Coral for some time, the old man behind the counter makes a proactive decision. "They're clearly frightened by something, Lenny. Son, let's let them use the phone to call."

Raven's mother picks up the phone on the first ring and I can tell she is not amused. She has been searching for us everywhere since arriving home and she is about to call the police. She even went over to find Lana and found our house deserted. As punishment, she hikes down to the store to fetch us instead of driving, determined to teach us a lesson for leaving her house unlocked and the gate unlatched. She is furious. "I've been worried sick about you girls!"

"Thea, you know we have a rule about you coming over when Raven has a guest." She sighs and gives us a look of resignation. "Coral, I guess you're about ready to be taken home, huh?" Coral nods and keeps silent for most of the way back to the house.

"Thea, your parents aren't home. Do you know where they are?" I shake my head no.

"Okay, I guess you'll have to come with us then."

Internally, I am so relieved. I am terrified to go home. Once we arrive, everything seems to be in place. No pots and pans have fallen to the floor and there is warmth and the delicious aromas of Lacy cooking wafts up the stairs to Raven's bedroom. Her black cat Pepper lies in her arms purring loudly and Nutmeg their Golden Retriever is thumping his tail earnestly against the porch in happy greeting. Coral leaves and Raven refuses to speak about the incident as much as I want to compare notes.

When it comes time for me to return home, I don't want to go. I know my parents will not believe a word of what I have to tell them, and as it turns out, I am right.

Soul Song: Dissonant, Dark, and Profound

8 years–Forbidden Shadows

"For what is evil but good tortured
by its own hunger and thirst?"

— KHALIL GIBRAN

A NIGHT OF SHADOWS

Can the soul ever fall? I don't know, but sometimes I notice the soul goes quiet, becoming a solemn observer, whilst the body takes over: experiencing, grieving, growing, exploring, and falling victim to the unknown. In my eighth year of life, a shadow creeps in, slithering through the darkest night to bring fear, and far worse than ghosts to mind.

Lana and Searle are headed out for a date night and leave me to hang out at home with my favorite babysitter, Raul. I regularly play a secret game and pretend to be in deep slumber when they return. As they usually check in on me in my bed, I stretch out languidly in a somewhat exaggerated posture with my mouth wide open and my eyes rolled up under hooded lids.

Searle has adopted the unfortunate habit of lifting my eyelids to see if I am sleeping or not, but I have discovered if I roll my eyes up or around to the back it satisfies his curiosity and he believes I am truly sleeping. When Lana catches him doing this and questions him, he tells her it is safe to assume I am asleep. Inwardly, I growl at his meanness. Some part of me laughs that I have him fooled.

Bard would never do such a thing, I think to myself angrily. Lana tolerates this practice as she does most of Searle's detestable actions nowadays. I wish my Tata-dog was here to sleep on my bed and protect me.

After letting my sitter Raul go, my mother chooses not come in to check on or kiss me. Sometime later, someone else does. I dare not open my eyes and nobody lifts my lids. The shadow-man breathes heavily above me, carefully lifts the covers off my frozen form, and cautiously hikes up my nightgown. I can smell the foul alcohol in his beard, close to me. I hold my breath not daring to look. Big rough hands scrape their way across my skin and pull my panties around my knees.

As I lie in a death grip of fear, not daring to move, all my senses are switched on red alert and I find I don't need eyes to see. His sour scent is familiar as he leans above me and his head lowers to the tidy bare mound that my floral panties have covered only moments ago. I peer under half-closed lashes to see a shadowy head in the dark bend over me. As I squeeze them shut, I feel the warm tongue of the devil lick and suck at my virginal flesh. I am trapped in my body with no way out. Here, I remain paralyzed as a cold rigor mortis seizes me like a long-lost friend. Some ancient shred of knowing makes me aware that this is dangerous territory and any movement could be disastrous.

I am only eight, yet I feel sure I know his identity. His unmistakable scent betrays him when he descends on me. I lie in silence as the distasteful violation of my little body drags on for what feels like an hour, yet is probably only moments. Fear swallows me whole. As suddenly as I am defiled, I am covered again, and the shadow of a man turns away, leaving me and my room in silence. The silence of a lamb that has been slaughtered in its manger – the wall and the ceiling the only witnesses to this gruesome act.

How is it that at this moment I cannot feel my guardians? There are no angels or others to comfort my crying self. A special part of me, the part that is innocent and hopeful, drops like a silver dollar slowly sinking to the bottom of a dry well where no one will ever find it. I scream at the bottom of the well where no one can hear. My innocence has slipped away, leaving me in shambles.

SNOW WHITE

Later, I find a way to share my experience with Lana, mustering all my courage, fidgeting in the chill of the hall at the entrance to our kitchen. She stands outlined in the window with her back to me as she washes dishes. I feel weak and am ashamed to tell her what happened, but I muster the words anyway. When I mention that I think the shadowy man who has violated me is Searle, she whirls around indignantly. "What did you just say?"

I mumble something incoherent, feeling upset by her wild gaze that searches my countenance as if I have said or done something frightfully wrong. Silence yawns like a dark chasm between us, as I do not waver in my gaze. You did tell me to tell you if ever any man did this kind of thing or touched me in a place I didn't invite them to, I think wildly to myself.

Finally, she breaks the silence and scoffs at the idea of it all. "That's a big claim to make, Thea. I'm sorry, but if you can't say more than that, it was just a dream, Thee, just a dream," and she turns back to drying the dishes and staring out the window at the nondescript wintery skyline.

The way she speaks and her uncomfortable body language brokers no argument; there is no question in her flat monotone. In fact, it is a statement. When I protest behind, "But... Lana, it isn't a dream!" she becomes aggravated and breaks her silence to shoo me away. "Stop this now. What are you saying? Do you know for sure it was Searle? No. Okay then, enough. Just leave...me...alone."

I now feel guilty for upsetting her and become angry, sad, and sullen all at once with the huge injustice of it all. Nothing is going to be done. The pain is too much. I move slowly to the backdoor. Once outside I heave deep breaths of the salty sea air that has blown off the bay, fighting my tears and trying to forget the entire thing. But night must fall, and over and over I await the visitor, wondering what next?

To cleanse myself, I design my own innocent rituals of purity. I shower with the door locked now. It is the only act of self-preservation I can come up with. I train myself to fall asleep in bed, awakening in the same position as the pictures of the pure-hearted Snow White and Sleeping Beauty I have seen in my hand-illustrated storybooks. I lie resolutely on my back, feet and legs tied together and swathed in the bedclothes or tucked neatly into my long nighty with hands crossed over my breast as I pray to my collection of stuffed teddies, asking them to watch over me. The unicorns, kangaroos, walruses, and whales stare at me with glassy eyes and I believe they are listening.

I sleep like this for several months, safely, until the discomfort of lying bound this way becomes unbearable and the evil memory slowly loosens its grip. Perhaps, the man-shadow was drunk and did not know what he was doing? What more can I do, and how else can I cope? My mother's blatant denial causes me to resolve any shame. I know with every fiber of my being I am not to blame. I resolve unconsciously to melt and dissolve this fear, pain, and confusion. I attempt to divorce the shadows and live for the days ahead.

****

FAMILY OF ONE

"Why can't I have a brother or sister?" I pester Lana as she lies in recovery on the couch after an operation. She tells me her tubes have been tied and forlornly explains what that means.

"I won't be having any more children, Thea." A tear trickles down her cheek.

"But why not?" I ask, worried for her.

She shares that she has decided she must not have a baby with this man Searle who might one day take the baby away, and she would not be able to protect the child from him.

"But, what about me?" An array of emotions bombards my senses as I wonder why I have not been considered.

"At least he can never take you away, sweetie, because you have a father," comes her weak reply.

"Really?"

"Searle might try. You know how he gets when he's angry. I won't let that happen to you."

I am not impressed or relieved in the slightest. I reason inwardly that *I* am still subjected to the reign of Searle's unchecked terror and so is she. I am still traumatized by his brutish actions upon my mother and now myself. I do not feel safe. What is she thinking by saying she won't let it happen to me? I nod to appease her, as she looks deflated and tired. Deep down I feel hopeless, lost and betrayed.

At night, I have trouble sleeping and I develop an unfounded fear of death. The image of the world exploding from within keeps me up until my eyes become too heavy to fight it. I am terrified that the explosion will hurt me and I can barely breathe the deeper I look into the inferno. I am plastered to my position each night, watching and trembling under the covers. For all intents and purposes, my world has ended.

At times like this, and every birthday, I wonder where my "real parents" are. I fantasize about my birth mother gathering me in her loving arms and smiling down at me through happy tears. I imagine the fiesta we will have once we are united, and how I will forgive her for giving me away, because she probably had no money to keep me. I wonder where my birthfather is; yet oddly he doesn't feature much in my concern. I can't "picture" him at all. I begin to ask Lana for information. She shows me the papers in "Thea's Adoption File" in her bedroom. The papers say my birth mother was a beautician, and my father a factory worker. They say he had hazel-green eyes and is short and stocky of Mexican descent, and that she had brown hair and eyes and is also fairly short. *Little do I know it is Marla who has green eyes and Jose's are brown like my own.* I hunger to know more. I wish I could remember…

I begin to fantasize that I am nothing like Lana or Bard. I tell myself they are much smarter, and much taller, and therefore more capable. My adoptive parents appear to be formidable giants whose lives I have stumbled into unwittingly. At night when I am less distracted by daily activities, I hear echoes of my birth trauma whisper, "You'll never measure up… you'll never be like them."

Soul Song: Native, Cultured, Pure

9 years—Empathic Protection

"Say not, 'I have found the truth,' but rather,
'I have found a truth.' Say not, 'I have found the path of the soul.'
Say rather, 'I have met the soul walking upon my path.'"

— KHALIL GIBRAN

BAJA, CALIFORNIA

On one of many holiday trips along the desolate desert roads in the far south of the State of California, I sit in the middle seat near the front of the VW camper van watching the tumbleweeds blow across the road and sing songs with Lana and Searle to while away the journey. In the early part of the day, Searle pulls the van over and hikes off the road to relieve himself.

There, inside the bones of a dried-out desert cactus, he spies a scorpion. He carefully lifts the skeletal remains of the plant with the scorpion inside and carries it to the car to show Lana and me what we must look out for. He explains that this variety of scorpion has a sting that is potentially fatal: the smaller the scorpion, and colorless, the more potent in this part of the world, he explains. I can't believe that something so tiny is so dangerous. This is my star sign! Maybe I can also be dangerous? I think to myself.

Later, we set up camp on the edge of a lagoon. In the distance, a host of Winnebago are parked in lines in a trailer park across the sheltered lagoon. As Lana and Searle start building camp and getting supper ready on a gas-powered stove, I slip out of my shoes and run down the beach to explore the myriad of tide pools, happily gathering seashells for an art project Bard has engaged me to present to him the next time we see one another.

As I search the beach for treasures between the rocks and tidal pools, I see what appears to be the creature Searle showed me earlier. I squeal excitedly and run to drag Lana to the spot to confirm it is what I think it is. In her reluctant, obligatory way, she allows me to pull her by the hand. Once at the site, she gives it a perfunctory glance, turns on her heel, and calls back to me over her shoulder, "Scorpions don't exist on beaches, Thee, it's only a shrimp of some sort. Come on Kiddo, it's time to wash your hands and get ready for dinner." She waves at me from afar to join her with chores at the campsite. I mimic her in a falsetto under my breath, "It's only a shrimp, Thee."

I feel distressed that she dismisses my find so quickly. You didn't even look properly, I grumble angrily to myself. I'm sure it's a scorpion! I give the creature another hard look. I know what you are, I tell it silently. Now, just stay where you are!

That evening, a small crowd of campers gathers to sing and play music around our campfire. Searle is like a traveling bard and master percussionist. He and Lana have dragged a huge woven hessian basket full of cymbals, bells, and percussion instruments with them on the journey. Song, dance, and stories float on the air until late at night. I become drowsy and head to my sleeping bag that has been stretched out upon the glittering moonlit beach. I tuck myself in and I am lulled to sleep by soothing songs at the fire, and the gentle waves of the lagoon lapping on the shore nearby. I am wearing a beautiful white Guatemalan dress to bed with meticulously hand-stitched scorpions embroidered in cyan blue all along its neckline and sleeves. I snuggle deeper into the sleeping bag, gazing up at the constellations in the southern hemisphere above, feeling content and happy in the world as I slowly turn over on my pillow.

Suddenly, a sensation as hot as fire erupts on my face. I scream out loud, "Bloody murder, fire, fire!" Lana is the first to rush over with a torch as I scream and bolt upright, pointing to my face and nose to indicate where it is burning, unable to speak. Searle anticipates the cause immediately and instructs me to be very still and breathe slowly as he searches my face with keen eyes in the torchlight. Simultaneously, he reaches down another giant hand to part my hair and turn my jaw. His eyes narrow on my neck.

"Listen to me now. Thee, I want you to breathe very slowly. Turn your face to the light. This way."

"What is it, Searle?" Lana demands to know, peering worriedly over his massive shoulders.

He motions her to stand back. Then with unexpected dexterity, his big fingers clamp down and pluck a pale arthropod off my neck! He flings it forcefully into the brush near the campfire as Lana calls on our camping neighbors to run and bring ice for my rapidly swelling face. I am told to sit very still so the poison does not move too fast around my body. Lana and Searle zip their sleeping bags onto mine and we gather close to sleep together in the cold desert air. The following day my face is red and swollen, triple its normal size. I am in agony. The neighbor's ice is finished. It is time to go.

We pack up and head down the long straight road to civilization. On the way, we come upon a Mexican hitchhiker and decide to pick him up. He sits in the back of the car facing me. His eyes rest gently on my tear-stained cheeks. I have a cold towel wrapped around my head. The man cannot communicate well in English. He moves to the front of the camper van and confirms one word, "Alecran" – Scorpion in Spanish to Lana. A short time later he instructs my parents to stop the car. Hopping out, he begs my mother and Searle to wait for him as he walks off into the dry desert scrub.

"What's he doing?" Lana and Searle wonder impatiently. We take time to get out of the car to stretch. Lana wants to get me to a doctor and the city is still far from this deserted place. We swelter in the midday heat, as we have no air-conditioning in our car.

At last, the hiker returns with a big stalk of beautiful yellow flowers in his hands. He presents me with the bouquet to hold. I say, "Thank you" and catch Lana rolling her eyes in exasperation, but he shakes his head and points to his mouth.

My mother shakes her head at me. "Don't touch it, Thea; we don't know what that is. It could be poisonous."

The man nods yes, I should do it. He is asking me to eat them. Lana throws me another warning look, but I feel an intense desire to trust this man. Finally, he plucks a bud himself and sips nectar from a small tube at the base of one of the flowers. Searle starts the engine. It is his way of saying it is okay. If the man is eating them then the flowers won't harm us.

I take the stalk of flowers, holding one small bud in my hands. The first sip of nectar is ambrosia, as if I am drinking straight from the River of Life! It tastes so sweet, earthy and smooth, and all my senses lift in joy. The hitchhiker nods encouragement, a big smile upon his sun-weathered face as I begin sipping the whole gigantic bunch one at a time. In the front seat, Lana and Searle grow curious as they watch the swelling drain out of my head within half an hour. This is the time it takes to reach civilization and our friend departs with a friendly wave, requesting to be dropped off on the road just outside of town. Another human angel dropped into our midst says hello.

MEXICO

Several months pass and the scorpion sting fades from memory. Our next scheduled trip is a journey to Mexico with Searle's brother and sister-in-law as well as my maternal grandmother. We camp on unpeopled white sand beaches and celebrate Christmas unconventionally. My mother, ever the irreverent and quirky one, sticks a bushy twig in the sand at our beach campsite and decorates it with baubles she has brought from home. She stands back to admire her handiwork as the adults toast each other with Mexican Dos Equis beer and compete to see if they can ring the base of the tree with their empty bottles and large fan-shaped beach shells we collect as they wash ashore.

After Christmas, we drive up a steep hill above Mexico City, and find ourselves behind a truck overladen with boxes of ripe oranges. The going is slow and Searle rides the clutch and handbrake expertly revving the VW camper van as we lurch uphill. Suddenly, the truck swerves off the road avoiding another motorist coming the opposite direction and overturns on the edge of a cliff. Oranges tumble down the hill and poverty-stricken bystanders rush to steal crates of the juicy fruits, unconcerned that someone may be trapped within.

The cab has overturned awkwardly, pinning the driver inside. He is unconscious with a pulse and Searle rushes to see if he can pull the man to safety out of the wreckage. The cab is hanging precariously over the edge of the cliff and Searle works quickly and carefully to pry the driver out. Lana jumps into action and begins pulling our camping gear out of the back, creating a makeshift "ambulance bus" bed in the stowage area above the engine. Once reorganized, there is only room for my grandmother in the middle seats with bags piled high on her lap. I am required to squeeze into the back compartment with the injured man. Searle lifts him like a ragdoll and props him up, moaning, and bleeding inside. My mother translates and asks him questions in broken Spanish as he comes around and starts to tremble in shock. Lana rushes to snatch up blankets to keep him warm. He is mumbling feverishly for us to contact his family but there is no way to do so, and pay phones are few and far between, way down in the heart of the city.

My young eyes are fixated on the blood gushing out of a puncture wound in his thigh, soaking the shirt we have wrapped as a tourniquet around his leg. The blood seeps beyond the tourniquet onto the mat at the back of the car. I point shyly for Searle and Lana to see and they take turns trying to staunch the flow of blood to no avail. Eventually, Searle grabs a piece of clean clothing from Lana's hands and stuffs it into the wound. Finally, in desperation they ask me to kneel and hold pressure on it with all my might and not let go no matter what the man does. I climb in beside him and apply pressure. He cries out at first and then goes silent. Our car speeds off as we search for a hospital, careening through the city streets and stopping only to ask locals the way. The sky turns dark and my arms ache as I hold tight and connect with the man whose blood is seeping past the cloth under my hands.

I whisper soft words of encouragement under my breath and a calm descends around me as the panicked voices in the front of the car fade from my awareness. Strength radiates down my arms and it never occurs to me to flinch when I see the man's eyes roll back in his head. I choose to hold true to life…

I participate instinctively. Although time seems to stretch an age, we finally arrive at an emergency room where Lana tries to contact his wife. That night I curl up next to my adopted grandmother and her smelling salts in a dingy hotel bed and wonder if the man has any resemblance to my biological father, another Mexican who may look like this man we saved today.

POINT REYES

Bard and Viv get married in a private ceremony in San Francisco and move across the windy waters into an old refurbished Victorian apartment in the bustling San Francisco Polk street district. At their very informal wedding ceremony, with a monk officiating, Viv allows me the honor of being her flower girl together with her sister's daughter. Though she tries to hide it, I can feel her reluctance to include me. She makes veiled comments to her sisters and friends as she dresses and I feel further from my father than ever as he fauns over his new niece and greets adults I have never known.

On 6th Street in Berkeley, Searle's larger-than-life approach looms above all else, igniting a call in me to stand up and be more. The next hiking trip Lana organizes for me will test my will and safety to be alone with him. Lana senses my sadness at Bard's more frequent absences. Other than occupying me with summer camp and allowing my cat Befir to have kittens that I must look after and later sell, she is determined to remedy my melancholic spirit by having me spend more time with Searle. Searle truly wants to see himself as a father figure and jumps at any opportunity to redeem himself in my eyes.

We hike away down a California trail at Point Reyes, a large State-run park full of trails, campsites, and not far from home, with backpacks strapped firmly to our backs and hard, boiled lemon drops tucked snugly beneath our tongues. Lana stands next to the old VW wan at the trail head and waves a teary-eyed goodbye. As we enter the woods, she calls out one last time, saying she will meet us at the other end. I look back and see uncertainty and hope outlined in her posture as she waves. I turn my eyes forward and ignore it. We are to be gone for three days.

Once enveloped by the tall trees, the bonding time begins. We hike side-by-side along the man-made path and share mutual appreciation of the flora and fauna hiding in shrubby thickets along the edges of the trees. Searle begins singing and I eventually join in, our voices matching well, filling the coastal air, and mingling with the distant sound of the sea birds on the wing. The songs distract us from any awkward feelings we may feel alone in the other's presence. Oddly, I feel safe with Searle in this context. He appears different alone in the outdoors than he does at home. Here he is in his element. No demands or expectations are leveled at him other than physical survival and he merrily assumes the role of protector not perpetrator.

In our tent at night, he dreams up stories of outer space landings that tickle my fancy and we giggle ourselves to sleep as I nestle down in my sleeping bag and beg him to make the sound of a spaceship coming to Earth. Although he is a bit of a taskmaster, sternly forcing me to participate in chores such as wood gathering, campsite cleaning, dish washing, and rolling up the sleeping bags, it is what I am used to at home and this is a mesmerizing environment to be in, so I find I don't mind being put to the test.

On the last night of our hike, the hairs rise on the nape of my neck and a prickly sensation crawls over my skin. It is as if someone is spying on us, yet we have not met more than two people on the trail the entire time we have been in these woods. As I comb my long hair and put it in braids before sleep, I feel like we are being watched and something is waiting to pounce. I notice Searle's nervousness too as he pops in and out of our tent in the gloomy twilight of our last night in the woods when he hears a cracking sound in the bushes near our camp. I pretend to sleep as I watch him stand outside to listen intently several times an hour. When I ask him what keeps him alert, he responds vaguely, "Oh it's nothing Thee, go back to sleep. I'm just watching the fire die down." After this, the forest is quiet. In the early morning, Searle wakes me up for breakfast and then keeps pace with me as we hike side-by-side, mostly in silence.

Lana is waiting at the other end as promised, and since we are a bit late for the rendezvous, she decides to walk inland a few kilometers to meet up with us as a surprise. As she walks along the dirt track, she begins to have a similar unsettled feeling of being observed. Her brow furrows in consternation as she walks, bandana-ed head held high as her eyes dart back and forth, scanning the path ahead and seeing nothing but the blue Pacific coastline, dark green bushes, trees, and a cliff to her right. She nearly jumps out of her skin when at last Searle and I appear triumphantly around the bend and I run toward her with my hiker's pack bumping against my bum. Tears of joy and relief shine in her eyes as she embraces us and puts her seemingly insignificant concerns aside.

"I was worried about you guys! Where were you?" she gushes. "How was it?" "You got a tan!"

Searle and her share a long kiss and I look away toward the sea knowing the car is not parked far away and wishing to get this heavy pack off my hips. Lana offers to carry it but I say no. I am determined to finish this journey strong.

The following day, headline news informs the public that the park is shut down due to a murder investigation. A couple has been found savagely slashed and murdered by a knife not far from the trail where we had our family rendezvous. The killer is caught days later stowing away on a ship in the San Francisco Bay. "I knew something was wrong. Oh, I'm so glad you were safe!" Lana exclaims, hugging and kissing me fervently on the head. I have a weird feeling that Searle is responsible for our survival. No one with any sense would challenge his menacing appearance. Deep down, I now feel safer with him than I'd care to admit.

Learning of this brush with disaster teaches me to cast my awareness wider. I knew something wasn't right in the woods. I begin to hear the sound of my life, the strength of the song that comes to sing to me in dreams. I regularly forget this music in my daily life yet it is ever-present, protecting and guiding me as needed.

Soul Song: Fragmented, Muffled, and Mellow

10 years–Saying Goodbye

"Why do you go away? -So that you can come back. So that you can see the place you came from with new eyes and extra colors. And the people there you see differently, too. Coming back where you started is not the same as never leaving."

— TERRY PRATCHETT

THE OTTER

Lana has just received the exciting news that she has been offered a position as an Associate Peace Corps Director in a developing West African country: Niger. We will be moving to the capital city Niamey within the year. She is thrilled. This offer marks her potential for a long and illustrious career in government, filled with perks, money, and adventure. Her heart lusts for travel. Her formative were years spent on the move with her roving teacher-parents and younger brother, living in exotic locales, such as the Amazon in Brazil, the Virgin Islands, and all over the Continental United States of America.

A natural linguist, Lana is fluent in English, Spanish, French, Portuguese, and Italian, and from her time with my father she adds a bit of Greek, Yoruba, and Swahili to her impressive repertoire. Wishing the same for Searle and me, French tutoring is on the cards for our family almost immediately. We are headed for the Francophone world, after all, so we had better get a taste of the language.

Though the rampant abuse by Searle continues, she cannot bring herself to leave this man and we fly to Hawaii so she can marry him on the black lava shores witnessed by her mother Jan, who, though several years widowed, still works and owns a twenty-acre farm on the Kona coast above Capt. Cook and Kealakekua Bay. Searle must now become Lana's husband in order to travel with us as her dependent to Niger.

The pair cast a regal outline eclipsed by a tall Hawaiian priest with white flowing hair who chants his blessing and protection over the couple in a very small unconventional ceremonial circle blessed with the blowing of a conch shell to the North, South, East and West, but I scowl at their side. I do not feel happy about this union. My mind travels out across the water and under the sea, wondering where my dolphin companions are.

My mother wears a blue and green pantsuit with bell bottoms and Searle goes tanned and topless with white pants cinched low on his waist. I walk barefoot on the hot lava after the ceremony and surprise everyone when my feet do not burn. Secretly, I am burning away the private pain that threatens to engulf me from inside of my raw molten core.

When Bard hears I will be leaving the United States, he is devastated. Although our times together are short, and I don't see much of him, the bond is still strong between the two of us. His home is the sanctuary and safety net I crave to balance my feelings of uncertainty in my life with Lana and Searle. Bard's home is always peaceful, contained, and generally filled with creativity and fun.

My father has recently begun having shamanic dreams. They are ancestral and otherworldly in nature and he begins to share them with me. We are best friends, after all. During these encounters between souls, Bard relates that he feels time-altered as he opens himself as an adult to a world I play in on a regular basis. The odd things he tells me don't faze me; instead they fascinate me as I lean in, listening with wide-eyed intrigue. His experiences open up permission for me to also engage in exploration of the unseen and unexplained. His new understanding validates my own innate understanding and vivid dreams.

Lana and Bard have always shared their dreams with me and consider them to be important parts of life to look at, analyze, or acknowledge, but what I share with Bard are more than regular dreams. This sharing gives me a glimpse into the inner world where his soul walks when he seems faraway. I, too, walk in a world akin to his at times, and the difference between us is only the degree to which we escape.

Bard begins as any scientist would, methodically researching encounters by others similar to his own, delving into shamanic lore and seeking out teachers and indigenous elders from traditions ranging far and wide across the globe. He explains to me that Shamanism is seen not as a religion, but as a particular kind of spiritual practice that harvests energies, honors the earth, and the universal mystical laws of the cosmos. He warns me that it is ritualistic in nature and such rituals are sometimes risky to a person's sanity when that person isn't mentored appropriately. I am fascinated by his discoveries on "dreaming journeys" that he shares openly with me when I come to visit.

Bard recounts experiences in East and West Africa where he has come to touch upon what people of that vast continent know in their bones. The lore and practices that are taught to those born into recognized shamanic lineages and tribal traditions are sometimes fraught with peril and other times heal people emotionally, psychically or even physically and evoke freedom. He says we have lost sight of our own lineage in the Western world as well as many of the sacred traditions. Most Americans and Western Europeans who are re-learning the ancient ways are focused on popularizing Native American or South American herbal lore and wisdom. Bard discovers from the various teachers he seeks out or comes into contact with that the "spirit realms" are considered real and there are wise messages to be received if one opens up and allows this crossover of experience, information, and listening.

He quickly learns how to journey to different dimensions at will, that exist parallel and within our own. We have conversations about his experiences and he doesn't need to tell me not to break the confidence. It is our special time together, and I know better than to tell others, like Lana, who may think we have both gone crazy.

It is the end of summer, so Bard, Vivian, and I travel to our favorite getaway retreat in Tassajara, Big Sur, California. One night, sheltered in one of the monastery's stone chalets, perched over a gurgling mountain stream, my father creates a sacred ceremony with my solemn permission to journey to the shamanic underworld to retrieve my power animal. I learn that the power animal, in shamanic tradition, is our protector guide and matches our being. It chooses to be with us for a special time or for a lifetime and the benefit of retrieving it and embodying it, is meant to harmonize with its good intentions for our protection from physical, mental, and spiritual attacks that could be headed our way. Bard teaches me that people may have many power animals for a season of their lives, however there is usually a dominant species that tends to emerge more frequently than the rest.

Bard, being an artist, is visually oriented and does not need mind-altering drugs or plants to take him into a deep hypnotic trance. He and I lie side-by-side, touching arms and legs, and Vivian agrees to be our drummer, our link to this world, by clacking two toothbrush holders together in a rhythmic beat to assist the journey. The monastery has no electricity wired to its guest accommodations so the mood is set with a low burning oil lamp beside the bed on which we lie. I close my eyes and feel secure, tucked tightly against my father's left arm. Soon, I feel his body go rigid and begin to pulse as it twitches gently next to mine.

After what seems only a short time, he sits up abruptly gasping for air. Viv stops clacking and murmurs to me that I should remain still while he kneels beside me cupping his hands either side of his mouth, blowing heated breath into my torso, my chest, and the crown of my head. I feel as if a warm golden liquid is filling my body, infusing me with a euphoric sense of wellbeing. The sensation swirls throughout my body and deep inside of me. I feel magically blessed and wonderful.

"What did you find down there?" Viv and I chorus in mutual curiosity, anxious to hear his story, and captivated by the wide-eyed wonder shining on his face.

"It was a river otter, as tall as a man," he recalls, now kneeling on the edge of the bed, cocking his head thoughtfully as he looks at me. "It showed itself twice and I thought it might be a serpent as it was undulating in and out of the rippling pond before me, but I didn't feel fear so I waited until it emerged from the pool to stand on the bank. It was as tall as me! As I greeted the otter-being, it embraced me and I brought it up to the surface of this world." He turns to me, smiling triumphantly, "Thea, it lives in you now."

Oddly, though I keep this magical being a secret, in the days that follow people at the Zen Center start to tell me how much like an otter I appear, swimming in and out of the mountain streams, sliding down well-worn mossy waterfalls into rocky emerald pools and bobbing to the surface. I feel the otter in me. I play, dive, twist and turn, and am fearless and shining, dipping my long dark hair underwater, emerging into the sunshine sleek and smooth. As we drive home through the quaint tree-lined streets in the artist's town of Carmel, California, my father stops the car suddenly and ducks into a jewelry store where he miraculously reappears with a golden chain on which a tiny golden otter holds a pearl between its paws and dangles delicately. He places it ceremoniously around my neck. This is to be my new amulet of protection. How beautiful it is! I feel the otter spirit turn over gracefully inside of me.

I feel blessed. I'm suddenly a little shaman-girl initiated and wandering the dream time of this world, and Bard and Mother Nature have chosen me! The lens of my perception has widened to include much more than the visible. I know this is a solemn occasion. It is also the first piece of gold I own.

We all return to my father's home sunburned; however, Vivian's back is on fire from too much time on our last day in the hot California sun. After taking a shower and changing into pajamas, I am drawn to my father's room where I find him massaging a soothing balm on Viv's skin to soothe her burns while she wriggles in pain on the bed and cries out for him to stop. I meekly ask if I may try. My father nods, only too glad to be relieved of this duty and hands me the tube of gel. I climb up on the high bed and kneel next to her gently touching her shoulders. She relaxes and her breathing eases almost immediately.

"Ah, Thea," she enthuses, "You have a healer's hands! Bard, did you know she has healing hands?" I feel my heart stop and flutter open in this moment. She is speaking directly to my purpose to tend and heal...*You must tend, nourish, validate*...The whisper of the Light within is strong this night. Her rigid exterior cracks open, just this once, as I lay my tingling hands gently upon her taught red skin.

This rare tenderness between the two girls he loves clutches Bard in his heart. He reaches out to me and asks for a hug. As I come in to his embrace, he chooses to shower every ounce of love he possesses upon me. I hear him heave huge wracking sobs for our spirits being torn asunder. We won't see one another for almost a year as I am headed to Africa and he must stay behind. His sobbing pierces my heart. It is the first time he has ever shown me the depths of the way my life touches his.

At the age of ten, I don't know what to do except return the embrace and be a strong container for his giving. The presence of my father's arms, his tears without shame, are far more precious to me as his daughter than he will ever comprehend. No matter what happens in the future, I will always keep this love as his greatest gift. I feel the river otter dancing playfully inside of me as I sink into his arms, unaware that events will cause me to cry for this moment a hundred thousand times in the not-so-distant future.

Soul Song: Imposing, Wild, and Exhilarant

10-11 years–Homecoming

"Listen to your heart. It knows all things because it came from the soul of the World, and it will one day return there."

— PAULO COELHO

NEW EXPERIENCES

Lana, Searle, and I rise to leave early in the morning, some day in the month of September 1981. My prolonged farewell to my long haired tabby cat Befir is far harder than the goodbye to the scary old house. I am not attached to the memories and moaning ghosts of this place and I long to be away from all that on this great new adventure. Raven, with her mother and brother, are up at the crack of dawn to wave goodbye from their back porch. This close friendship has been an enriching experience, and all the special moments we shared, I must now leave behind. As she fades from view, I eagerly anticipate the excitement of travel, and somewhere deep down I feel something tapping on the border of my Soul. It is an ancient yet indescribable feeling, as if an elder is tapping his walking stick on my bones and murmuring, "Arise Thea, arise and walk to your home." I listen and wait for the unknown.

Circling in the airplane above shiny tin roofs scattered amongst the burning sands below, I point and turn to ask my mother, "Is this where we're going to live?" She shakes her head in disbelief, her thoughts far away in her distant memories of Nigeria. "I don't know, it could be..." she murmurs absently.

We are squeezed on a tight smelly flight from the burgeoning metropolis of Dakar, Senegal, on the far Western shores of the vast African continent where we have just spent a few muggy days acclimatizing.

"Lana?"

"Hmm?" She looks over at me and suddenly registers my question.

"No, Thee," comes her quick reply. "I don't think this is it. Niamey is much bigger. This must be another collection stop on our way."

As it turns out, she is right; we are stopping in Bamako, Mali on route. More passengers swarm onto the already stuffed plane along with a scraggly goat that is allowed inside, bleating and crying the whole way. Sour milk and the pungent odor of nerves and perspiration waft past our noses and are sucked into the chilly air-conditioning flowing throughout the cabin.

Eventually, the captain speaks in French over the loud speaker. "Next stop Niamey! We will arrive at our final destination in the next ten minutes... please fasten your seatbelts." The looks of nervous anticipation shared between my mother and stepfather gives me goose bumps. This is it, our new home in the desert. I can't help but feel a wave of excitement and adventure rush through my body.

Arriving to the dry heat and the jostling of porters, beggars, and pick-pockets, thrusts me into the harsh reality of life in a third world country with a jolt. The stench of feces and urine from the open sewers hangs heavy in the air. Beat-up old taxis and cars line the exit of the small grimy airport. There is a need to stay close, and for the first time I am aware of the fact that my skin tone is distinctly different and noticed by the masses.

The American envoy from Peace Corps meets and greets us, and his driver bundles us into his white Government car against a press of sunbaked bodies jostling for a ride or a bribe. I do not have time to process it all while I follow my parents into the big white 4x4, absorbing everything and my spirit keeps singing, "Africa, I'm here and I love you!"

Our first stop, before being taken to our semi-furnished home, is the Grand Marché. We are told there is nothing in the house save a few emergency items, such as some cutlery and a bowl or two. The Grand Marché is an enormous sprawling marketplace full of the smell of dead fish and fermenting fruits. Pickpockets and beggars line the entrance, and easily follow our light skins and "exotic" hair throughout the makeshift stalls. We need fresh vegetables and fruit and a few other things the vendors are selling, but we are warned not to buy lettuce or anything without a protective skin, since it may be contaminated by dirty river water.

Searle becomes an attraction in the Marché, towering above everyone else like a gladiator in the dusty sun. His first prerogative is to buy a big basket woven wide-brimmed hat, which makes him stand out even more!

Lana has shared the history of Niger that she learnt in the government halls of D.C. while on a briefing for the job she is to undertake. It is one of the poorest countries in Africa, previously under French rule and occupied from 1900 to 1960. Its nationals have a high rate of mortality, eking out a living under militant governmental regimes and Muslim sharia law living as a suppressed collective of ethnic peoples from various backgrounds.

From 1960 up to now there have been several attempted coup d'états and many of Niger's presidents have come and gone through military ousts against one another. It is a challenging place to inhabit, with many generations and tribes born into slavery and bondage to their own race. The main ethnic groups, with exotic names my mother has me pronounce aloud to her in the car, are all represented in an array of colorful dress styles, rolling jaundiced eyes at us or flashing white teeth set in pink or blackened gums, as we travel along the dirty streets. Melanin ranges from burnt umber to deep mahogany and gradients of ebony.

The Muslim West African Hausa-Fulani, Djerma, Songhai, and Kanuri squat or stand with baskets of food or tea wares on their heads, colorful shiny robes and wraps draped expertly over their rich brown skin. They lead fairly sedentary lives in agrarian villages and the capitol is teeming with their flocks of sheep, camels or cattle. Men hold hands with other men in kinship as they walk slowly in the late afternoon sun, embroiled in deep conversations down the wide earth-packed walkways and treacherous sewers that line the tarmac. There are no sidewalks here. I am told holding hands is considered traditional and appropriate and does not signify a sexually inclined preference to one another.

Our guide gestures with a nod, "Over yonder, you will see the lighter-skinned Tuareg, Tub and Diffa Arabs leading camels out of town." I look out the dusty window and see women covered from head to toe in swathes of indigo. These tribes are known to keep slaves and wander the deserts and fringes of organized society not mixing much with other groups. They are traders and merchants of the Old Way. I am told to avert my eyes and not look directly at them or they could take offense. They do not like cameras that they say steal a part of the soul. I am warned that should I stare innocently into their eyes the men may see me as a wife and claim me. Swords are concealed in their garb. I steal quick glances at their dark smoldering eyes under sun-faded blue turbans and secretly wish to be stolen away. The women sport beautiful hand-wrought silver bangles on their wrists, geometric patterned earrings dangle heavily against slender brown necklines, and their fingers are full of intricately carved silver.

In the first two days of living in Niger, and recovering from the long trip, we are trundled off to the Sahel, an inner region of sandy Saharan desert lands, to open a stagier house. *(West African lingo for a Peace Corps hostel.) My mother must make her first appearance and speech as an Associate Director of Peace Corps, speaking in two languages: French and English. We arrive at the event, which is being staged in a hotel in Agadez, Niger's original desert capitol, and I swim and play in the slimy green pool, unfinished and rocky at the bottom. I enjoy organically grown roasted peanut snacks and sweet orange soda in glass bottles imported from France.

That night as I head to our room, I discover someone has left the outside porch light on with the door ajar and there are thousands of grasshoppers and giant cockroaches crawling all over the walls of our room. I scream and cause mayhem at the end of my mother's speech, running, slipping, falling, and shrieking as the insects jump into my hair and onto my clothing. Lana and Searle race to my rescue and try their best to swat at the swarm of bugs, but there are too many, and finally, exhausted from the excitement, we turn out the lights. Lana and Searle work swiftly to tuck my quivering body under white sheets, head, toes and all. The "beasts" stick themselves to the mosquito netting, jump on top of us, and cling ferociously to the walls. I can hear them clicking and buzzing all night long. The only thing to do now is to try sleep with them jumping on my linens. In the morning, almost all of them have disappeared and I have survived. Africa welcomes me with a feast all her own!

HARDSHIPS ABROAD

Back in the capital city Niamey, Lana hastily enrolls me in a French-run international school, Coeur de la Fontaine. I can barely speak a word of the language, except a few phrases and words learned in a few weeks of tutoring in Berkeley, California before coming here. *"Je ne comprends pas"* becomes my favorite phrase, meaning, I don't understand. Needless to say, I do learn to read body language fast! I am the tallest girl in my class and the most developed, already blessed with budding breasts, a trim waist, and rounded hips. I am singled out immediately and labeled by the students as a dumb mute. I am teased, tormented, and laughed at by the French-speaking students on a daily basis. Not only are my peers a challenge, but also, I must endure three reprobate teachers in succession who make my learning and daily dose of ridicule even harder to bear.

The first teacher is excessively rude to the students, especially a small French waif who looks like a European street urchin in his over-sized white starched shirt and khaki trousers hanging off an emaciated frame. I watch his dark eyes widen as she bellows like a buffalo getting ready to stampede, and raps her metal ruler impatiently on the hardwood desk, where she presides at least two steps above on a raised dais in front of the class, constantly scolding us all for unfinished homework. After bellowing for thirty minutes and wringing her thick white hands in exasperation, she jumps up angrily and unpredictably whacks the boy next to me several times with his loaned stack of hardcover books.

I am shocked at the way she treats him. I reach out under our double desk and touch his wrist softly. He brushes me aside and holds his other hand up to his reddening cheek, not daring to face her. But she insists he hears her and looks. As he does so she performs the act of hitting him in the face with the books three times in succession. The next day she moves me away from the dark-haired boy and creates a buddy system, bullishly insisting I change seats daily to be babysat by the other kids as if I have a disability. This further reinforces what I am sure they are already are convinced of:

that I am a simpleton. Fortunately, she never dares to lambast me personally, and soon enough we are informed that "the beast," as we call her at home, has been sent out of the country due to mental collapse.

The second teacher is self-contained, anorexic, authoritarian, and austere, but has way too much ground to catch up due to her predecessor's mistakes along with a handful of mistrustful students who have begun to lose respect for authority. She doesn't last long. I don't know where she has gone, but one morning I find a third teacher in the chair at the front of the room.

This one is heavyset and matronly and speaks haltingly to me in English. Unfortunately, she has little time to catch me up on all I have missed. She has a jovial nature, but is more interested in proving herself to the faculty than in my problems in the classroom. She hasn't long to go before the term ends.

The headmaster of the school is chauvinistic, short and brutish. One day I watch him reprimanding two boys in the schoolyard. The pair are notoriously rambunctious. The boys get themselves in trouble by kicking a soccer ball into a long line of glass windows by mistake. Mortified, they don't know what to do, so stand there, looking at the glass and pointing fingers at each other until he is called to decide their fate.

The headmaster stalks across the yard with a murderous look on his craggy face, unhappy that he has had to be called out of his air-conditioned office. He stomps up to the boys and grabs each one by the ear. Bellowing once or twice in abject red-faced fury and spittle flying out through clenched teeth, he hauls both boys' heads back and crushes their skulls together without warning. After this, he marches off without looking back as they drop to their knees in the dirt. One of the boys falls flat on his face into the sand where he convulses and lies unconscious. The other one holds his head in his hands and moans for a long time. The teachers move in to assist only when the Principal has vanished from sight. I am horrified! This would never happen in my school in America.

When Lana hears of this incident, she makes an appointment to berate the man in French, but he waves her away in disgust that any woman could dare to challenge his authority and warns her he can expel me in an instant. She realizes I could end up being punished for talking to her so her next move is to send Searle in with my African home tutor as his translator. The headmaster snorts derisively at their attempt to speak French and quickly dismisses them both from his office. He thinks he is better than any African or American for that matter, and uses this to his advantage, belittling any of their half-baked attempts to correct his offensive behavior.

Making my way to school everyday is a mission. Sometimes I hitch a ride with my mother on her way to work, or Searle chauffeurs me when his car actually works, but more frequently than not, a taxi man picks me up and drops me home. The Nigerien taxi driver comes from the commercially driven Hausa tribe and he is paid monthly by Lana to return me directly home without stopping for other customers. Time and again he breaks the contract, and instead, we tour the sandy city in his sweltering car blaring the local music and picking up all types of local passengers to line his pockets further. When Lana eventually finds out, she changes the taxi man, but before long the cycle starts over again with the next.

Finally, run down and suffering mentally and emotionally, I become physically ill with various flus, stomach viruses, and other unknown bacterial infections. I struggle to wake up in the morning as my nights are consumed with listening to mosquitos whine haunting melodies in my eardrums and thumb-sized cockroaches clicking and scuttling across the floor of my bathroom. I don't dare get up to use the toilet. Childishly, I stuff every crack in the bathroom tiles with paper toweling and masking tape in the hopes that I will starve these buggers in their holes. It doesn't help. I still hear crunching noises at night. When I dare to turn on the light and peek into the bathroom on tiptoes, I find I am only feeding the infuriating little critters. They have eaten right through the tape and paper!

I miss my father, my friends, and my cat, Befir. In the mornings, Searle and Lana revert to the unkind tactic of dumping ice water from a glass onto my face when I refuse to rise, insisting they mean business in getting me to school. When I complain, Lana coldly offers me to attend the Niamey Government School in our neighborhood, where I may be the only white person and am unable to speak any of the three West African languages spoken there. I consider it for two days, but I chicken out when I see the way the neighbors sneer at us and throw their kitchen slops and grey water over our compound wall just outside my bedroom window to spite us as being from a higher income bracket and light skinned.

Subconsciously weighing my options, I am aware that adding racism and ignorance to my struggle will not help my current situation, and my apprehension stops me from choosing this path. I continue to endure the

French School, where I am bullied on a regular basis, and lured by crafty bored European students, who entertain themselves by locking me in the toilet stalls and laughing hysterically when I turn up late after class.

Tensions in our home are mounting. Searle becomes a ticking time bomb in the making. Lana has all the limelight and prestige in our small expatriate community, and in our first year in Niger he is a stay-at-home husband. He is no linguist and he is not a seasoned African traveler either. This experience is as new for him as it is for me. He takes it in his stride as best he can, but feels lost and inadequate at the best of times. None of us fits in with the rest of the American community. We belong to the US Peace Corps family of diplomats whilst other expat American families belong to the US Army or Embassy and seem to have an unspoken distain for the liberal-minded Peace Corp community. They have big fancy homes and extra privileges while we eek out our existence closely on par with the locals. This means even though the home we have found in the government budget has a swimming pool, we aren't permitted to fill it.

Electricity goes out for days on end and we make do without a generator and light, using candles, kerosene lamps, and torches. Once, an undereducated worker mistakenly dumps DDT in the main water supply and our sprawling desert town doesn't have fresh water for weeks. There is a mad dash to the supermarkets where all the bottled mineral water is bought up on the first day. We quickly make a plan and start boiling filtered drinking water in the kitchen and hording ice-cold filtered water in huge clay vats next to our showers in the event of a shortage. We shower using big tin mugs of the water to wash off the soap and shampoo.

There are some perks.

In the first few months of arrival, an au pair is hired who comes to sit with me in the afternoons. Her name is Djemila, meaning beautiful one. Her smile lights up my loneliness. Djemila and I sit side-by-side and draw colorful pictures together. I try to make heads and tails of my French school homework with a male Nigerien tutor who barely grasps the concepts himself, while Djemila amuses herself on the couch humming softly and drawing elaborate and vibrant quilts of color for me with my felt-tip pens on blank sheets of paper.

Several times, the door in the dark hallway slams shut by itself and the waterspout switches itself on at the back. This is disconcerting and causes the house staff to startle, but is nothing new to me. Djemila, nonetheless, is convinced the house is bewitched and finally leaves my mother's employ due to her own insurmountable superstitions. I am very sad to see her go. She is my one friend and my link to Nigerien society. If she had only waited long enough, she would have been a part of our move to a nicer home.

The new place boasts a traditional tiled and covered entrance patio and a cool dark lounge with no hallways and zero ghosts. Local musicians that Searle befriends occasion the patio on weekends to play traditional music and dance in traditional tribal circles with us late into the night. Lana isn't always keen on having these strangers at our home. I can tell by the way she hangs back and insists that no one come inside the house during these front yard jam sessions, and we serve food and drink on the walls of the patio. We don't have a guest toilet so they must use my mother's en-suite bathroom and are escorted one by one if the need arises.

Too exhausted from her long hot office job, Lana hits gold when she hires a "houseboy" from the neighboring coastal country of Togo. The thirty-something Dramane, with his broad smile and round face, knows how to bake French butter croissants with soft chewy centers and crispy flaky exteriors; he cleans and sings songs in our kitchen, and brings his whole heart and soul into every task, caring very much for me. Prior to his hiring, there are other workers who have tried out for the position; however, none are as honest, qualified or caring as the big-bellied Dramane.

Fridays are spent at the American Recreation Centre; a hired outdoor space with huge gardens, warehouse kitchen, big covered eating patio, and pool. Here, I practice my gymnastics on the enormous open lawns and my diving technique on the small diving board in the small pool next to where we watch movies in English or subtitles on a big screen using a projector on movie nights. I meet other American kids here, and one evening, I find the cutest little wounded hedgehog and lovingly nurse it back to health as some boys with sticks have injured one of its little legs.

TRIBAL MURMURINGS

Tribalism in West Africa is rife. Everyone is superstitious. Voodoo spells are par for the course. People eat cats and perform rituals in the night against their neighbors. Most believe in spirits and possession. Our neighbors don't like our skin color and our perceived affluence. We need to protect our cat, Basho, who prowls everywhere in the night. My mother finds a leather cowrie shell pendant pouch at the market, rolls up a tiny Sanskrit scroll inside, and ties it around the neck of our cat. No one touches him now. She laughs at her genius!

My father, Bard, halfway around the world, begins to believe in protection through a different means. He tells me he is in the midst of a spiritual awakening and attributes his latent abilities of time travelling to an initiation he had years ago while we were in East Africa. Now a mostly self-taught student of shamanic lore, he readily shares his experiences over our monthly telephone conversations. One day, a gift arrives from my mysterious father through the post and with the gift comes a story. I am enchanted!

My father is wandering down to his department in the lower halls of the University of California at Berkeley, when a youthful looking Native American man, tribally dressed, and out of context in one of the long hallways of the university stops to greet him. The handsome man reaches out and grabs my father's forearm firmly and presses a silver amulet into his palm. The man tells him a story about fleeing from a giant yeti in the northlands. As he touches my father his visions are transmitted through pictures to Bard telepathically.

Bard gets the impression of a giant primate humanoid, with shaggy hair that keeps steady pace with the car the man of the First Peoples is escaping in. The man remarks that, "The Eternal Mother gave me this amulet." And Bard notices how he had it in the car with him and believes it protected him from the Yeti. He'd held onto it tightly throughout his ordeal and it had saved his life not once but twice.

"Your daughter will need this," he murmurs cryptically yet with an urgent sincerity. "Give it to her." A stunned Bard nods in acquiescence.

"I will do so, but what..."

The man shakes his head at Bard sternly. Shushing him and brokering no argument, he sprints away around the corner. Upon gathering his wits, Bard moves quickly after him in the same direction, but when he peers around the corridor, he finds no trace of the brave. The talisman remains behind, a real piece of proof in his hand so he finds a leather thong for it and quickly sends it off to me.

Soul Song: Tumultuous Longing

11 years–Life in the Sahel

"God takes everyone he loves through a desert...it is his cure for our wandering hearts, restlessly searching for a new Eden...the protective love of the Shepherd gives me courage to face the interior journey."

— PAUL E. MILLER

INTO THE SAHARA

For many months, we do not have air-conditioning switched on. The heat becomes so intense that I can no longer concentrate on my schoolwork in the afternoons and lie listless in bed under a mosquito net with wet sheets on top of me. We swelter in temperatures of 48°C/120° F. Finally, Lana has air conditioning sanctioned and installed.

We live in a neighborhood without tarred roads. It is a collection of homes with two to three-meter high walls that shelter a series of red Saharan mud and daub style compounds, some with Tuareg guards standing outside. It is well known that if the Tuareg find a prowler on the property, they kill the person then and there. We are told that one American government employee awakened one morning to find her guard grinning proudly at her door with the head of a thief in his hand.

Lana piles me into the car every month, fearing to leave me alone with Searle and possible altercations at the French school. She realizes that there is no way I could miss anything worthwhile since the schoolteachers there have long since decided to fail me. Traveling out of town into the hot Sahara sands with my mother becomes a ritual salvation every other month. It is her duty to visit Peace Corps Volunteers (PCVs) under her watch in far-flung villages who are teaching the locals Nigerian village kids and adults English, math, agriculture, and various other subjects using foreign aid money to do so.

Lana always carts a big cooler box loaded with as many hard-to-get commodities as she can carry, and gifts them to the lonely Peace Corps volunteers who host us. They must live without the basics of clean running water or electricity on par with the villagers in the small agrarian towns in the middle of nowhere. Butter, soap, hair products, fruits, vegetables, and toilet paper are stuffed into every corner of my mother's bags. American magazines, letters from home, notes of encouragement from fellow volunteers, and pots and pans are always gratefully received and coveted. Having been a PCV in Nigeria year ago, my mother knows how much they will appreciate these things and having them will soften any news she must convey from their bosses. One volunteer in the furthest reaches of the desert confides that she has resorted to using the last of her American magazines as toilet paper when she runs out.

Desperate for any excuse to get away from the French school Coeur de la Fontaine, which I fervently consider is the bane of my existence, I leap at the opportunity to travel with my mother and visit these remote dwellings in the desert. Travel times are carefully calculated as wind and weather reports are crucial for navigating the dirt tracks that link distant towns and villages to one another and the capital. We must travel when the Harmattan winds aren't blowing too hard, otherwise the roads will vanish before us in a haze of red sand and dust.

The tall handsome Hama, our Tamasheq* driver, knows how to handle the white government issued Toyota Land Cruiser expertly and traverses the disappearing desert roads with finesse. As we drive on, the Harmattan winds blow sand into every small crevice of the car, and we find ourselves putting on bandannas and head shawls like foreign Bedouins to keep out the dust and grime.

---

* Tamasheq Tuaregs - a small group of nomads that raises livestock such as goats, donkeys, cattle and camels for subsistence and trade in the Sahara Desert.

Hama falls for me and offers my mother camels for my hand in marriage more than once when I am only 11 years of age! I am secretly flattered. Smitten by his intense glances in my direction, I smile demurely out the window as he peers at me frequently in the car's rearview mirror. My mother snorts wryly in her seat next to him and tells him to keep his eyes on the road. Coping has become survival and I turn into a recluse, left alone watching the other children play during the class breaks on the school grounds but, in these remote villages I am the daughter of a prestigious government agent. I am tanned and slim with a flat tummy and lean muscular arms. Budding breasts are stuffed tight into a variety of African-tailored sundresses, and my head is crowned with sun-streaked braids of thick Spanish hair. I feel intimately connected with these tribes people.

Though their women folk are tattooed at a young age and play subservient roles, I witness a simple freedom in the women's swaying gait. I pause to admire the fierce strength that lights up perceptive kohl eyes that miss nothing. Their pride is bound and coiled within their traditions and elaborate hair-dos hidden beneath indigo veils. Jewelry woven into their hair and dark blue, black or red tattoos that adorn their perfect bodies celebrates their individual status.

The Sahel takes its toll, sandblasting these tawny skinned women, who are expected to keep bearing children year after year, looking after their brood and carrying pots, firewood, and household goods as they hike across the burning sands for kilometers with babies on their backs, dragging tired donkeys and children behind the long caravan train. Alone, they soldier on while their men ride ahead together or alone astride the camels they all rely upon for their survival.

These women illustrate to me the epitome of how a human spirit may thrive even under extreme circumstance and hardship. They are warrior women in their own right, perhaps not fully empowered yet they subtly claim respect and status in their own way. The men grow proud at the amount of beautiful strong wives they have and the quantity and quality of the camels in their train. A desert woman is enduring and weathered. She lingers in the wind, letting it blow away the longing for an oasis of love to slacken her thirst on cold winter nights beneath the radiance of distant star clusters. Her beauty remains even as she ages early in the dry and harsh conditions.

In a mud and daub town to the north of the capital I find myself brazenly studying one old Tamasheq woman as she rests her tired bones in the shade of a compound wall. Her wry mouth is uncovered, though a cloth veil loosely falls about her head and shoulders. In the shadows, her lips curve ruefully upward; top bare, while her lower half is covered in a ragged and worn dyed-cloth with masses of silver jewelry decorating even the ankles of her outstretched limbs. She lifts her chin seeing me watching and milky grey-green eyes flash almost angrily in my direction. In sudden irritation, she flips one long sagging breast over her right shoulder and tucks the other behind an ear in defiance of the dust, heat, and flies. I quickly avert my eyes.

It is in the desert, tasting exotic recipes, learning how to build adobe ovens for baking bread and millet cakes, seeing and hearing about the process of soil erosion and importance of clean water and waste disposal, that I learn the importance of teamwork. I am impacted by the culture and the way it sculpts society. I learn through direct experience and observation.

I see firsthand how religion carves into society. The belief system in Niger revolves around the Koran, yet I notice that it alone cannot penetrate a people's superstition, their belief in magic, oral traditions or medicines of the Earth so long ingrained in their past. The people here blend religion with traditions far older than their grandparents. The religion of the Earth is poignantly compelling to those who face death on a daily basis. They live by the rules of the state, the rules of sharia law, but more often than not they fall back to the rules of the land.

Mosquito nets are a must for survival everywhere we go. Malaria is rampant, and before long Searle suffers a near fatal attack of cerebral malaria. I find it funny that a small vulnerable female insect is the one to lay him in hospital for such a great length of time. What do we call this? Karma. I dare not share my inward thoughts with Lana, who is currently occupied with saving his life, hassling the hospital officials, bringing him clean bedding and water every day. Lana keeps mosquito repellent with her everywhere now and we ingest anti-malarial tablets daily. This life-education is more valuable to me in understanding the world than the rote learning I receive at the hands of the French expatriates.

As I squat for my ablutions over latrines where snakeskins dangle from dark pits, and cockroaches run rampant; or when I sleep in pitch black homes with windows without glass, open to the night air and the bats that swoop in and out overhead, I am overcome with a new sense of appreciation for life itself. This is not the appreciation of my American lifestyle, where I have enjoyed the creature comforts of a perfect temperature and no bugs. Instead, I have cause to lean into the rhythm of Africa and her magnetic pull. Nigerien culture begins to tug at my artistic sensibilities. Despite my light skin and upbringing, I share something unknown with this land. I feel a part of the sand and the music. Africa welcomes me spiritually and my body sways easily in time with her dancers. I am drawn to the camels that smile craftily, ready to spit or smack their lips in my direction, and the distant stars sprinkled like sand in the indigo skies overhead.

Soul Song: Tender, Provocative, and Brave

11 years–Dying for Love

"In the spiritual journey, you cannot be a wine taster; you have to become a drunk"

— MOOJI

BACK TO AMERICA

At last comes the day I have been waiting for months to arrive! It is summer vacation and time for me to leave Niger to spend two months with my father. Searle has begun roughly manhandling me when I step forward and shout at him to stop threatening and attacking Lana physically. His rage knows no boundaries, and is disproportionate to any slight against him. I am frightened, yet some part of me radiantly rebels. I guess I have nothing to lose as I witness Lana looking in terror into his eyes, still terrified of what it will do to her. It is like a death wish she has, but cannot complete. I know she must be saved. I must be strong enough to do it.

In moments alone with the Searle monster, I am learning to sit still and absorb his toxic and irrational tirades. "You take up so much space, Thea," he complains in irritated tones. I look up at his face and see thunderclouds brewing in his disapproving eyes that are full of bitterness and hatred for my being. I do not fully understand his meaning, yet I sense there is something greater to grasp in his words. He speaks about energy. My energy. His words don't feel complete, though half of what he is says rings true in the back of my mind. I take myself further inward, closing up like a clam, closing down and dimming my light. I don't want to "take up space."

The difficulty of living within this self-created shell, and my constant battle with illness all fall away when at last I make the long journey back to America as an unaccompanied minor to visit Bard and Viv. The French airline bungles my fights in Paris. However, I am fortunate to have my wits about me and sneak out of the dank area where the officials hold me together for hours with other unaccompanied minors. I employ the little knowledge of the French language I have picked up and make it to the gate in time to board my plane. Bard and Vivian are relieved to find me as I exit at last in San Francisco.

I am welcomed into their new home graciously. Nevertheless, the longer I stay, the more I feel the awkwardness of being a visitor in my father's home even though I have been given a room of my own to enjoy, set up with my books, stuffed toys, and a few familiar figurines from years gone by that decorate the shelves. It is very comfortable here, but different than it was before. Something has changed. My father is distant and subdued. Vivian is in charge of almost everything. She is hypersensitive and jumpy.

My summer days are spent mostly at an art college. My father has enrolled me here to keep my occupied. I spend long hours and days at the college and then a lot of time alone, reading and resting after school while my father winds up his thesis projects at the university. Viv works in her physical therapy practice splitting her clients between a room at home and an office downtown. Generally, it is peaceful and we chat over tasty meals my father cooks up in the big kitchen at the back of his house.

I want to see old friends and rekindle them, but they have moved on after ten long months apart. They make it clear through their parents that their lives are too busy to include me. Their rejection opens up a well of sorrow within me. I can't understand what I could have done to deserve my childhood friends' rejection. Why won't they accept my gifts or see me? I saved up all my allowance to buy exotic Tuareg bracelets and beautiful handmade leather goods for my Caitlin and Celina, but these things are returned through their parents.

Adult friends surmise they are jealous of my experiences. I am doubtful. We never used to be jealous of one another. Why start now? This becomes a lesson in letting go in the face of something I do not understand, and it is not easy. I do not let go easily. There have been so many changes and losses in my young life that I suddenly feel the need to cling to the known. Feelings of hurt and confusion take root and clutch me in their grip seeking to bind me.

I feel strange and awkward, and soon realize that I don't fit in at the art college where older girls bully me and call me names at the bus stop. My dress sense is not up-to date with how older girls dress here and I am singled out as different. After weeks of this, I have had enough. I finally turn to one of my tormentors and attack her physically, easily using my strength to pin her to the bus stop wall and warn her not to mess with me again. She quickly learns to leave me alone and respect my space.

Bard applauds me for taking charge. Viv uncharacteristically starts helping me to fit in. She ties up my hair in pretty modern style ponytails and helps me pick out some different clothes. I still wonder what it means to be Hispanic, and imagine what it would be like to live with my Mexican family. How different would it be? What if I have brothers and sisters somewhere who would protect me? Would I fit in with them? Right now, I don't know where I fit best.

IN THE UNDERWORLD

When the summer course ends, Bard spends more time with me. I am allowed into the research rooms at the university where he is busy creating the illustrations for his thesis and he shows me how to draw faces. After awhile, we bond again as if we have never been apart and he eagerly invites me to partake into a new type of shamanic ceremony to retrieve another regal animal protector from one of the known spirit realms. Last time he was the one to perform the retrieval. Now, having just been initiated to womanhood and starting the painful process of menstruation whilst visiting friends across the bay, Bard asserts I am ready for the journey. I have recently told him that I felt my otter slip out of my body and said goodbye while I was swimming in a communal pool on protected American grounds in Niger.

I willingly agree to take part in the new ceremony and begin my own journey on the seeker's path. No drugs or sedatives either natural or synthetic are used to produce the trance state I fall into with ease. I simply lie down on the bedroom floor and follow the rhythmic pounding of Bard's rawhide drum breathing gently and opening my awareness through my third eye as instructed.

Though in a trance state, I do not find it easy to leave my body. There is a natural significance to me being in this body that is hard to release. My physical presence is a miracle, after all! I naturally want to honor it, but the drumbeats pull me upward and eventually I break free.

Instantly, I enter the airy bedroom and fly out the window, soaring like an eagle to my favorite spot above the earth where I alight and quickly enter a fissure in the rocky sand of a real river cave I know. I spiral down into the heart of the loamy earth, going deeper and deeper, sliding like water through the cracks, inhaling the muddy mineral rich sand and rock as I go. My consciousness melts through stone and suddenly I am breathing in the dense rich air of a dark tropical jungle. I recognize this to be the place my father travels to and I am in his dream so I visualize light shimmering through huge roots and elephantine leaves in the tropical undergrowth. As I gravitate toward the light that is shining invitingly beyond the trees, I find myself stepping nimbly to the edge of the jungle where an expansive field of coarse golden reed grass stretches as far as my eyes can see. A hot golden sun is radiating dry heat, low in the sapphire sky.

A pathway opens before me and I feel compelled to walk along its tawny clay-baked track. I remember now that I am here to seek out my power animal. As I enter the trail, I note that I am instinctively hesitant to look behind. The reed grasses wave slightly in a breeze high above my head making a gentle shushing sound and I can no longer see any horizon. I feel as if I am being watched by something predatory in nature. Nonetheless, my sheer curiosity to see what comes next propels me forward.

The path winds like a giant anaconda through the grass. I cannot see anything new ahead or behind, except for more tall grass and the winding path. I can hear the faint thudding vibrations of my father drumming to the rhythm of my pulse, but that all seems very far away as I look around for my spirit guide.

Something catches my eye and I know that despite my misgivings I must turn and look over my right shoulder. I glance back, right and down, and there he is. An ebony-skinned tribal man with a shaggy mane of Rasta locks crouches on all fours and grins up at me with a mouthful of ivory teeth. He sports a necklace of lion or tiger claws around his neck and very little else save a loincloth, and other beaded garments and accessories lashed to his lean black form. I take immediate fright, although he does nothing but to keep grinning. I leap into flight mode and fly past him, nimble as a gazelle, sprinting back the way I have come, then fly on great wings up and out of the cave tunnel, above the cities and trees, back to the room, back to my body, and back to Self.

I sit up with a start and leap into my father's arms, shaking as I relay my story. Bard looks at me speechless and baffled. This is clearly outside the realm of his experience. Viv enters the bedroom and demands to know what happened. Bard sits on his haunches and muses that maybe if I had stayed longer in the underworld the power animal would have revealed itself.

FORCED PENANCE

Days pass and the magical experience blends in with everyday life. Vivian's cat is a menace. It has a nasty glint in its green eyes and lies in wait to ambush me on the steps up to the bedroom landing. As I pass by, the bad tempered black cat makes a game of lashing out with sharp claws determined to scratch me. She seems to lie in wait everyday as I return home from art class.

One hot summer day, I decide to teach the cat a lesson. I kick out at her with my lean tanned legs as she prepares to lunge from her perch on the middle stair. She yowls in fury, bringing Vivian immediately out of her room to the landing at the top of the stairs. "What did you just do, Thea?" she demands to know. "Where is El Negro?"

All my own suppressed anger and hurt seethes to the surface as I scream back at her, feeling downright justified in my actions. "Your cat deserves to be punished!" I yell and I slam the bedroom door in her face. This is what she has been waiting for. She runs to cradle her traumatized cat and when Bard comes home she has him with her as a witness, gravely determined that she is going to teach me a lesson. As we talk, I think I can outsmart her by denying any wrongdoing. All of a sudden, Vivian pounces and flings me across her lap like a small babe thwacking me as hard and as many times as she can muster, pulling me toward her every time I try to escape. My bum and my pride are burning when at last she storms out of the room. Bard, who has never hit me before, sits calmly on the floor, cross-legged, amazed and, yes, I think, oddly smug. Old embedded voices come to my awareness."Rejected, undeserving, useless, manipulative, stupid, victim." I am furious and saddened that my father does not stand up for me.

Instead, Bard calmly states that this is also Vivian's home, married as they are, and that I have behaved inappropriately and deserved her rage. "Why don't you just apologize?" he wonders out loud in consternation.

"But Dad, you don't understand!"

"You know what Thea, that's enough, I don't want to hear anymore." He unfolds his legs and stands abruptly, going for the door.

After he departs, I quickly stand up and lock the door. I stay cloistered in the room for a full 24-hours. To distract myself, and escape facing the demons that laugh at me mirthlessly via the scraping of the tree branches on the window outside, I make myself too busy to notice as I internalize a constant replay of events. To take my mind away, I reach up to the shelf, find the biggest book there, and read the entire epic adventure of *Watership Down* lying on the big comfortable queen-sized bed or sitting on the floor for hours. The universe speaks in much kinder tones teaching me what I must learn through this special story. My guides and guardians settle in around me as I read pages meant just for me. *Watership Down* by Richard Adams is the tale of rabbits that escape the desolation and ruin of their home to seek a new burrow all while being provoked, tempted, and challenged every hop of the way. I refuse to come downstairs to eat or drink anything until I have finished reading the novel.

During this time alone, I seek solitude of self, searching for solace in my soul that hides elusively beyond reach. I don't belong here. Do I belong anywhere? I realize that I, too, am lost like these rabbits and I scream inwardly, tears falling down my cheeks as I connect with the rabbits' struggle to survive against terrible odds. I turn over on the bed clenching my pillow and roar my agony into the downy feathers beneath me. Suddenly, a light comes silently to the outer edges of my grief and takes my hand. She empathizes and sits by me lovingly smoothing my long wavy hair through her fingers as I lie on my belly with it fanned out heavily across my slender athletic back.

CROSSING OVER

A time comes, near the end of the summer visit with Bard and Vivian, when I become nervous and worried about returning to Niger. I am terrified of going back to the French school. I can't face another three years there. I am scared to go back to feeling sick all the time. I have been in good health since staying with Bard and Viv. Most of all, I am frightened of Searle and his unpredictable outbursts. I am hurt that my mother has continued to allow him to threaten, physically hurt, and scare us. I am mad at him for not caring to control his insane temper. I have become an adept at compartmentalizing my separate lives so neither parent has any idea what really goes on within the other's time with me. Shockingly, although it has been happening for half a decade, my father knows nothing about the abusive relationship my mother is in nor the effects it is having on me.

One evening, Vivian, Bard, and I drive downtown to see a James Bond film. As the credits roll and people swim across the screen in the nude, I suddenly become uncomfortably self-conscious and refuse to watch. I begin to rise out of the seat. "What's wrong? Thea, sit back down. We'll leave when the movie finishes," Vivian hisses at me across my father.

I squirm uncomfortably in my chair, but it seems unnatural for a girl of my age to be watching this, so finally I decide to leave and storm past them, causing them to get up to follow me. As I march down the street, I can hear my stepmother loudly calling out my name. I ignore her deliberately and march out my sudden rush of emotion and anger, unsure myself what is happening within me. Hormones are raging. This infuriates her and the familiar power struggle blooms between us once again.

Bard abhors confrontation and follows in silence, withdrawing into himself as he takes long strides to keep up with us along the sidewalk. He has not been a daily part of raising me and so he second-guesses his own methods now. He has never trusted Lana, and he now believes that his personal experience of her as a willful manipulator has passed to me, so he allows Viv to take the lead. She reaches for me but I step back easily avoiding her, ready for more abuse. Bard stills her hand and whispers something in her ear that makes her get into the passenger side of the car and he gestures sternly for me to get in the backseat. Vivian rails on and on about my behavior as we drive home in the car.

I stop listening to her. I begin to operate only from instinct. I hyperventilate and breathe in long angry breaths in the back of the car. All sounds are drowned out as I follow the surging patterns of my breath and increase the intensity and timing. Soon, I become dizzy and numb and discover one goal: I do not wish to live one more moment of this current reality. I have no idea that I can truly expire as a result of this thought and the energy and focus I put into it. The two adults in the front of the car don't think about this either.

As we arrive home, I feel myself being dragged into the house, where I collapse weakly on the floor at the base of the stairwell to their surprise and my own. I am semi-conscious, and then suddenly… I enter another realm.

All physical reality is removed, and it is as if I am far away, floating gently in a tube-like chamber of misty light and soft shadows, magnetically pulled toward a glowing light in the distance, yet close too, I can't really tell. It feels as if I have all the time to get there. It is of no consequence. I am very aware of my smallness and the soft swirling spaces.

Out of the walls of mist, twelve holographic god-like faces appear, six on one side and six on the other. They are wise and omniscient. Their eyes track my passage in silence and some turn their heads toward the soft light where I am enigmatically drawn. They are unsmiling yet I feel compassion flow and ripple through the air around them. I continue my forward movement through the grey misty tube and I am so far completely unafraid. The faces become twelve planted cedar trees, six on one side and six on the other as the surface beneath my feet begins to vibrate and then becomes more solid. I know I am connecting with sacred ground. I walk respectfully forward into the light and stare about in wonder.

Before me lies the most beautiful garden that words of this world are truly unable to describe. Every part of this space is sentient, full of vibration and song. Flowers, birds, and butterflies are drenched in the most brilliant hues of light. As the butterflies fly across my vision, they leave behind crystalline trails of shimmering light, dazzling like fairy dust, or how one might see multiple exposure frames, flying in and out of many dimensions all at once.

The garden is intimate and there is a swing covered in roses in a bower of green to my right. My awareness picks up on a vast world and mountains to the east beyond this garden and I feel an overwhelmingly powerful and creative presence throughout the land. All of the sounds that come to my ears and resonate throughout my other senses are symphonic harmonies of the purest source. I stand mesmerized amongst the radiance and feel that I, too, have a place in The Eternal Song.

I turn to my left and glimpse a circular opening in the grass. Out of this hole, luminous light is spraying like a fountain from the ground. In its iridescence, I see all the colors of the rainbow and additional colors I have never seen in this life on Earth. Even so, the light fountain is as white as the moon and stars. As I stare at the flowing brilliance, a tall man emerges through this channel in the soil, glistening in robes of white. His hair is white and waving like a halo around his head, combed and sparkling to perfection, and I recognize him immediately. He takes the form of Lana's father, my only acquainted grandfather from this lifetime, whom I have not seen since I was four years of age. He greets me happily and we embrace. Then our spirits communicate at length.

"What is this place, Grandpa?"

"It is The Song, Thea."

I have stepped out of linear time. I experience our conversation from every angle like the facets of a brilliant cut diamond. I am at once inside my body, while also outside my body. I am watching the scene as if in a movie, while simultaneously from inside my Grandfather's being, looking through his eyes and out of my own. In this way, I can feel what he feels. He communicates using a language of love in a way we have no memory of here on Earth. He tells me that I must return to my parents. I plead not to leave this beautiful place. The Song...

He puts his hand out gently to cup my cheek. "You cannot stay here long," *he sighs gently.* "You, my dear, are destined for so much more. You have more to discover, more to be."

"What more?" *I sob, pushing my cheek into his hand and even deeper into his heart.* "More of this hardship at the hands of my parents?" *I complain worriedly.*

As I struggle with this idea, he indicates for me to turn around. "Go, now, Thea!" *he says firmly. As I lower my gaze to the grass beneath my feet, I hear him say,* "They love you..."

From this moment, I am propelled very fast through time and space, flying forward as if an enormous hand is firmly and positively pushing me away. I snap with a painful jolt back into my body, which has been laid out on the floor where Vivian is straddled over my chest and Bard is kneeling beside my head. All sense of four and five-dimensional reality disappears, but this current dimensional reality is anything but flat. I hear their voices leaning over me loud and clear. I push gently on the inside to open my eyes and breathe.

"Is she back, Bard?"

"Yes, Viv, it seems to be over" comes his shaken subdued reply.

Vivian lets out a sharp breath. In violent exasperation, she mutters unmentionable expletives to Bard as she leaps to her feet and I can hear her feet pound upstairs where the bedroom door slams shut with a wild crack.

Bard stands at the base of the stairwell, clearly shattered and alone, firmly beckoning me to come with him. I follow him as he escorts me step by step to my own bedroom. I fall weakly to my knees and crawl on all fours, but he holds back not showing any care for my antics. My body is still trying to integrate what has happened and what has changed in me forever. My cells are reintegrating. I feel extremely unstable and vulnerable.

What should I do now? What do I know now?

I now know there is a Heavenly Realm! I know there is The Song. I know The Creator of The Song accepts me unconditionally. I somehow know that the golden presence I have been immersed in is akin to the presence people feel when they pray, meditate, and focus on their calling. It is one and the same essence and something greater than being in human form allows us to perceive.

I am now keenly aware that unity, love, wholeness, and connection exist beyond this reality. Re-emerging as me, I am suddenly grown, and aware that time exists only as a concept and a construct of our human minds. I know that there is a reason to live, but crawling up the stairs to my bedroom I don't remember what that is; only that it is important to honor all life. I am no longer afraid to live or die…it is even better on the other side.

136

Soul Song: Low, Hushed, and Serious

11-years–An Alternative Choice

"Choices are the hinges of destiny"

— PYTHAGORAS

BATTLE LINES

It is not long before we have forgiven each other, if not understood each other, and Vivian and Bard take me out to dinner where I am given the chance to tell them about my life. I tell them of some of the abuse I have witnessed and experienced. Vivian blanches in her chair as I speak. Bard is mute as he sits still and asks me to repeat myself several times in stunned disbelief. He steals a look across the candlelit table at Viv, his eyes questioning. She nods slowly and they both turn to ask if I wish to stay with them. Surprised and full of relief, I say yes without hesitation. I have been nervous to return to the strange and difficult life with Lana.

The next day, Bard sends a letter out from his lawyer to Lana that reads, "I'm taking Thea." He has no legal right to take full custody of me in this manner, however he sends it anyway. The battle lines have been drawn. Faraway in Niamey, Niger, ten days later, Lana opens the letter at her desk and explodes into action. She takes leave without hesitation and books herself on a plane, believing I am being kidnapped.

She arrives in California and hits the ground running. She organizes court dates and races to collect me to stay with her at her friend Eva's home. As I am ripped away from my new home with my father, he tells me he has no choice but to let me go as she has full legal custody over me. My decision at the court and in conversation with her will affect everything. I assure him I will come back to him. I convince him that I will tell her that I cannot live with her anymore.

Before Lana's arrival, Bard and I had visited potential public schools for me to attend. They are full of grime and graffiti and tough looking kids who wear dark clothes, slouch in their chairs, and chew gum. These institutions are a far cry from the sheltered world of private school I have been accustomed to! At least the miserable French school in Niger has big windows and groves of trees planted in the sandy yards outside my classroom. These concrete prisons are a culture shock, but I had stoically hidden my apprehension away from my father, scared to disappoint him.

Lana arrives with all her familiarity, upbeat chatter, hustle, bustle and the police. She fawns over me and bundles me swiftly into a car to travel to her friend's house, casting an evil eye of disapproval over her shoulder at my father who stands helplessly see thing in the doorway of his home. I let her chatter until at last she pauses long for me say meekly, "Mom, I don't want to go back to Niger."

Tears spring to her eyes, but she brushes them away from under her glasses as she drives.

"Thea, oh my God, I can't live without you! I just won't make it," she declares, staring at the road and waving a hand in front of her eyes, a nervous tick she has developed denoting irritation and overwhelm.

At her friend's home and left alone, she draws me into her arms, sobbing. I feel like I did when I was five. Torn by her pain and my own, split in half once more, I know deep in my soul that I do not want to cause anyone anymore agony. As much as I resist and regret her arrogant, wacky, and judgmental approach, I fall under a spell when she displays this sad crumbling persona. I hold her in my arms as she weeps, trying to stand for my young self, but tremble inwardly, unsure if I can.

"*They love you, Thea.*" My grandfather's words echo in the back of my mind. How I wish I could be standing in the heavenly garden of Song right now. I feel cheated to be here, but at the same time the remembered words bring me a sense of calm, and bolster my courage.

"Well, Mom," I sigh, as we break our embrace. She grabs a tissue from her sleeve and blows her nose noisily as I wait, staring at my toes. My legs are tingling and my lips feel pouty and numb as I stumble over the words that must come out next, "I don't want to go back to the French School and I'm not going back to Searle... the way he hurts and scares us all the time."

"No, Thea. I can't let you stay here. I'm in charge of you. I made a promise that I'd never leave you. I'll do anything, please, don't do this to me," she begs, with fresh tears rolling down her face and silent sobs wracking her body.

I sit observing her, feeling myself withdraw while at the same time wanting to comfort her in some way.

"Searle isn't that bad, really, Thea. What did you tell your father?"

I shrug my shoulders indifferently, unsure my answer will be accepted. The abuse and neglect have been all I have known for years and I am not aware of the danger she has fought while I have been away. She inadvertently reaches to her throat as she remembers him asphyxiating her and nearly breaking her windpipe only a month before. She gathers herself now for she sees every word she speaks will be critical. I sit still in my chair and listen.

"Thee," she continues in a more measured tone, "I have some good news. I've been working with some other Americans to start an International American School in Niamey. It was going to be a surprise for you. If you really don't want to attend that dreadful French school, you can do correspondence school this year and go to the American school next year. I've got it all set up! I have found a tutor and I'm even willing to buy you a camel or a horse! Whatever you want, sweets. Just come home. I'd just die without you."

I look down at my feet, again, flushing. I have given Bard my word, but how can I leave my poor mother in this condition while she threatens that she might die? What if something happened? Could I ever forgive myself? Something quivers in my heart. I want to hide, but I stay awake. I want to mourn, yet I keep quiet.

I feel the world swirl and spin around me. What whirlwind have I created? I want to talk to my father alone: just the two of us, without Lana, Vivian, or any well-meaning interference from friends, yet this is not to be. I am not allowed to see or speak with him alone again. I have no one to talk to except my inner self.

The counselor at court who is hired to mediate the situation pulls my parents into the office as I wait nervously outside, not knowing what is to become of me. Hating being the cause of renewed fighting between my parents, time slows as I wait apprehensively to see their faces when they come out. My mother is busy behind the closed door I stare at, playing her final card; lying about the magnitude of Searle's abusive behaviors. My father is accusing her of subjugating me to Searle's instability. When they emerge with the court counselor, Bard looks rattled, sickly and pale, and barely acknowledges me with a nervous weak smile. He glances at my mother with a deep displeasure that leaves me with a queasy feeling inside. My mother's eyes are glittering with unshed tears and something which looks like a manic desperation that makes the queasy feeling in my stomach drop deeper in my bowels. I stand up shakily and go inside with the counselor-lady on my own.

The woman and I sit opposite each other in the small couched room in which my life will change forever without an ounce of compassion or grace. Her style is corporate and unkind. I sit sullenly withdrawn, responding to her sharp questions with one-liners. She snaps out words abruptly like a yappy dog. She never asks me about if I have been abused. She argues with herself as she questions me, and I do my best to try to answer her. Finally, I seem to hear her from a distance.

"...you're responsible for deciding where you want to go, after all, young lady," she cautions bitterly.

I glance up as her words reach my brain and fall into my consciousness like bricks, one for every year of my life. The heaviness I feel extends each minute. I had counseled myself in the car on the way here, hopeful the adults would resolve the issue without me having to take sides. Everything goes dark as I face this woman who is now beginning to look like the devil incarnate.

"You have three minutes to make up your mind and tell me your decision so we can all go home."

She drums her fingers impatiently on the wooden table beside her. No compassion and certainly no love for a child in turmoil.

Hard pressed for answers, I surrender to a greater power. As a way to seek guidance, I evoke a childhood counting game and sing silently to myself,

"Eeney, Meeny, Miny, Mo, catch a tiger by the toe, if he hollers let him go, Eeney, Meeny, Miny, Mo" and end up on the whispered word that echoes in my mind: Africa. Interestingly, I remember another part of the rhyme goes, "my mother says_____," and then you are supposed to land on the final decision in an either/or scenario. I am not sure there is a middle ground here.

In a quiet, little voice I finally give the court counselor my answer, "Africa... I guess."

She mirrors it back to me, "Did you say Africa, little girl?"

I nod in acquiescence.

"Aha! So that means with your mother. Is that correct?"

I shake my head in the negative. For me, Africa means Africa. It does not mean choosing my mother! How can she say I am choosing one parent over another? I would never do that!

"Africa is where I choose to be," I murmur sullenly, privately contending with a pounding heart that will not stop doing backflips in my breast.

The counselor refuses to be sidetracked from her mission by any semantics.

"Okay, little girl, do you have any idea what trouble you have caused here?" She points her finger at me accusingly and I notice her yellow nails.

I don't dignify her with an answer.

"It's settled then," she huffs. "I thought you'd come to the right conclusion. A child must stay with her mother. You need to go and face your parents and tell them your decision right now."

"What do you want me to tell them? That I have chosen Africa over America?"

"No, young lady, that you're going to live with your mother, which is the right decision if you ask me."

I nod miserably, quiet and subdued, wrapped in the fear of my decision as we step out into the lobby.

I find both Bard and Lana sitting on the edge of their seats in the waiting room. The pert little lady in the tweed suit informs them she has got good news. They will not need to go to court as I have decided, which I am prepared to voice now in front of them both.

What? I am in no way prepared! However, seeing no choice, I tell my parents the news so quietly they have to ask me to repeat myself. I fidget nervously and then repeat myself.

Lana looks triumphant. Bard slumps back on his seat and does not argue. He looks at me with a terrifying mix of confusion, hurt, disappointment, and disgust on his face. His chest caves inward as if a dagger has pierced his heart, and in this moment, I witness his identity draw an invisible line in the sand. I do not fully comprehend, but I shall soon enough. He hugs me once, ruffling my head with his warm hand, and leaves the tiny reception room immediately.

Soul Song: Intense and Sustained

11-13-years–Initiation

"You have been told that, even like a chain,
you are as weak as your weakest link.
This is but half the truth.
You are also as strong as your strongest link.
To measure you by your smallest deed is to reckon the power of the ocean
by the frailty of its foam.
To judge you by your failures is to cast blame
upon the seasons for their inconstancy."

— KHALIL GIBRAN

RIDING THE WIND

O n the plane to Niamey a few days later with Lana I wonder what is in store for my future. I dread facing my stepfather. In the weeks that follow, Bard makes a few attempts to protect me, sending Searle messages telling him to keep his hands off me. Searle is incensed at Bard's intrusion into what he considers to be his right to discipline in the home and he demands to know what *stories* I have told my father. Enraged, he presses me hard into the living-room couch, pinching my collarbone fiercely between his gargantuan fingers, while his right knee pins me down. I squirm and cry out helplessly. He tells me that he will truly hurt me if I do not agree to contact my father directly and tell him to desist. When I don't respond, he squeezes harder, causing all the air to exit my lungs as I nod yes under duress.

Rage burns within me like a furnace. It burns murderously low and deep like a hot burning coal, fanned by an intense passion against abuse of the defenseless. As soon as he releases me, I scamper to my room and shut the door. Fuming indignantly, an ugliness rears up inside me and I pluck a red pen from the cup on my desk. I use the felt tip to slash hateful words across the pages of my journal. I bray to the world in the only place I can, what he is to me. My mother comes home from work and hands me a letter from my father, Bard. She now opens and reads my mail adding to my sense of raw exposure. She warns me it contains ten pages of lectured scrawls full of blame, telling me how I have ruined Bard's life and the life of his wife by bringing undue stress and pain in their lives with my summer antics. She toys with the idea to give it to me or not until I demand to see it. My heart is crushed anew when I choose to read the contents.

According to him, I am the cause of Viv's recent miscarriages! Lana angrily tells me that I am not. I feel trapped in a web of perpetual violence and pandemic perpetration from every corner. There is no safe place for me to crawl. Internally, I draw my own line in the sand. These people are not parents or role models. They are monsters, I tell myself, and I will bide my time until I can escape and run away...

Lana follows through with her promise to keep me away from the French school. I begin correspondence lessons with a tutor and a cyst appears inside the flesh of my left breast, over my heart, born out of all this fear and turmoil. It is hot and painful but thankfully benign. My twelfth birthday arrives and to mark my newfound strength I have my long wavy mane chopped off to just above my shoulders. I decide to make it shorter as if this will somehow make me a new person.

I am relieved to share some of my pain with my American tutor Joanne who helps me remain focused on my education. She is a kind, loving, and patient soul with a big Southern drawl and ravishing smile, and I flourish under her patient tutelage, making up two years in one and feeling more confident in my studies than I have ever achieved previously. We have fun in the breaks, making real southern style corn bread and eating it with hot butter while dangling our feet in the crystalline waters of the pool in her perfectly manicured backyard.

I find some freedom and joy taking part in the French-run Equestrian Centre's activities. The Muslim community in which I live do not believe in gelding horses so we, as riders, are forced to handle persnickety stallions that bite, twitch, and kick vociferously. Stallions whirl, dying to turn their heads into the wind. As the breeze increases they became ever more agitated and vicious toward one another. The little Arab horses and their Anglo-Arab thoroughbred cousins show a respectable absence of fear for the giant crocodiles that plague the slower waters of the river. The grooms saddle my aging black stallion Taco and we walk off into the dunes with the others. I kick him into a galloping canter once we reach the dry ridges and escarpments above the wide Niger River.

These moments on his back, feeling his boney musculature under the urgent pressure of my thighs are times of solace. Songs in my soul croon to me in the language of the desert astride his unforgiving black back. Most times, I forget the saddle and ride bareback along the arid plateaus and plunge daringly down steep ravines. As I stare off into the undulating dunes, for a time, I can completely forget my personal pain. Here, I am a princess of mystical origin, sitting tall astride my Arabian steed, tanned arms holding worn leather reins, powerful in my own right atop the vastness of this red sandblasted wasteland.

Once home, I write in my journals to release some of my feelings and an imaginary warrior-soul emerges like a savior out of the pages. Together, we ride great white stallions through the stars and we are as inseparable as spiritual twins: at first seen laughing and playing in meadows full of wildflowers, and then, in mature writings well beyond my age, I describe a future us, his strong arms wrapped all around me, overlooking snowy purple mountain peaks and valleys lit vermillion by a majestic setting sun. In these imagined moments with my imagined warrior-soul mate, I find peace of mind.

TRIAL BY FIRE

During this time of heartache and distress, Lana's deceased father George remains in touch with me through my dreams, and we take walks arm in arm under the acorn trees at the Zen monastery of my childhood in the Ventana Wilderness of Tassajara off of the Big Sur coastline of California. One night, as I lie asleep tucked in under my new blue mosquito net in my tiled Nigerian bedroom, another dream, stranger and hauntingly prophetic, comes unbidden to my consciousness. This dream is just as clear as the others, yet it seems foreboding, adversarial, and even scary:

I am at the edge of the world. Everything has turned varying shades of blue and grey. I am completely alone in the stillness, overlooking a tiered-town at the edge of nowhere. Instinctively, I make a move to leave the house I am in, without locking the door. As I begin walking through the deserted streets of an unknown town, a feeling of dis-ease overtakes me, and I push it away consciously as I make my way through the houses and neighborhoods of this strange place. At last, I arrive on a street full of sunshine. It is the only street in my dream that is awash with light, but the light feels harsh and stark. I feel safer in the cold blue shadows, but nonetheless I keep stepping forward on the pavement.

All the white picket-fenced houses appear to be abandoned either side of me, and one, in particular, on my left catches my eye. I am too nervous to call out in this quiet space. I will my feet to take me to the front door of the house that I find myself focused upon, and the door unlatches with a "click-clack" sound as various locks slide open before me. What seems a welcome, now feels like a veiled threat as I see no one is there. I enter hesitantly, holding my fear at bay, and nothing happens. The interior is a familiar space and design. I am reminded of my mother's best friend's home in Berkeley, the place where my dog Tata was lost years before.

Suddenly, and without warning, the door slams shut behind me and locks itself, with a huge array of nuts and bolts now seen closing by themselves and trapping me inside. I decide not to panic and begin to walk calmly up the stairs to the second floor. As I trail silently across the landing and into the first bedroom on my right, I peer inside, and notice the air of the room is the same gloomy grey and smoke-blue as the village at the edge of the world. There is a wolf sitting inside the gloom staring at me with big intelligent eyes. I am not afraid of the wolf, whose glimmering yellow eyes search and penetrate mine.

Someone is sitting next to the wolf in a hooded robe, and when the wolf glances at me, the figure also looks up, revealing a pale wrinkled face with no eyes. This is disconcerting, but I feel no urgent fear, just a gentle warning not to interfere with whatever process is occurring in the room. Perhaps this stranger is seeing through the eyes of the wolf?

The figure gets to its feet and I recognize a feminine quality to its movements. It floats past me like a ghost into the hall, sheltering something in its shadowy arms. Other versions of the hooded one also begin to file out past me whom had not been apparent when I first looked into the room. The wolf precedes the hooded woman padding stiffly past deliberately allowing its wiry hair to brush along my calf. I feel compelled to follow them, still undecided if they are friend or foe.

They turn into the guest bathroom on the upstairs landing and I observe the wolf disintegrate in midair, and watch as the first figure bends, bathing some ugly frightened creature in the bathtub. Something is very wrong. I don't know what it is, for I do not wish to wait to see or hear more. What I am seeing seems to belong to occult business so I turn away more feeling than hearing the cries of something beyond my comprehension. I run instinctively away, as the panic sets in. I reach the ground floor of the house and run for the door, only to find it bolted with many strange locks that will take me too long to undo.

I turn around slowly to face my plight and become aware that the floor has changed into the black and white tiles of a chessboard. I am now being pulled by a hoard of people, with glazed vacant eyes, into some kind of chess game on the tiles where a huge fiery creature is dancing at the center of the room. Music booms over a loud speaker. The fire creature is randomly picking individuals from the crowd who are dancing. He burns and consumes them in his arms.

I see that to survive we must all dance carefully, only stepping on specific tiles and never attracting the creature's attention. I keep hiding behind others as they are swept away one by one to theirs creaming demise. The fire creature dances closer and closer as the crowd thins, and soon its flaming eyes turn and lock with mine! In its eyes I see a fire stallion rear up in the blackest of night. Shaking, I awake relieved somehow that I withstood the power of this demon and wondering what it means.

SCENE 21

Soul Song: Reedy, Fragmented, and Worn

12-13 years–Bent Yet Unbroken

"Maktub (It is Written)," she said.
"If I am really part of your dream, you'll come back one day."

— PAULO COELHO

MORE THAN COPING

Searle occasionally takes me for driving lessons down the sandy alleyways near our home in his beige and chrome VW bug as if trying to make amends. When I turn thirteen, he optimistically tries to teach me to maneuver a Moped motorbike through the thick sandy roads. This scares me and ends up in arguments. I resist his attempts to reach out to me, being deliberately bitter; unforgiving in my lack of affection toward him. *If Bard is to be replaced it will not be with this man,* I swear to myself stubbornly. One minute he is teaching me tennis and showing me chords and harmonics on my acoustic guitar, and the next minute he is smashing up our property and overturning the dining table at supper when Lana and I refuse to practice French with him at mealtimes.

Bard insolently refuses to have me come home after the debacle the year before. The entire year I have endured reading his ten-page essays berating and lecturing me on my poor choice and "emotional blackmail" as he sees it. The letters are sent via post containing drawn out personalized assessments of our relationship and who I have become in his eyes, and he continues to blame me for stressing Vivian to the point of depression and despair. I feel the sting of his words and to survive, I fortify my exterior.

Despite his rejection, I choose to go ahead with plans to head home and spend my second school holidays at a summer camp in the hills of Southern California, where I learn to play the guitar, take acting classes, synchronized swimming lessons, learn archery and tennis, bond with girls in my cabin, and afterward choose to stay with Searle's large extended family, and spend some time in Berkeley with friends of my mother's. I never contact my father or Viv while I am on holiday, choosing instead to force myself to forget their existence. When he finds out through the grapevine that I am in town he is startled to discover I have traveled alone and never contacted him. *You either have me 100 percent as your daughter or you don't,* I think to myself angrily. *I'm not a grey area. I'm a person with feelings and you have chosen to neglect those feelings and overlook me as your child.*

Returning to Africa after the summer in California, I attend the newly opened American International School of Niamey full time with three other permanent age-mates in my class, all boys. Lana plays a pivotal role in making this new education a reality. There are twenty students enrolled permanently in the school overall, and in the afternoon our little group is joined by other American kids our age who are supplementing their education at the French School. We spend all our time together and our social lives increase dramatically.

I spend afternoons with a small group of American friends, hanging out in their expat-styled homesteads walled off in more exclusive neighborhoods than my own. I jump at the chance to get away from my own home for sleep overs or run along deserted sand-swept roads in the suburbs at night with my new best friend Kay, a feisty, athletic and confident girl my height and age. Kay and I innocently share our hopes and dreams, watch romantic comedies and videos, and make a mess of her mother's large fancy kitchen. We climb telephone poles in order to run together along the vast network of six-foot-high compound walls that the affluent populations share with the poverty-stricken ones. Saturday or Sunday mornings are spent in earnest tennis practice with Searle as our coach waking up at the crack of dawn before the heat forces the entire town to lie down beneath trees, fans or air conditioners. I enjoy softball in the late afternoons with the stationed US Marine recruits and Embassy staff, and my flesh turns a deep bronze from diving and swimming at the public and private pools.

My immune system has finally kicked in and I am physically at my best. At home in my sparsely decorated bedroom with a cupboard full of books, an old wooden school desk, and a single bed with blue mosquito net, I read voraciously, write and draw pictures, or practice folk songs on my newly purchased guitar. Sometimes, I sit alone in the afternoons after school playing the turntable in the dark lounge away from the afternoon heat and practice singing to the words to my mother's collection of songs by the famous 70s folksinger-songwriter and political activist, Joan Baez.

I still search for a door back into connection with The Song, which continues to feel so far from my reach, and I long to return to the embrace of the heavenly garden. Living in an atheist home doesn't nourish my spiritual sensitivities nor does it keep me connected with the near-death experience that has so recently changed my perspective on life. I want nothing more than to keep this memory alive, yet whom can I talk to? Lana gifts me a book on the ancient mythology of the Greek Gods so I instinctively began to pray to these deities for guidance, knowing no others. Athena, Hestia and Zeus, Andromeda, Poseidon and Hermes are regularly featured as I stand in the center of my tiled bedroom and bow my head, clasping my hands in earnest supplication.

I try on the middle name "Daphne," a Greek naiad (nymph) that foiled Apollo's attempts on her virginity and was turned into a beautiful Laurel tree for protection. The story captivates me and I begin signing all my writings and artwork as journals: Thea Daphne. My adoptive parents have never graced me with a middle name, and this, for a time, feels like the missing link. In primary school, I had once tried on the second name Maria, thinking it sounded like the perfect Mexican name, but when my schoolmates chanted "Tia Maria, Tia Maria," I was deeply embarrassed and dropped it.

At last, it is time to leave the deserts of Niger, but the departure comes just before the end of the school term, so I beg to be left with friends so that I may conclude the term. My friends' parents agree for me to be a guest in their home so Lana and Searle agree to leave me there. They catch a plane and head to Europe where we are to rendezvous in Greece in a few weeks' time. I am excited to visit the home of the gods that I feel so connected to. I have been praying for over a year now, and now here I am, on my way there.

Soul Song: Chromatic Diminuendo

13 years–Dissolving My Innocence

"When it hurts to move on,
just remember the pain it felt to hang on."

— ANONYMOUS

THE GREEK ISLES

I t is an early spring morning in April 1984 when I finally alight in Athens, the city named by the Greeks after the Goddess Athena and today's modern capital of their country. I shiver uncontrollably under my thin cotton blouse wishing for a sweater. I have endured a harrowing turbulent journey complete with a grounding of our plane in Algeria and being held and searched for the pilot's mistake of accidentally flying over restricted airspace. The temperature drop from West Africa is extreme. When I left it was one of the hottest days in history and well above 100 degrees Fahrenheit, and when I arrive in Greece it is a cold and windy afternoon. My blood has thinned considerably to cope with living in the desert and my body is not prepared for such a shock.

Lana and Searle are there to fetch me at the airport and we head straight for the Old Plaka, a historical stone market district in the older part of town before making our way to the hotel. Wandering amongst the various hawker stalls I choose a periwinkle-blue sweater as my first purchase hand-crocheted for months according to the pushy lady vendor who wants us to buy more of her wares. However, she is no match for our aggressive haggling experience in the Nigerien marketplaces, and in the end, we get the deal we want. Lana is eager to show me the back alleys of Greek life, have me taste Greek dolmades, souvlaki, spanakopita, and baklava, visit their historic museums, and browse the antique shopping havens in the lesser-known parts of town. We hike on foot all over Athens.

The sadness of the Parthenon in ruin and disrepair on the magnificent Acropolis hits me in the gut. My mother tells me years ago when we visited with Bard it was not in such a terrible state of erosion. The restoration works that have begun are estimated to take huge resources and years to conclude.

The vision of the Parthenon on the Acropolis looming over Athens and hiding the original tribute to the Greek gods who I consider my saviors, fills my heart with shame. Within me a quiet note emerges out of The Song. The note shows me a vision of polluted cities, lost memories, and lost skill, all muffled beneath the sound of crumbling marble elements, bas-relief facades, and giant colonnades built by gifted trade-masters and designers, blasted down by men at war. Some of the ancient works still stand up defiantly, but most lie about us on the mount. They signify a fallen time, a fallen race, and fallen principles, all replaced by mankind's corruption, greed, and malice.

"Thea?" My mother awakens me from my reverie.

"What?"

"Hey, don't answer me like that. What's going on, kiddo?"

"I want to go back to the hotel. Please can we go?"

My feet are suddenly aching and I need to take refuge in my bed and write out my thoughts in private. This is almost too much to bear. I take my leave, suddenly realizing the demi-Gods I have been praying to all along are actually disempowered.

At eventide, we walk through the streets of the Old Town, having finished an enormous traditional Greek meal in the Plaka, and we happen upon a street-fight between two men. A crowd has gathered in a narrow alleyway and they are jostling each other downhill into a tight circle hurling taunts and jibes at two men circling on another in the center. Searle immediately steps in and pounces on one of the two who have begun wrestling and flings him away from his quarry into the ravenous crowd. There is a tussle and then, almost too late, we see a flash of steel glinting in the moonlight. A knife appears in the hand of the main perpetrator. Instantly, he turns toward Searle. I cry out a warning as Searle leaps back, moving quickly for his size, dodging the blade expertly and grabbing the wrist of the man in question, struggling physically to overpower him. The bloodthirsty crowd is thrilled for more action. The man is no match for Searle, who is huge in comparison, but I can't see what has happened to the blade.

Lana yanks me out of the crowd and pushes me up the cobbled street toward the inn we are staying at, leaving my stepfather to fend for himself. "But Lana, we cannot leave him there alone," I plead, very worried. As much as Searle has been the perpetrator of violence in my life, so too is he a gladiator of men. He has kept us safe in many situations where we would have been overpowered as women.

"Well, what exactly do you think we could do?"

Lana insists it was Searle's own choosing to be embroiled as we could simply have walked away and not gotten involved in the first place.

I realize her point and follow more slowly uphill.

Finally, I hear his pounding footsteps coming up the steep incline behind us, sweating and only slightly agitated at our hasty retreat. Lana clucks pokilyat him, but she is clearly relieved he is unharmed.

"I saved a life tonight," he manages to gasp huskily as we walk. "That guy was going to get stabbed."

"Yeah, Searle, and you could have been badly hurt or killed yourself," Lana retorts. He looks at me, shrugs, and winks behind her back.

The next day, we sail to the Greek Isle of Rhodes. Here, the lanes are choked with artisans and dancers. I find myself deeply attracted to the features of a beautiful fine-boned Greek artist with smooth dark curls, soft olive skin, and lips that curl sensually upward as if he knows a secret that I do not. I sit for him in the street as he pencils a likeness of me and we stare for over 45 minutes into one another's eyes. I feel tempted to draw him!

He captures my sad, soulful eyes with a few deft-handed pencil strokes on a blank canvas before adding watercolor and charcoal. I imagine spending days with him and that he desires to touch upon the mystery embedded in me as well. Then, just as I feel myself becoming uncomfortable in his gaze it is over and I am free to see what he has created. The art piece shows the determination in my jaw and a sullen uncertainty in my gaze.

The artist touches my hand lightly and holds my glance a moment more, committing me to memory when my mother and stepfather aren't looking. We are, in this moment the two who become united beyond time and language into a magical space of flow. I allow him to catch a glimmer of my spirit and he allows me the freedom to dream of a perfect lover in his quiet rendering of pencil, charcoal, and blue. He almost looks like my imagined partner of the future whom I continue to write about privately in secret diaries that even Lana can't find to read. Somewhere between woman and girl, I hover impatiently, waiting to cross the threshold.

"I saw the way he looked at you! He liked you, didn't he?" she prods, goading evilly. I am dying to leave her company and retire to my island hotel balcony filled with geranium pots set against white sunlit walls. Thankfully, Lana allows me space to rest and dream. Later, we walk through an old cemetery: more fodder for an imagination run wild!

As our family of three explores the ancient cultural island of Rhodes, I become highly embarrassed by the company of Lana and Searle. I find them to be loud and overtly curious, always stabbing their fingers at people or things and talking loudly to anyone who will engage. The locals laugh at their audacity. I trail behind them at all times, furtively meeting the eyes of the seemingly refined Europeans, and the Greeks who sit, entertained in their front row seats perched in doorways, on their neighbor's balconies or at the harbor's edge in quaint cafés to watch the crazy tourists who alight upon their shores. In the morning, we journey to a different place where we rent a small villa on the beach, and we are joined by Searle's brother and his wife.

Here, I spend time quietly reading in the villa, talking with my step-aunt and Lana as Searle and his brother practice free diving for Octopus with the local fishermen who come back amazed at their ability. Once they return, they hang their small catch up in a tree before turning it into calamari and roasting it proudly on the grill.

Our time in Greece must come to an end all too soon, but before we leave, Lana surprises me with a visit to The Oracle at Delphi. Here, I am able to slip away from all people and end up facing The Oracle alone. "I am here!" I whisper quietly to the Oracle. In response, the wind stirs the wild blooms on a rock nearby. Nothing else speaks to me, yet I get the feeling I am heard. I have no clue what to ask for, but I feel as if I am floating in a place of memory from a time long past. I share with the Oracle that not knowing where I was taken during the two months prior to my adoption is a strange thing to feel, as if something is missing. No matter how ideal a process I am afforded, it is a singular type of learning curve. To get used to "something missing" as away of life, I am still exploring how it feels to be disconnected. An insight comes in this moment alone at the shrine. My experience of who I am need not be defined by history, genetics or memory. It is a fleeting impression but I fold it into my heart for future review.

FIRE AND ICE

Back on American soil, Lana has purchased an orange Volkswagen camper van with a pop-top tent. We tour the East Coast and begin a sightseeing trip across the United States. I am bored here. I have had enough of all this adult stuff. I just want to talk to people my age now. In Maryland, I do meet some young adults five years my senior. They own horses and invite me for a ride in the backcountry. These young people are big bold and American-bred. They are born patriots and know nothing of the world outside, nor do they seem to care. The boys' ride bareback with shirts off cowboy-style, while their older sister rides in blue jean cut-offs, long brown hair, and cowgirl hat flapping behind. She takes me under her wing and smiles widely at my dressage approach to riding as I try to work out the unfamiliar western saddle. Finally, we take it off so I can ride bareback. We ride for hours, bonding together in the rolling grasslands, and picnicking under shady oak trees, laughing and teasing one another mercilessly. Later, we swim and tan in the complex, where my parents and I are guests at the invitation of one of our Peace Corps friend's townhouses. My new friends cavort and splash around with one another in the communal pool until late in the afternoon. In the evening, I am invited to a party at the boys' apartment.

My parents agree to let me go, having had assurances from the older sister that all is well. However, when I arrive it turns out there is no party planned. I find myself in a situation that I don't know how to manage. This is a double date and they have already started drinking beer and watching a movie on TV. I have been chosen to be one of the boys' partners. The idea is that we should perform sexual acts in front of one another and the girls must entertain the boys. As my tipsy partner reaches down to kiss me, I draw back, concerned for my own wellbeing. I am sober and he is not.

"Oh come on, don't you want me?" He leans over me, turning on his cute smile, with charm oozing out of every pore. I am scared. I have never been with a boy and this is practically a man. He is old enough to drink legally. I want the experience, but I don't want this guy. "Come on, let's have fun. You don't have to take your pants off. I'll show you what to do." And he does a good job of that as soon as his buddy leaves the room.

My parents are asleep as I let myself in. I lock myself in the bathroom and wash away my tears. The incident leaves me feeling incomplete and ice cold inside. I have not given up my virginity, but my childhood has vanished before my eyes in a flash.

Lana and Searle have no idea of the profound shift that has occurred in me. Thankfully, we leave shortly thereafter, but the further West we travel, the tenser the journey becomes. Lana and Searle bicker and fight at night, and finally he explodes, becoming verbally violent and physical with both of us in an isolated camping park on a moonless night. We hunker down, nursing our bruises and endure the emotional and physical pain with clenched jaws as usual. I don't know what Lana is thinking. All I want to do is escape. She pinches me hard in the dark, telling me to keep my mouth shut, as I mutter angrily under my breath. For me the internal fire is back, the one burning deep inside. The same volcano I felt when she married this man in Hawaii years ago is heating for a blow.

Soul Song: Allegro, Brassy, and Canned

13 years–The Onion

"We hardly realize that we can cut anything out of our lives at anytime, in the blink of an eye."

— CARLOS CASTANEDA

BERKELEY, CALIFORNIA 1984

The small university town of Berkeley is buzzing and alive with students from every corner of the world, for it is a hub for all things alternative. The shops and cafés that line the streets are universally eclectic, imaginative, and magically bookish. Cultural diversity thrives here. Writers, professors, lawyers, yogis, artisans, magicians, 'yuppies' and nerds all mingle freely.

Telegraph Avenue is the hangout spot where people my age and above go to meet friends, listen to musicians that play on every corner block, or shop, scarf down the best pizza, frozen yogurt, health food takeaways, and haggle with street vendors for gyros, shawarmas, and Chinese take-away. It is summertime and the leaves are green and wet with morning dew, and the skyline reflects a rose gold sun above the San Francisco Bay in the afternoons when the air is filled with smog that casts ribbons of burnt orange and bruised plum between the man-made bridges and skyscrapers.

Bard and Vivian allow me to visit them in their home down the road as time has eased some of the pain between us and they are in a charitable mood, willing to let down their guard a little. I am eager to get to know my stepsister Baby Cerise with whom I fall in love immediately. She bonds with me, too, and I help her climb up and down the stairs of their home as she is transitioning from crawling to walking. We soak together in their newly established backyard hot tub complete with shoji screens and wooden deck, and I feel grateful for this time to share experiences.

I won't have long with them, as we are about to settle in a town called Corrales outside Albuquerque, New Mexico, in the American Southwest so that Searle can enroll in a degree program there where he is finally taking himself to school. Lana has been applying for more jobs with government agencies overseas and tells me that whatever salary she gets will be based on the previous job, so if she can't find work now that gives as many perks as the Peace Corps one, she will get less than she earned in Niger. This is not ideal so she plans to bide her time waiting and let Searle increase his employment opportunities. She is confident we can live on her savings, while my child support money from Bard and her rent from the house on 6th Street will cover our day-to day needs.

Just before we are ready to move out of town, Bard and Viv invite me round for a simple meal with old friends. It is awkward to be in this space that I abandoned when I was eleven, and I feel like I am tiptoeing on eggshells. My room is no longer my room. It has been transformed to a room for Baby Cerise. Vivian is warily monitoring every word and step I make, while Bard is cagey with his attentions on me and ill at ease. He can't believe I am a full-bodied young woman, having grown large breasts and gained inches in height since he last saw me.

In the big airy kitchen, we are prepping the early summer meal. Bard is making his favorite chicken dish with rice and Vivian is busying herself preparing garlic bread and salad. I ask what I can do to help. I am told to dice an onion. I quarter the onion and begin chopping. My father notes that I am cutting against the grain. "Thea, this isn't how you chop an onion."

"Well, this is how I have always done it," I challenge him, thinking how I have been cooking for Lana and Searle since I was eight years old.

"Hmmm."

He glances toward Viv who tightens her jaw and holds her tongue while prepping a salad, then comes to my side where I burn in frustration and tears, less from the pungency of the onion and more because of the sting of words that seem to land with barbed irritation twisting angrily into the vulnerable spaces of my psyche. What I hear in between the lines sounds more like: *Thea, you're stupid, good for nothing, and unworthy.* The sting of these thoughts is excruciating.

Bard begins to instruct me anyway.

"This is how I chop an onion," I mutter under my breath, trying to take a stand for myself, pushing back at the thoughts that cause my eyes to prickle with unshed tears as I continue to chop. Inwardly, I can't understand why it matters so much how I get to the end result since it will be diced either way.

Then Vivian's clipped command barks out from behind, cutting through the air like a knife, "Thea! Just chop the onion the way he tells you to. Geez. Bard, I don't know why you just don't put your foot down. She can't get away with this!"

"Why can't you just leave me be?" I whirl and scream at them both, feeling all the years of judgment, blame, and pain they, Lana and Searle have heaped on me. I shake violently and feel as if I am ready to explode the dam of suffering I have endured alone for the past thirteen years.

You people think you're akin to gods. I run from the kitchen barefoot, after dispensing expletives at them, and out the front door into the summer lane. I run and run on the hard concrete, then veer out onto the real streets, burning my feet on the scorching hot tarmac. I am so fiery within that it does not seem to matter. I ignore the scalding sensation on my feet.

After thirty minutes of running and fuming, I finally cool down. I roam like a lost animal through the winding tree-lined neighborhoods, avoiding the bright sunlight and trying to gather my thoughts that are burning holes in my head. At last, I manage to calm down and become aware of the explosion of green leaves and young people chatting as they walk quietly with friends in the late afternoon sun. I hear gentleness in the sighing of the wind that brings the evening mists in off the bay.

"You're our beautiful child. You have a place in this world. It isn't in the way you cut the onion." The trees seem to hum warmly. I breathe a huge sigh of relief. I think of all the times I have needed my father and he has not been there and how abandoned I have felt in recent years. I decide his approval is a big deal. My soul is intact. It means a lot to me. I prepare myself to arrive home to apologize.

I return just as our guests pull up and wave hello. I meet and greet them happily at their car. My father is out in the front of the yard watering plants and calls for his wife through the open front door. He ushers the guests to come in and tells me I need to stay outside for a chat. The guests look puzzled at this strange turn of events but acquiesce and enter the home. Bard's words are harsh. "You're no longer welcome in our home. You have confirmed to us both that you're your mother's child. You have confirmed everything Vivian has ever said about you."

I stand before Bard feeling stripped of dignity and shamed as a heated flush works its way up my neck. My feelings of humble appreciation vanish in an instant into thin air. I argue with him on the sidewalk as all the mutual feelings of disappointment; loss and anger spill forth in a bubbling fountain of righteousness between us. My soft meander through the trees is forgotten. Anger, indignation, hurt, and pain turn me lightheaded and my veins sing war songs in my arms.

Wild thoughts whiz around my brain. *Why won't you be a father and stand up for me? Am I truly your weakest link to be discarded after all? I have idolized you my whole life defending your actions to anyone who said anything wrong about you. How are you now disappointing me and making my mother's unwelcome prophecies that you cannot be here for me come true?*

Vivian comes to the door. "Hey Bard and Thea!" she yells forcefully to get our attention. "You two don't come in this house until you've got your act together!"

"You can't tell me I'm not welcome. It's my father's and my house too," I retort, angrily.

"Thea, contrary to your belief, this is my house and you're just a visitor since you gave up any rights to live here long ago, and Bard, if you know what's best for you, you'll get her out of here, NOW! I've had it!" Vivian slams the door.

Abruptly, and without warning, Bard grabs my wrist and drags me toward the car. I refuse to go, leaning away and making my whole body heavy.

Bard clutches my hair as I continue to resist and takes me by surprise. Grabbing hold of my head, he yanks my neck back and pushes me roughly into the car. "Don't you move!" he shouts angrily, pointing his index finger at me through the window. For a moment, I see furious energy exploding all around his body as he crosses the front of the car to get in the driver's side.

The impact of my usually placid, soft-spoken, father taking such physical action stuns me. Bard jumps in the driver's seat and tears off down the road with me in the passenger's seat. There is silence in my head throughout the short journey as if I have been short circuited. I am so hurt I cannot speak more. "You had this coming, you know," he lectures all the while in patronizing tones. My lips remain sealed. My legs are trembling. I know I have gone too far and there is no turning back.

Bard drops me outside the house that Lana, Searle, and I are house sitting. Bard does not want to get close to Searle and remains in the car, forcing me to get out and ring the doorbell. Searle, who has never met Bard in person, comes forward and waves, wondering what I am doing back so soon. Lana is away on business. He can see my face is dark as thunderclouds and tears sparkle brightly in my eyes. He glances up at the idling car with Bard at the wheel, frowns menacingly, and hikes up the slope a few steps until he is nearly touching the vehicle.

Their paternal roles shift as Searle suddenly takes on the form of my protector. "Hey, what's going on?" He knocks on the car window and shouts after Bard who revs the engine, throws the car into gear, and drives off like a coward. I turn and enter the house. Once inside, I sob bitter tears of frustration and Searle asks if he may intervene. He has been privy to the years of hurt feelings and wishful thinking I have endured in relation to my father. I come to my senses then, declining his offer, knowing the impenetrable walls of the emotional fortress Bard has built will only be reinforced by more aggression or contact. I instinctively know that fighting fire with fire will not help in this case. Only time may ease the way.

Bard's anger and frustration at his messy past with me and my mother smolders like hot coals stoked by the even puffs of my stepmother's words. Searle's anger at not being able to replace Bard burns hot and bright and crackles like a bonfire, though I know it will eventually burn out, replaced by his softer side before long. I will never peel or chop an onion again without recalling the pain of this day and I vow to myself never learn to do it "right."

Soul Song: A Tragic Trashy Anthem

13-14 years–New Mexican Blues

"A gem cannot be polished without friction,
nor a person perfected without trials."

— CHINESE PROVERB

CORRALES, NEW MEXICO

Lana, Searle, and I take a week or two to unpack and move into our three-bedroom adobe home on a large two-acre grassy lot in the small sprawling agricultural town of Corrales, in the State of New Mexico. We are financially strapped and the pressure to survive is mounting. Suddenly, we have no roots, and we are living in a state where none of us knows the local customs or terrain. I attend a private prep school at the center of the city of Albuquerque and it is a fairly long commute from our new home. Corrales is an old farming community and many of the homeowners still raise livestock or keep horses on their plots. I ride horses with my next-door neighbor Catalina, an attractive Hispanic who becomes my bosom buddy straight away. She offers to let me ride her mounts as long as I agree to exercise them and help her groom, muck out their stalls, and feed them. Catalina and I hack out on long out rides into the Rio Rancho suburbs, which are still being built on a manmade ridge high above our more rural neighborhood. When we get bored of the ridge we ride along the tree-lined ditches and drain-off areas toward the Sandia Mountains.

Catalina's father, Raul, is a runner and takes us jogging for an hour every weekend, so my fitness returns in no time. Catalina's mother is the queen of Mexican cooking and bakes us hearty tamales, chicken enchiladas, and toasty warm tortillas with pozole in their kitchen. I make myself at home in their house imagining how my own biological family might be living and cooking somewhere this way.

Something is terribly wrong with Searle. He is more agitated and aggressive than before. Instead of a monthly episode, the violent encounters between him and Lana become weekly affairs at home. He is drinking more. They both are, but Lana has always held her intake to a few glasses of wine. One day, she picks me up from school in a dark tinted car and we flee across the city of Albuquerque to stay with a kind old couple that hides us away while my mother figures out what to do next. Searle's aggression has escalated to epic proportions and I think she is worried he will kill her. We cannot go home for fear of his explosive temper.

I am miserable, studying eight hours a day after school, and the intensity of the homework takes its toll, as I must also worry about losing our home and our public standing. I fall into a state of overwhelm, and although I am young, and more resilient than my mother, who is crumbling before my very eyes, I am not bullet proof. I begin to lose confidence in life and myself. To make matters worse, Lana inadvertently runs into Searle one day in town and tells him where we are staying. He comes over late one afternoon when the old couple isn't around to entice her to come home. Frightened by his menacing presence, she hides behind the burglar bars while he tries to reach in and then threatens to burn the home down. Our cover is blown. Lana lodges a restraining order against him and we return home. The day the order is lifted, he bursts into our home, waking us up, and yanking Lana from her bed. There is another terrifying fight between the two that is so loud that our neighbors' phone for help and the police are called in.

I am unable to cope at the prep school anymore, and it is an expense we can do without, so Lana gives me the choice to attend the public school near to our house in Corrales. I start anew with a counselor who is assigned to me.

I find the atmosphere at Cibola High School to be more supportive and less critical toward individuals than Sandia Prep. It is a much larger school and they don't have time to follow up every child and their problems. I discover if I stay under the radar, nobody cares. I am successful in trying out for the junior squad of the gymnastics team and begin meeting peers in class who, like me, come from broken homes.

I meet a lot of tough, hardened peers here, many of whom take illicit drugs and party every weekend. They seem suave and knowledgeable about life and I am immediately taken in by their edgy exteriors and cool body language. It inspires a rebellious streak and a tenacity I didn't think I had. Being preppy doesn't work at this school that looks and acts like a prison with its oversized square concrete brick and mortar walls and small windows.

Looking around, I realize to protect myself from being bullied I will need a strategy and look for some strong peers who appear streetwise and know the ropes. I pick two older girls in my classes who take me under their wing as long as I help them cheat in their exams. They copy my notes, borrow my clothes and jewelry, and in return I gain some much-needed protection. I am not teased or harassed on the school grounds anymore. I learn what's "in" and what's not.

I discover it is cool to smoke weed, "feather" your hair, wear tight faded blue jeans (the more tattered the better), leather jackets, studded belts, garish dangly earrings, and lots of rings. Neon is in. It is cool to bring out my Hispanic roots and I find myself fitting into the image of "tough-girl" easily.

Still, everyone takes note of me as an attractive newcomer and looks for weaknesses. The boys look for ways to date me, and the girls for ways to bring me ill repute. After riding the school bus and arriving late a few times, my mother arranges a deal with my Science teacher who lives down the street. His daughter is two classes ahead of me and owns a red mustang convertible, and she picks me up every morning with her engine revving. Now my "cool" status gets a massive boost and I am on time for class every day!

REBELLION

I begin sneaking out of the house in my first semester of the second year of high school and steal my mother's car, a maroon and chrome 1970s Volvo. I am fourteen now and old enough to hold a learner's permit. I push the heavy sedan around the circular drive outside her window, up the drainage ramp to the street, and a few yards down the road where I pop the clutch and ride. My friend Lysa and I have found some older male friends in their late twenties who are small-time cocaine and marijuana dealers. The naughtiness of hanging out with them thrills me. I give in to the pressure of smoking weed for which I never pay, and drink copious amounts of their alcohol, but I adamantly refuse to take any pills or cocaine, even though I think Lysa does so behind my back.

I lie to Lana and Searle about where I spend my weekends, saying I am going to stay with my girlfriends. My girlfriends tell their parents they are going to stay with me. In actual fact, we stay at the flat of these older men. Just before I turn 15, I am date raped in the bathroom at the men's flat by a friend of theirs –an overwhelmingly handsome Italian-American boy called Toni with a New York accent. I realize I am in trouble. Fortunately, before he is able to impregnate me, I am rescued by one of the housemates and he is thrown out into the street.

Not fully aware of what is happening to me, Lana has a flash of intuition and takes me to a clinic where I reveal that I am sexually active. The doctor who examines me and prescribes contraceptives, gives me the whole story about sexually transmitted diseases and reproductive cycles, and sees I have scar tissue forming from the broken glass bottle Toni used to "open" me in his drunken stupor. I remember the bleeding and the soreness. I am ashamed and embarrassed by the doctor's discovery and refuse to discuss it at length.

I find myself sitting solemnly in a Catholic Church with my friend Catalina and her family on Sunday mornings feeling like a penitent imposter. I just want to be loved and think that impressing boys and men is the way to get it. I fail to register my true emotions, but physically I am competitive as I continue to beat my classmates both male and female on the track at school and attend competitions around the state with the high school gymnastics team. I refuse to smoke cigarettes with the majority of my peers. In English, I devour the Iliad and the Odyssey, imagining myself back in Ancient Greece, and I begin reading Richard Bach's books that strike a chord deep within.

During this time, I meet a tall handsome boy with clear mesmerizing blue eyes who teases and then befriends me in English class. Moments spent absorbed in his presence feel like a breath of fresh air. I know he has a crush on me, but I am looking for a true friend, not another lover. I flirt generously with him to keep him close. We walk, talk, and ride our bicycles in silence down the country lanes of Corrales, and together we contemplate the passages we are both reading in Richard Bach's book, Jonathon Livingston Seagull. This is the real me, the me I love, I tell myself. Nevertheless, my life and my personality branch off in many streams, and I am at odds to keep up. I date boys from my weightlifting class and am courted by many.

After a gymnastics accident takes me out of the team, I am in the gym to rebuild my core. The accident occurs while in my sophomore year as I freeze midair while flying between the uneven parallel bars and land on my tailbone. The cracking sound of my tailbone smacking into the bar brings the whole gymnasium to a hushed standstill. As I slide off the thin bar of wood still in shock, my legs buckle beneath me, and shooting pain rushes up my thighs and spine. More frighteningly, I am unable to feel anything for 15 minutes and I am rushed off the gym floor on a stretcher.

My recovery takes shape slowly but I manage to be in school, though the pain slows me down. The strength that flows through my muscles is the strength I wish to feel inside of me. My body is so strong yet I quiver and quake at the fear of failure, and the fear of not measuring up to some notion of perfection. My grades are dipping and I live with this duality on a daily basis and become known as "Rocky" on the school grounds when an aggressive street fight breaks out between me and another girl two grades my senior. Outwardly, I am tough as nails, yet I am sad and foreign to myself within.

The boy with the clear blue eyes bends impulsively to pensively kiss my surprised lips, then awkwardly before I can reach up to connect, he runs away. He deliberately makes an excuse to make himself scant thereafter and the strength of my inner world of magic and make-believe folds in and collapses completely. Later, he tells me he can no longer see me, and refuses to say why he must abandon our friendship. I am secretly devastated, as we pass one another in the packed hallways between lessons and he awkwardly averts his beautiful eyes from mine. I am too proud to cry. I tell myself I don't know what I saw in him anyway. I walk around with my leather jacket in hand and tight jeans on, cheering as my Latino boyfriends impress and break dance, spinning faster and faster in circles on the polished floor.

Soul Song: Atonal Preponderance

14 years–Nowhere Left to Turn

"The world is a dangerous place to live; not because of the people who are evil, but because of the people who do nothing about it."

— ALBERT EINSTEIN

DEFILEMENT

Searle has befriended a man in Albuquerque who is a single parent with a daughter my age named Laura. We attend a potluck at their home one weekend and she and I get along well. I am invited to spend the night, and when the party is over, Laura and her Father Jerry open up a sleeper couch for me in the living room and she goes to sleep in her own room. I wake in the early hours of the morning to find someone with large pasty white hands groping my breasts and fumbling into my nightclothes. I squint my eyes open to slits and look outfrom under my lashes to catch a horrifying glimpse of an ugly hairy beer belly and white underpants hanging off a pea-sized erection below.

My first reaction is to freeze; the horrors of my past reaching up to clutch me. Then slowly, I begin to turn away onto my belly and moan as if I'm having a bad dream. I worry he might have a knife. My movements interrupt the man who abruptly pulls his hand out of my top, hovering above the bed and then decides to leave. I quickly raise my head squinting past the gloom and see it is Searle's friend Jerry, Laura's own father! I can see him clearly now outlined against the light of his bedroom door, tottering off, bumping into the walls.

A few moments later, after somehow dozing off again, I hear my friend cry out faintly in the next room: "Oh come on, leave me alone. Stop, stop, leave me be."

I sit bolt upright under my blanket. I desperately try to remain awake long enough to see what happens next, but the stress has overwhelmed me and my eyes keep closing, as fearful as I am. I feel drugged. A few hours later, I attempt to get out of the bed. I can see the light on in his room. I hatch a plan in my head to run away in the night. The problem is, I don't know where I am.

Nevertheless, I step gingerly down onto the wooden floorboards of the lounge. The floor snaps spitefully and groans as I apply more pressure. My heart pounds as I imagine I might bring more attention to myself, so I quickly hop back in bed. I decide it is better to stay awake and stay put. My vigil lasts a few more hours and then I fall into an uneasy sleep, whereupon I awaken to find the man and his daughter making a large pancake breakfast as if nothing has happened the night before.

After brushing my teeth and dressing hurriedly in their bathroom, I tensely request to phone my mother.

"Sure, the phone is right there. Go ahead." Jerry points to a shelf with a telephone a few paces away and his beady eyes follow my every move, causing my stomach to curdle. Laura appears cold and distant. She is not the same girl who I felt so comfortable getting to know the night before. The atmosphere is charged and there is no privacy. They stop talking and I feel their attention riveted on my every move.

I take the chance. I make the call. *I have to get out of here!*

Lana is half awake and picks up on the other end.

"Hi Mom," I say, unable to keep the tremble out of my voice.

"Good morning, Sweets. Why are you calling so early?"

I try silence.

"Thea?"

"Yeah?"

"Well, what do you want?" She clearly isn't catching on.

"Speak up, sweetie, I can't hear you."

"Yeah, Mom," I say through clenched teeth, wishing she would pick up the difference in my attitude, "I just remembered I need to be picked up early today."

"What for?" she asks, genuinely awake now.

"You know, that show."

"No, I don't know. What show? Really…" She takes a moment to yawn.

"Thea, are you okay?'

"No, not at all," I say, falsely laughing and smiling to fool the two pan-cake-makers who are glaring at me across their syrupy plates.

"Shall I come and get you right now?"

"Mmmhmm. Yes, please."

"Okay, I'll be there in 30 minutes. You say you're not okay?"

"Nope."

I sit in silence with the duo at their table, barely able to make eye contact or eat a bite. Finally, Lana pitches up alone in her Volvo, and we thank them for their hospitality and drive away.

"Do you want to tell me what that was all about now?" she demands.

"He molested me."

"What?" She slams on the brakes in shock, and then pulls the car onto the gravelly shoulder of the country road back to Corrales. Lana is so incensed by this defilement that she contemplates turning around to go back to give Jerry a piece of her mind. "No Lana, I'm not going back there!"

"But why not? I'll go give him a piece of my mind!"

"No Lana, please just take me home."

Once we get home, Lana pulls Searle out of bed and accuses him of knowingly leaving me with a sex offender. I don't want to keep discussing it with either of them and jump in a hot shower, but Lana insists on us doing something so we all head out to a restaurant in town, off the beaten track, and low and behold, there they are, the father and daughter right in the same restaurant!

Jerry and Laura glance at us disdainfully as they walk in and shove past an aisle down from ours to sit in their own diner booth without saying hello. I am flabbergasted. I feel betrayed and I am convinced there is no coincidence, but that Lana and Searle have arranged this entire charade to check if I am lying. I feel my gorge rise as I get up and storm out. Searle then awkwardly insists on the man being invited to his birthday party a few days from now. I am horrified and furious that Lana would even consider it. I say that I will not be present if this man comes near our home. All faith in my mother leaves me and my ire at Searle's disgusting behavior is tripled. It is at this time I remind Lana of when I was 8-years-old, and he molested me in my bed at the 6th Street house in Berkeley. I can cite other *incidences too, where as a teen he has inappropriately grabbed and squeezed me.*

I feel as if I am falling faster than Alice down the rabbit hole.

A GIRL ON THE RUN

One cloudy day, after a particularly bad episode involving the police and Searle, my mother and I find ourselves checked into a grimy women's shelter. We arrive on a Thursday, and I am instructed by the matron to earn my keep by looking after the little ones in the playground while battered women and Lana share a group therapy session in the conference room. We are locked in this shelter trying to figure out what to do next and it feels more and more like a prison everyday. We are, of course, impounded for our own good. I ask myself why are we all caged in, while the perpetrators like Searle roam freely in the streets? It hits me hard that there seems to be nowhere left in the world for us but to come here. How disempowered we are!

Other women in the shelter look much worse off than we do. They are pale, with sallow skin and black eyes, broken bones recently set in casts, and scraggly limp hair. Some are drug addicts or lesbians. Their kids are dirty-faced with dark, haunted orbs for eyes. The play in the playground is devoid of laughter, and games are played furtively and urgently as if this is the one chance to climb, swing, and slide and it could be interrupted at anytime.

What I cannot escape from noticing is that no matter what end of the spectrum of life we are from, we are all shell-shocked and afraid. Fear seeps into every pore of this dingy place and smells as sour as The Plague. Women swap stories and nightmares with morbid fascination, commiserating with an almost desperate desire to hear a story worse than their own, while some victims refuse to speak. The most hopeless ones rock and hold their own thin battered bodies tight while their eyes say all we need to know.

Lana takes me out to a movie a week into our stay at the shelter in order to break out of the depressive energy of the place for a while. After the movie, I want to do something else… anything but go back to our shared apartment. "Come Mom, let's go get some frozen yogurt to take back. Aren't you tired of cooking?" I suggest hopefully. She shakes her head. "Aw, come on, I know a great place around the corner from here!" She acquiesces, but reminds me we have a curfew and will be locked out if we are not back to the shelter in time.

I insist on finding a frozen yoghurt place I know. I am feeling upset with her lack of lack of cheer and I dawdle. She snaps and becomes frantic when I insist on getting a burger when we find the yogurt place closed.

"God dammit, Thea, get in the car! We're wasting time!"

We do arrive late and they have closed the gates. We have to beg and plead to get in. Lana is crying hopelessly and the guards take pity on us as the heavens open up and rain pours down overhead. They let us in and we hurry to take refuge in our room. I am enraged. How could my mother put us in this living hellhole? There is a badly battered woman sharing our little apartment. She is skinny and frail and looks like she abuses drugs. The previous night she regaled us with stories all night long and moaned in pain in her bed for hours. Medics arrived and gave her painkillers to keep her quiet during the day. I am not looking forward to seeing her again now.

As I rush to climb up the outdoor staircase to our apartment, holding a wet grocery bag in my arms, a strange premonition crawls across my skin. Upon reaching the landing I enter a gloomy under-lit hall and find the door to the room is ajar. Peering cautiously inside, I notice the bathroom is light on and hear the bath running. The battered lady is not in her bed. My mind rapidly computes the fact that this fail woman was not able to move on her own previously. Could she possibly be taking a bath by herself now? What is wrong with this picture?

Lana lags behind, fumbling with the grocery bags and her umbrella outside the hall as I take this all in. I put down my bag and retrace my steps calling to her impatiently, "Hurry up, Mom." I have taken to calling her Mom or Mother recently and it feels better than using her first name. "I'm telling you, there's a problem here."

"Oh boy, what is it now?" comes her tired and exasperated voice across the driving rain.

"I don't know but it doesn't look right."

"Be careful, Thea," she warns me as we steal across the threshold into the sparely furnished apartment. Gingerly, I tiptoe toward the light in the bathroom and call out tentatively, "Hello?"

We open the bathroom door and find a nightgown in the bath. The water is about to overflow on the floor, and the woman is gone! Lana calls for security and I immediately discover our little stash of money is missing and my best pair of blue jeans is gone. After the security leaves, I wail murderously at my mother.

"This place isn't safe, I hate this life, I hate you, and I want you to get us out of here right now!" I yell at her in a sudden fury. Her face reflects terror and a brokenness of spirit at my violent outburst.

"But Thee," she pleads frantically, "where will we go? I don't have another place for us! Please, don't do this! I don't have money for a hotel, and besides, the gates are locked… how do you propose we will we get out, huh?"

Her reactive response takes me over the edge. Worse are her tears. How dare she cave in now?

I forcefully slam the door to my heart and turn on my heels, leaping up onto the badly tiled roof outside, my flight mechanism strong. There will be a place to go because I say there is. I use my gymnast skills to sprint across the slippery angled rooftops and climb out of the heavily walled and wired shelter in the wind and rain. I drop two stories on all fours onto the dimly lit street below and run out into the desert storm of the terrifying night. I ably splash down empty streets in the dark as rain pelts cold and hard on my back, soaking my black t-shirt and adding the perfect rhythmic sound to my misery.

Real homeless folk are wedged under cardboard boxes sheltering beneath bridges and call out menacingly as I pass, "Come here girly girl and give us some!" I leap aside, spry as a desert jackal as they reach for me. Somehow, I manage to navigate the unfamiliar streets of Albuquerque, until I find myself at the door of a boy I once kissed whose home is next door to my mother's friend Lenore's place, but I guess I know these streets better than I thought.

It is pure Providence that has brought me here. I do not know how I knew to find the way. The boy's parents take me in, put me into a hot shower, and give me a thick fuzzy robe to wear, and after hearing my story, they hand me some hot soup for my grumbling tum. We watch a horror movie together as I fall asleep in some semblance of normality on their couch. The next day, they inform Lenore where I am and she calls Lana to come to fetch me.

"The Police have been looking for you all night," Lana admonishes weakly, trying to save face before the others. True to her character, my mom, ever the "action woman," has found a way. She's made another plan for our security by attaching a renewed restraining order on Searle and we return to our home at last, safe as long as he remains cowed by the law.

In the lull of this drama, I decide to end my life. I study myself in the mirror and pop the pills in my hand, a cocktail of over-the-counter drugs for headaches and pain. I have tried to call Bard many times to take me out of here but he repeatedly tells me I used my only chance long ago and he cannot and will not help me now or ever. I have decided there is no other way out of what I perceive to be a useless life, so matter-of-factly I down the whole lot, head to school, and wait for the effects to take hold during a class. I take the decision lightly, choosing darkness over emotional pain.

It starts with a ringing sensation in my ears, and then, I am drifting. I lie down alone on the grassy knoll overlooking the track and field, where I have previously out-sprinted my opponents and won and imagine this is where it will finally all end. I look toward the Sandia Mountains as the dizziness overcomes me and my speech begins to slur as I hear myself mouth my goodbyes to the spinning clouds above in the cool desert sky. My ears are now ringing in time to the school bell. My heart beats wildly as a quiet panic overcomes me and I try my best to withstand the unpleasantness I feel but nausea as I dry-heave on the grass. Then suddenly, out of the blue, I feel the urge to fight for my life. I ease myself onto my elbows, but I can't get my body to work. It's gone numb.

Suddenly, an acquaintance is by my side, talking to me, but I can't hear her. Oddly or not, it is one of the girls I once fought against in the car park for the whole school to see that earned me the name "Rocky." I mumble some incoherent words as she bends over my prone form. She forces me to my feet and bundles me across the grass, determinedly dragging me into the big grey building. She drops me off in the nurse/counseling department where I sit for what feels like an hour slumped against the wall of the waiting room as she disappears to class. My lips are numb and a welcome darkness enfolds my aching mind.

I awaken in the blue-curtained room of a hospital. Lana is there talking to a doctor. She insists we go for family counseling, which proves ineffective but interesting. The counsellors have no skill to help me out of the dark hole I am in. They can only listen and echo my pain. We get nowhere, and I cannot see a way out through these people. I cry myself to sleep every night, but I don't try to take my life again. Instead, I rebel against the emotional pain that I awake to every morning and burn little fires on the terracotta tiles of my bedroom floor letting the firelight swallow some of my anger, and avoiding home as much as I can. As the latest country pop star Dolly Parton says, "It is hard to be a diamond in a rhinestone world."

SCENE 27

Soul Song: Sentimental, Soothing, and Sequential

15 years—Living for Love

"I once asked a bird, how is it that you fly in this gravity of darkness? The bird replied 'love lifts me.'"

— HAFIZ

SUMMER LOVE

The hot summer storms bring old family friends to our door in Corrales, New Mexico on a move back to their old family home in Isla Vista, California. Jack and his second wife Belle arrive on our doorstep with their compassionate and refreshing outlook on life. Jack is the man who lived a summer with us after my mother divorced Bard, and I used to play with Jack's son Jesse on the Northern Californian beaches at Stinson and Bolinas. Later, I met the beautiful Belle and her two older children from a previous marriage: Ali and her younger brother Chris who is two years my senior. We all became fast friends and shared frequent visits between our families in the days before mine moved to Niger. Lana is more than happy to have a break from our turbulent relationship, so she readily releases me to travel home to the California coast at the invitation of Jack and Belle.

Once we arrive at their small beach cottage by the sea, I am overjoyed to see Chris, Bell's handsome surfer son, who beckons me with his engaging smile, magnetic stare, and statuesque golden physique. He must be of Nordic descent and oozes chivalrous confidence and charisma. An electric desire springs up between us and takes us off-guard. His distinctive scent of coco-cacao mingles dreamily with the salty beach air and my vanilla rose. In between tall eucalyptus trees we experiment with intimate moments embraced by damp grass and the summer sun. His gaze intensifies, and I am mesmerized by his teal gaze that turns varying shades of violet while staring into my amber orbs.

The attraction between us lacks tangibility. I never want it to end. I feel humbled by his constant unwavering attention. I wish I could see myself through his eyes! His validation clears any negative self-talk I have going on in my head. My emotions are eclipsed by sensation and I regain my confidence enfolded in his embrace.

Out of the blue, my father Bard decides to send me a ticket to visit him in his remodeled home in Hawaii to spend a couple of weeks with getting to know my young stepsister Cerise and to visit with him and Viv. My maternal gran still lives down the road from their house and my mother's brother, who fought in the Vietnam War, has also returned home to the Big Island to work on my gran's property for a while I ready myself for a spiritual homecoming.

KEALAKEKUA, HAWAII

The day is bright and warm and I mull over what to do next. I've spent time with my gran, my little stepsister and Lana's brother, who has taken me to the gym to pump weights and swim laps in the heavily chlorinated indoor swimming pool. Bard and I travelled a distance across desolate lava lined roads to the largest white sand beach this side of the island and spent a day tanning and swapping stories in a prolonged father-daughter bonding session that nourished and soothed my mind. Our time together has helped me assuage the feelings of nervousness and wrongdoing I constantly feel in Bard and Viv's presence, knowing that any wrong move or word might spell disaster in our precarious relationship. Time spent with my stepsister Cerise is carefully monitored by Vivian who does not seem to want us to be too close, but immediately we are. It is, in fact, like we are from the same soul-tribe and that blood has nothing to do with our sisterly bond. I recognize love for this child and she easily shares space with me and holds my hand.

There are no young people my age for me to hang out with so I ask Bard to take me to the closest beach so I may journal by the ocean's edge. When he drops me off and disappears from view, I am befriended by a flaxen-haired drifter known as Gabriel who has made his home in a VW camper bus and he gives me my first personal introductions to the art of meditation. We sit together in silence listening to the waves lap and crash against stone and sand and spend the rest of the day playing Frisbee on the beach. The sea sparkles and beckons me to play in her waves. This is the same water where the dolphin once rescued me! I feel genuinely safe here. The hours extend pleasantly and until I find myself joyfully body-surfing an emerald wave, completely unaware that I am swimming with an enormous white shark! I notice people begin to run up and down the shore shouting something and beckoning to me. I wonder what they are doing until I see my new friend Gabriel call to me using his arms and a big conch shell. When I body surf back to the sand, I am shocked to hear I was in the waves with a shark double my size.

"You must take note when people are giving you signs. That shark could have killed you," he reprimands me firmly, long blonde ponytail bobbing wildly in the wind.

I shiver in my towel and smile up at his worried face.

"That's okay, I'm not really scared to die," I lie, suddenly shy.

He looks at me sideways while performing a deep breathing yogic head-stand posture, showing off maybe, I think to myself.

"It didn't eat me, and here I am!" I declare, looking at him upside down. I am leaning over him with my hair dripping on my toes, bundled in a big colorful beach towel.

"Besides, Gabe, I've heard that the Hawaiians worship shark gods." I wait for his counter response but he keeps quiet, closing his eyes and still maintains his balance. "So maybe I was in the wave with a god?" I offer up mischievously, putting my towel on the ground and adopting the same headstand pose as him.

"Wanna play some more Frisbee until my dad comes for me?" I ask cheekily, sticking my tongue out at him now.

He knocks me over by tapping my ankle gently with one foot, without opening his eyes, and we both end up sitting cross-legged facing each other. One piercing yet compassionate blue-eyed stare quickly turns me silent and serious.

"Nah, I'd rather meditate with you." He smiles cordially.

"Come on, let's get back to my bus, the tide is coming in."

My father is waiting in the car park when I come out of the beach shower. He rolls a suspicious eye at the transient and moves to have a word with him. Gabriel stays back and I want to say goodbye but my father is in a hurry to get into the car. I never see the golden man in his magic bus again, however, I do receive a cryptic postcard from him. It is a picture of him, kneeling on a towel in his bus. "One Love, Thea" is all the words on the back of the card read. I understand. He is sharing the essence of The Song. The song of souls I have never forgotten since crossing over.

Soul Song:
Courageous Yet Savage

15-17 years–Emancipated

"I am the captain of my fate, I am the master of my soul."

— WILLIAM ERNEST HENLEY

MOVING

I return to the rural town of Corrales, New Mexico, rejuvenated, only to discover that in my absence, Searle has reunited with Lana and found his way home. His violent attacks on her personhood are now limited to verbal abuse and continue sporadically, but are rarely perpetrated in my sight. I spend much time locked in my bedroom on the pretext of studying but in reality, I am trying to escape the drama.

My fifteenth birthday is celebrated with only one friend at my own request. I pine privately for the feel of Chris strong arms, wide lips, and magnetic eyes upon my form. We talk on the phone sometimes, skimming over the surface, but we never mention our love relationship to each other or our families. At last, Lana gives up waiting for her government job to come and decides to move us back home to Berkeley since Searle has dropped out of his University course and was this was the reason we came here in the first place. Our support structure in New Mexico is slim and all our ties are in California, plus it is closer to Hawaii where my gran Jan still lives by herself.

I am so excited to live next door to my old bosom buddy Raven again! I wonder if our secret gate still stands. Will our friendship still be intact? Who has she become in my absence? More importantly, who have I become?

Back in the Berkeley home on 6th Street, I must stay in the house with tenants while Searle and Lana reside outside in the half-renovated garage studio. Eventually, the tenants vacate the property and Lana and Searle move back into the big Victorian house with me. I start the second semester of the 10th grade at the famous public school Berkeley High School, still wearing leather, faded blue jeans, and punk earrings, like a fashionable New Mexican, but I quickly discover that this impresses only the tough guys who are outnumbered by the school majority who happen to be middle class children of intellectuals. I decide not to be defined as tough anymore, so I begin dressing up in skirts, scarves, tie-dyed shirts, leggings, and soft off the shoulder sweaters that reflect the eclectic bohemian-style of my peers. I create myself a new here as a dancer and songstress in my spare time as I settle down to study.

I'm fifteen, and am drenched in love potion number 9, which is not lost on the boys. One such boy with full lips, dark tight-cropped brown curls, soft amber eyes, and mocha skin meets my gaze shyly across the room in our history class. It doesn't take long before he catches me smiling shyly back and moves across the room to ask if I will study with him at the big public library up the street. He introduces himself as Nafari. He explains that his mother gave him the name. His father is Caucasian and his mother's lineage is African American. "She's no longer on this Earth," he confides tersely with a sincere and heart-wrenching melancholy in to his voice. "I'll tell you the story one day."

Nafari walks me home and sits beside me on the bus. I feel secure in his presence and a gentleness begins to bloom in the core of my heart. *This is about healing,* comes the whisper in the back of my head. Though he is masculine, he is clearly a sensitive soul, and he opens a secret door to his feelings, hidden from the rest of the world, reels me in and shows me that he can connect with my angst and emotional pain. His body is naturally athletic and he is the perfect blend of man and boy that I need to feel safe. I learn about the turmoil that burns deep in his heart stemming from his mother's untimely death at the hands of her then-lover and the effect this has had on him. He was in the house when she was killed and he was only four yet remembers every detail and wants to take revenge if only he knew how. I share most of my experiences and heartaches with him.

Though both our lives are full, we seem to find hours to talk with one another on the phone at night. Despite these midnight conversations filled with heartache and pain, we also find joy in each other's company by the light of day. We share the camaraderie of our peers on the high school theatre steps and spend time walking all over town or at one another's houses on the weekends. There we hold onto one another, sneaking out of our houses and running home in the wee hours of dawn not daring to be seen by our parents. I feel myself and my age at last with Nafari, not having to be so serious and worldly with him as others.

Nafari has a stepmother who is curious about my life and takes me into her confidence. Nafari and I frequent the Berkeley High party scene in holidays and the weekends: raucous dance music, drunken party tricks, weed, wine, bohemian art and gourmet food. Invariably, someone's parents are away, and we all hear about the get-together's viva voce. Weed is present in almost every household and it seems almost normal for people to partake in nature's drug. It was one way of rebelling in New Mexico, but I find no particular need to rebel now.

It is easy to get around this small university town using public transport, libraries and bookstores to increase my awareness. I learn the bus routes and walk or use my bicycle to reach the furthest corners of the city. Raven and I don't see much of each other and she is now behind me in school by two years so we no longer mix in the same circles. Life seems to be looking up in comparison to the horrendous years in New Mexico, until one fateful night when the tables turn…

OUT THE DOOR

Searle launches into another one of his tirades, accusing Lana and I of some new transgression. He howls like a craven animal and throws us against the floor, where I am kicked to the bottom and Lana is thrown on top of me as he slams a pair of antique wooden dining chairs on her back, then body-slams himself on top, threatening to break our ribs. My mother entreats him to stop, but in his mad reticulating mind, he hears nothing.

An inferno breaks inside of me. I am furious! I try to get up but cannot. As he kicks at us and continues to pounce painfully on our backs, I pound the floor with my fist and scream for help. Our tenants below, Two women with guts of steel, spring to action. They run up the backstairs and pound on the door, demanding to know if we are okay. Lana says we are, but I say we are not. I slip past Lana and Searle in the doorway to reach these powerhouses and hide behind their hand-held skillets.

One of them questions my mother again, "Lana, are you sure you're okay?"

Lana hovers weakly in the doorway, nerve-stricken, and afraid to move. I know he is standing behind her, threatening something. I meet her eyes, begging her to come. She is simply frozen and refuses. She looks at me with a mixture of both admiration and irritation. Always there is blame.

How can I leave her alone to deal with Searle, and how can I be so brave as to stand up for my own rights?

"Come, mother." She shakes her head.

I can tell she is wounded that I am revealing our truth so callously. It wounds her, though I can see she is secretly relieved that I am not hurt physically and I am getting out of harm's way. We head down below and they give me the phone. We stand listening for more thuds upstairs and only once I hear her cry out. "Thea, will you call the police?"

I hesitate, considering, somehow knowing that this one action will change the course of my life forever. My heart is hammering in my chest. I know he could be actively suffocating her as I pause and we would hear nothing. I begin to tremble uncontrollably. My hand reaches for the phone and my fingers move numbly over the buttons as I dial 911.

After calling the police, I summon Nafari. He and his father come almost immediately to fetch me. The police take statements and agree that I will be better off spending the night elsewhere. They can see from Searle's records it is not the first time he has been reported for domestic violence. Safe in the backseat of Nafari's father's car, I stare listlessly out the window and notice the street lamps flickering, as I sob silently, feeling all alone even as Nafari rubs my back and pats my hand and his father pledges to be my safety raft through thick and thin, while keeping his eyes fixed on the road ahead. I resolve internally not to return home unless Lana gets rid of the monster once and for all.

PASCALE

A week passes by uneventfully as I stay sheltered, well-fed and loved in my new, but temporary residence in Nafari's family home. Nafari himself seems unsure how to handle the situation. He seems scared to talk with me, and our relationship seems distant during this time. I seek solace in the love, care and understanding I receive from his stepmother and his father. I am broken, damaged goods and I worry inwardly that Nafari may now think my lifestyle is too complicated for him. He brings a girl to our history class who he says is dying to meet me. "Here is Pascale. She used to play with you when you were five. Do you remember her?"

I can't believe my eyes. It is she, the little English-Peruvian friend I used to play with in the Berkeley Hills before we moved away and never saw one another again. She is a real beauty now with full lips tinted a natural shade of rosebud red, brown silky hair falling long and straight pulled back neatly off her moon-shaped face, and a perfectly rounded Peruvian nose. I can see Nafari is quite taken with her. She is exceptionally warm, grounded and seems genuinely enthusiastic to meet me. He leaves us in the hallway, sneaking off with his guy friends so she and I can talk. He has told Pascale of my predicament and I can tell she is very concerned for me.

"I told my parents," she confides gently. "I hope you don't mind?"

"No, it's okay, my life is an open book. I have nothing to hide."

"Have you been home since that night?"

"I only went to pick up some clothing and a few things." I sigh.

"What did your mom say to you?"

"Nothing much. She asked me, 'How can you put me in the middle? I'm not leaving him!' So, I told her, 'Okay Mom, in that case, I'm not coming home.' Then all she asked me was, 'Where will you stay?' I told her for now I can stay with Nafari's family, but I'll figure something out. Pascale, you understand, I can't just return home this time and I have no money to sustain myself. It'll keep going on like this forever and someone could get really hurt."

"Wow, Thea you are so strong. Do you have anywhere in mind to go?"

"No. Not really. I don't know what I'm going to do."

Tears shimmer on my cheeks yet suddenly I find I don't have the energy to wipe them away.

Pascale purses her lips, contemplating. The following day she invites me home.

"We've always wanted you to love and protect," her dark-haired mother says as she squeezes me tight with passion. "You're welcome to stay in the upstairs studio as long as you and Pascale don't disturb each other in your studies."

Pascale's father welcomes me too and wants to calmly discuss the practicalities of this arrangement. They insist on having permission from both Lana and Bard and they want a small rent and money for meals, which they agree to share with me. I will have certain chores and I am given my own key to come and go as I please. They put their trust me.

I am nearly sixteen. During the strained time living at his house, Nafari and I have broken off our affair. I still feel sad about it and share this with Pascale. She comforts me, and then I find out it is she whom he is secretly dating! Though I feel some pain at the discovery, I am more confused that neither one is truthful about the relationship with me. I resolve to quickly move on and make more friends. My friendships fill the void I have lost in having no family. Now I see I have the love and acceptance of many families. Nafari is fast gaining popularity for his natural athleticism and humorous personality. He is no longer the quiet attentive boyfriend I had once grown to love. I, too, am exploring another me: the creative one, who loves hanging out with musicians and artists who are living on the fringes of the unspoken popularity contest at school.

The view is incredible from my little loft upstairs in Pascale's parent's home. I can see the sunset over the San Francisco Bay. Many an evening I come and stand at the attic window contemplating life and listening to Paul Simon's Graceland track, remembering my ties to Africa and my childhood in this very neighborhood before Lana and Bard went their separate ways. I begin having visions of the lives of the Native Americans that once peopled the hills here and imagine this place without lights, sounds, roads, and shelters of modern-day reality. I lean deeply into my inner world and my imagination explodes with creative notions. I sometimes draw the images on paper and add little stories to the pictures.

I find a job in the next county cleaning cat kennels and packing shelves for a friend of Lana's. It is here I am casually introduced to a young Whoopi Goldberg who frequents the pet store buying 50lb dog food bags that I have the honor to carry to her car. All the other shop attendants go crazy for her autograph. She tells the shop owner that I have the best manners, and leaves me a handsome tip. If only she could know what this does for me every time she comes to the shop. The boss, who has known me as a baby, is proud of my humble work ethic and promotes me as she deems me ready to handle more responsibility.

Help pours into every facet of my life from well-wishers and do-gooders in the community. I am supported by my friends and their parents. Nafari's home is still open for me and every Tuesday night they host me for a family dinner. I still pen soulful love songs, while poetry flows freely onto the journal pages that I decorate and illustrate in jewel tones using pencil and watercolor. Soulful ballads erupt unbidden from my heart and sweet notes fill my voice and sweep across the strings of my guitar. The Song is back and moving in me, and my connection with Nature and the unseen realms returns tenfold to me, to bring me solace to what I deem is my singular despair.

BLAKE

Soon I meet a new boy, also from a single parent household. Blake has his own sad story to tell. He is like my soul-tribe member in a strange off-center sort of way, and he has tons of artistic talent that he attributes to a rich imagination, but I prefer to think of it as his magic. His father is homeless and wanders the streets, having lost a battle with mental illness and haunted by thoughts of a society that infringes incessantly upon mother earth whom he revers. He is frequently off his meds. Blake's mother, a scrupulous bookkeeper, does the best she can to provide a roof and shelter for herself and her only son and we become the best of friends.

Blake becomes my male muse. He and I spend hours exploring creative pursuits together and share a passionate love of adventure, magic, fantasy and nature. We seem perfectly matched for a time. Still, he's way too like me and I feel together our emotions run much too high and wild; our love threatens to overwhelm and take me places I am not destined for. His eternal desire to smoke cigarettes and other substances drives me away and into the arms of others. Though we appear well-matched, it is becoming unsafe for either of us to continue. I begin to pull back. He pretends to understand and we try to be friends, but our relationship becomes an addiction and we are constantly drawn back to each other.

One afternoon, I venture home to visit Searle, and Lana and complain that I am feeling very sad about a slight from my peers. Lana rebukes me without hesitation, refusing to offer me any sympathy.

"Oh, come on, where do you get off coming to complain and cry here?" she grumbles meanly. Her tone is twisted and bitter as she continues, "you opted out, so just get over it. That's life and there's nothing fair about it. I've told you that for years: life isn't fair, Thea. You'd better wise up and get used to it. That's the way the world is."

All I can do is stare at her, incredulous, and my stepfather Searle purses his lips and nods almost triumphantly in silent agreement. She's right, I realize immediately. I should not have come here for support or sympathy. I can't come here for much of anything these days. I beat a hasty and angry retreat. I am no longer welcome in my own home. I can't help but revert to the old thought that my biological family would never treat me this way.

Shortly after this, I am diagnosed with a supposed hereditary hypothyroidism disease that my doctor tells me will never go away. This is a hormonal problem that causes severe sporadic mood swings that threaten to pull me down while at school. The mood swings cause me to want to throw plates while washing them at the sink, or to sleep deeply during class, or to feel extremely high and only moments later very low. I begin scouring the healthy living shelves of residential bookstores when the thyroid drugs prescribed are out of synch with my bodily rhythms in order to find natural ways to cure myself. I am only 16 and can't imagine what it will be like to take pills my entire life.

I discover that exercise and iodine-rich foods can help my condition, so I begin running, cycling and eating seaweed, sesame, and honey candies daily. I wean myself off the prescription pills, and when I go for my next check-up the doctors are amazed that I have regulated my own symptoms. I sign up to be on the rowing team and practice rowing on a city lake in the early mornings with my Bolivian-American girlfriend Adelina. I also enjoy dancing modern dance in a school-based theatrical dance production that performs for members of the public frequently.

Unfortunately, my old back injury flares up and I stop being able to run. The rowing team coach drops me. I beg her to let me use the ergo meter, an indoor simulated rowing machine for my cardio training but she and the board of coaches for the city refuse emphatically, saying the team must run together in order to bond. There will be no preferential treatment. Deflated, I return to the expensive bodybuilding and gym workout solution instead. I am determined to keep myself healthy. I cycle and walk just about everywhere. I try to ignore the pressure that is molding me and grooming me without my own awareness. I feel all rough edges and I don't fit in anywhere and I feel unwanted and lonesome.

IT'S MY LIFE

Spring is here so I can't be melancholy for long. Birds are singing, Easter eggs line the shop front windows and afternoons are sunny. The trees are all in bloom along the main streets in happy pink, white and green finery and there is more movement outside the traditional cafés in town. I find a second part-time job in a warehouse consignment store and spend my afternoons working and weekends partying with school friends. In my loft in the hills with Pascale's family, I feel restricted and scrutinized. A rebellion swells and boils over in the home between Pascale's mother and me. I feel the spirit world stir in my heart and touch my consciousness softly as I watch the sunrise and see the breeze ruffle the leaves on the tree outside my window but I feel that I must now leave this comfort and prepare myself to pave my own way. The determination within may land me in trouble before long but I know no other way of helping myself, or stopping it.

Lana lands her dream job with the United States Agency for International Development (USAID) where she heads to our nation's capital to prepare for a year's training in Washington DC. She leaves Searle in charge of the Berkeley house and our pets. Am I an adult or a child? Should I tolerate Pascale's parent's demands? I have a car and two jobs and I am paying rent here although it comes from my father Bard's child support that will last until I am eighteen.

Pascale, ever the good girl, has begun to mirror my behavior and stand up to her dominant mother. I am gradually seen as the cause of this resistance in my friend. Pascale's gentle father who skirts around confrontation at all costs tries to calm his fiery wife. He speaks with me gently yet firmly, urging me to make a decision. This is deadly serious. I certainly do not want to be the cause of another family's break up.

I decide to leave and move back home to the outside garage cottage where Searle is staying in Lana's big house in the Berkeley flats. Bard cautions me against doing this, vehemently and rightfully declaring he will stop paying for my child support and will send me to a foster home if I return to live with Searle. He cannot see any logic in me wanting to return. Yet still he refuses to offer to take me in himself. The arrangement at Pascale's parent's home suits him since it means he doesn't have to worry or feel too guilty about my safety. It is a stable home tucked safely in the best part of Berkeley and while while I am still here he can comfortably carry on being a distant father, absent of all decision-making in my world.

Not long after I leave the comfort of the Pascale's home, I realize he is right about one thing: I am entering the dragon's den... The first two weeks, I think I am in Heaven. I enjoy having my own space in the garage, reestablishing my roots and feeling somehow free to be me. Then, one evening, Searle threatens me over laundry as I did not follow his instructions to hang it on the line and took a short cut by putting it in the dryer, thereby using too much energy. He demands that my child support payments be paid toward my room and board here as he purports not to be my parent since in the past I chose to leave. Bard doesn't trust my mother nor Searle to ensure I receive the child support for my own needs so I have now been given full access under Bard's friend who is a banker, who puts her name on my account and signs on my behalf until I come of age. Searle seethes about the expenses I am incurring and explodes about the clothesline. Fear of being the victim of his violence and instability makes me realize my mistake and that without Lana as a buffer, I am the newest target.

I call Lana immediately who instructs me over the phone from Washington, DC, "It isn't safe for you there, Thea– gather your things and get out NOW. I mean it, Thea, hurry. You can take my car, but you'll have to make an excuse to get the keys from the house. Meanwhile, I'll send my friend Eva to pick you up." My mother hangs up before I can say more. I rush to sneak outside. Before long, Eva pulls up around the corner and sweeps me away to her home for sanctuary. I flee in the night before he can discover I am gone. Once in the safety of Eva's house, I call Blake to let him know what is happening and where I am. He and his mother are very concerned.

Nafari's family comes to the rescue a few weeks later, whisking me away on holiday to the Napa Valley wine country and a spa with them, where I meet a female friend of theirs who is going through problems of her own. Roxanne needs a roommate, and I agree to rent a room in her tiny rental cottage just off Solano Avenue on the borderline of the county towns of Berkeley and Albany.

Throughout all of this upheaval, my homework, grades, and schoolwork suffer greatly. I am exhausted all the time. The hypothyroidism is my constant companion and my back aches so much I have to spend my savings to take myself to chiropractors that crack me back into alignment. I regularly skip the classes I have no interest in, driving to the beach instead, sitting on the sand, or gazing across the sea, wondering what is to become of me. Sometimes I take my guitar and sing love shanties to soothe myself, plucking the strings until my fingers almost bleed, listening to the ragged notes as they are torn away on the wind. Outside of school hours I take up more work babysitting for friends and for colleagues whenever I can. I can barely keep my eyes open in my favorite criminal law class, even though I am highly intrigued by the debates. Searle keeps coming to the school demanding to see me until the school counselor phones Lana and he is issued a restraining order that keeps him away.

Soul Song:
Radiant Rhythms

16-17 years–Unburdening My Heart

"Guidance may appear in all forms."

-ALIMA

MENTORS

I witness parents of my schoolmates shake their heads at my living predicament. Nafari's parents do not abandon me. They continue the now year long tradition of invites to their home for supper every Tuesday night, and Nafari's stepmother makes sure everyone is present, giving me a sense of family. She listens to me and offers advice where she can. I am invited on road trips and given a special place at the table. It is still a bit awkward between Nafari and me. He ignores me most of the time, so I am left to babysit his baby stepbrother and chat to the other brother who is two years my junior. Another friend, a psychiatrist called Yeshua, collects me every Thursday night, buys me dinner, and counsels me pro-bono one-on-one. I reach out for love and make fast friends amongst the single mothers of every boy I date, and I have long heart-to-soul conversations over tea at their houses once or twice every weekend. They are my unspoken heroines, heart saviors, and an integral support network for me.

Eva, my mother's good friend, is single and lives a solitary life after her own divorce years before. She is the one to whose home we have fled time and time again to get away from Searle over the years. She herself fled from Nazi Germany as a child and survived a scary relationship with an angry husband who also once tried to abuse her, but she tells me she picked up a toaster oven and told him if he came for her, she would have to kill him. Eva listens well and always offers me tea, lunch and her powerful presence, mostly giving me space to purge, nodding, listening, asking reflective questions and giving wise counsel.

Whenever I am at my lowest, I impulsively jump in my car and drive eight hours down the California coast to Santa Barbara to visit Chris and his family who always offer me love, comfort food and shelter, and put me emotionally back on track without asking anything in return. They simply believe in my ability to hold myself together and that one day I will make it. That belief alone gives me the resilience to carry on. The chemistry is still there and always makes time to spend intimately with me.

Across the San Francisco Bay are two practicing psychotherapists I once impressed and befriended as a little girl in past summers spent at Tassajara with Bard. They personally position themselves in my life as my lifeline of mental and emotional support, keeping me grounded when I think the world is tilting. They are strong pillars that validate, listen, and love me unconditionally and help me realize that though my sanity is 100 percent my responsibility, others have neglected their responsibilities toward my upbringing. The saying 'it takes a village to raise a child' now truly applies to me. They calmly reassure me that I am not fully to blame for my unusual predicament but that I do need to maintain my sanity.

Not one of my mentors ever offers me cash, which I really do need so badly right now but am too proud and afraid of rejection to ask for. Nonetheless, their ruminations are treasured and sacred. They reflect back my understanding like so many mirrors, each showing me new aspects of myself as yet unseen, keeping my confidence and faith high in times of strife. I soon become aware, under their constant tutelage, that this is my life, my responsibility and my choice to be on my own, albeit one that had circumstances been different I might not have needed to choose. It is assumed by all my friends that it is my parents' responsibility to see that I don't go hungry, yet some nights I do.

Summer months are always a welcome treat and I spend a lot of time working, but when I am not at work, I play as hard as I can. Leisure times are spent attending reggae festivals with friends and swimming under waterfalls with unknown bohemians... sometimes sharing a puff of the green stuff they smoke and laughing at everything they say. I am not afraid to be in the nude in front of strangers, as I am blessed with a trim muscular body, but I have learned healthy boundaries when it comes to giving myself over to just anyone. I have somehow come to the conclusion that I don't need a relationship to complete me.

I am clear that right now I am looking for happiness and not romance. My body image is intact and I enjoy adorning it with the heady perfumed incense and scented oils wayfaring concert gypsies massage into their skin. The boys at these concerts are gorgeous, tanned demi-gods with long unkempt hair, and the girls are bejeweled with rings, belts, braids, and colorful bags tied to their hips. The bohemian lifestyle captivates freedom of expression and I try losing myself in this wild riot of color, dance, and song. I soak in this amazing life, grateful for the natural world full of fire, rocks, plants, sun, wind, and rain.

After these little adventures of escapism, I always enjoy the return home. Home has become a sacred place to journal, read, and sleep. I fall asleep surrounded by the few material goods I own. During the week and after work, I spend most of my time in the company of my school friends Riva, Ethan, and Dan. They each have their own traumatic stories to tell and we ground and counsel each other over coffee, tea, and my favorite beverage: hot frothed almond milk in various coffee shops around town. On Saturdays, we party together, soak in rented hot tubs, or write music and sing to Dan's renowned guitar licks. I reserve Sundays for hiking with other high school friends. As spring and summer arrive to kiss awake the light, I take my bike and ride it up into the nature parks above the University campus with Blake and his friends.

We tote our guitars everywhere, singing and playing self-created melodies, writing poetry, and sharing dreams, drawing, painting and enjoying each other's company. Again, thoughts of my biological origins flash through my mind. Where is my real mother? Do I have a real father, too? Could they be amongst the homeless? No, not that bad, I pray silently to myself. One day I plan to find them.

YESHUA

Once a week my Rastafarian psychiatrist Yeshua picks me up in his fast sports car, buys me a healthy meal, and takes me back to his apartment for very unconventional pro bono counseling sessions. He is edgy, progressive, and cool, and we perform yoga poses as we sit on his living room floor discussing my joys and sorrows and designing steps to tackle the daily challenges I face. He never answers my pleas for help directly, but always points me back toward myself and the insights that live within my own consciousness. He asks penetrating questions that cause me to look for answers deeper within.

Not only is he a powerful counselor, but he also hangs out with me as a friend, showing me how to perform basic Shiatsu massage, unashamedly discussing spiritual matters with me, musing at whether all cases he has come across can be explained by mental psychosis and handled with drugs or if some are, at the very least, created by psychic or spiritual happenings in the person's reality. I find these discussions far more intriguing than my own over-hashed tales of woe, and throughout our time together he never falters in his quality of care for me. Like most of the other mentors in my life he assures me my maturity and sanity are perfectly intact and this gives me the confidence to carry on.

One day, he receives a call from my estranged stepfather Searle, who says he would like to meet with us to talk over our now non-existent relationship. After all, he is still married to Lana whom I do still communicate with. This is something I am not overly optimistic about, but Yeshua insists he will protect me if things get heated. I am dubious. He has never seen the wrath of Searle first hand. Lana is not for this approach either as she has become disillusioned and mistrusts him even more now that she has gained some distance and is living in Washington, D.C.

Searle drives up and walks through the door, all smiles, positivity and enthusiasm. This is the mask he wears in public and I know another side, equally intense, lies beyond the mask. I remain seated near the floor, eating my supper, watching cautiously as the two men chat. Finally, I put my plate down and consider the massive man I once knew as my stepfather seated across from me. Yeshua opens our dialog, setting basic rules and a tone for the talk and asks us each to contribute and listen to the other. Searle goes ahead and expresses his sentiments at having seemingly "lost his family" and Yeshua guides him with careful questioning, then turns to me for my thoughts. Searle does not like what I have to say. He is determined to gloss over the facts, becomes defensive and chooses to paint a one-sided story full of untruths, but Yeshua is smarter than that and continues to hold space for everyone to take ownership of their part. Searle feels he is losing ground and is not accustomed to owning anything. He thinks an apology without any promise or accountability moving forward is enough. Nevertheless, Yeshua insists on an accountability plan for all. He wants to know how this apology will guarantee my safety.

Suddenly, a vein pops out on Searle's neck. Uh oh. I can see the shift in his demeanor and posture as his voice rises. Yeshua tries to placate him, but Searle stabs an accusatory finger in his direction. "I know what's happening here. You are clearly sleeping with her!" he shouts furiously and leaps across the room bellowing and blasting hot air and obscenities at Yeshua's face. I freeze on the low couch and watch with my heart in my throat as Yeshua slowly stands to face Searle's wrath. His fist flexes into a tight ball at his side and he appears tiny in comparison to the looming form of Searle. Yeshua has woken the monster.

"Searle, you're way out of line. You'll need to respect me and sit down or else leave my apartment now."

"F—k you. You aren't going to get away with that. I'm not going anywhere. Just you *make* me!" He turns his venomous gaze my way. "Look at *her*," he sneers venomously, "All cuddled up smug." Searle kicks at my half-eaten plate on the floor. "You disgust me!"

I stay frozen, squatting on the low sofa and watch as the two men face off. I am inches from the telephone and imagine reaching out to call the police, but I am too scared to make a move. My body and mind are scanning the room for possible exits.

"Okay man, I believe it's now time for you to leave." Yeshua visibly controls his own outrage. Searle is beet red and spits in Yeshua's face while his huge hands flex uncontrollably, ready to strangle the life out of the lithe dark-skinned runner before him.

I watch in slow motion as Yeshua controls his own anger and begins to open his fist with measured effort one finger at a time. He must have realized he was clenching it by his side ready to take a swing. He is breathing rhythmically and seems to be in complete control of his own emotions.

"I said, it's now time for you to leave, my man," he repeats calmly for the second time.

I have never seen someone hold so much powerful poise in the face of such fury and wish that one day I will be able to do the same. I glance at the phone on the floor near my feet and wonder if I will have time to call the police if Searle decides to attack. I am shaking too much to do it.

Suddenly, Yeshua speaks up, his voice carrying above that of the bellowing maniac in front of him.

"Get out of my house now. GET OUT."

Searle leaps back, whirls and storms out as if a whip has cracked behind him.

I am in shock as I see him swing open the first screen door and slam the wooden one, then hear his retreating footsteps pound down the wooden stairs that lead outside to the street. Yeshua stands still a moment, then with dredlocks bristling he composes his breathing, and turns to ask if I am okay. I shake my head, surprised I can even move. Then we hear footsteps returning, pounding up the stairs two at a time.

Yeshua races to the door and tries to lock it just as Searle crashes into it. There is a power struggle as Yeshua throws all his athletic strength into holding the door shut and tells me to leave the room. I run to the kitchen. I know there is a door out the back. I am petrified and look for a knife but the kitchen is in disarray. All I can hear is grunting, pounding, crashing, and then nothing. I wait, trembling and alone in the kitchen.

"Thea?" My shoulders drop. It is Yeshua.

"Yes, I'm here."

"Well, that was something. I believe I have my answer. You won't be seeing that man again. I'll recommend he never comes near you in this lifetime. Damn, but he is strong!"

Shakily, I nod my head. The last thing we hear is the squeal of tires on tarmac.

Soul Song: Mysterious, Sacred, and Steady

17 years–Guardians

*"Don't depend on me too much, even shadows
disappear when it is dark."*

— THE KRAKALL

DARK SHADOW EMERGING

In Washington DC, Lana is having her own relational challenges. She instructs that a new restraining order be placed on Searle. The order has him staying at least 300 yards away from me at all times. She tells me that she is fighting with him over the telephone almost daily. She returns home to Berkeley once to handle business and finds another woman in our house who is equally as surprised to see my mother show up. Instead of demanding the woman get out, Lana purses her lips, heads up to the bedroom where she collects some articles of interest, including documents for the home that she is aghast to discover Searle has tried to forge her signature upon to proclaim himself the rightful owner of her property. At last, she is beginning to accept that this marriage is over and starts the legalities of divorcing him.

It is 1988. Leaves are turning red and gold and dropping from the trees. I feel overburdened and alone. Bard and Lana have both sent regrets informing me that neither one will be attending my graduation ceremony, one of the most important days in my life and the lives of my peers. I find myself constantly circling inward, barely managing to survive the feelings that rage and bubble at my core. Where are my parents? Who am I? What am I doing? How did life get so difficult? How did I go from an A/B+ average student to a wayward young woman without a family? This is grossly unfair and what will happen after I graduate? No one can guide me and I can't keep asking my community for help... people have their own lives to manage.

One night, feeling utterly alone in the world, I steal a bottle of cheap wine from my housemate's pantry and begin to write my sorrows on paper as I drink. I drink and drink until the bottle is finished. I look at the writing: red ink is scrawled haphazardly across several pages. Something is emerging. The writing starts out legible and tidy, but the words are hurtful, vengeful, and angry. I stumble into the small kitchen and extract a large butcher knife from the wooden knife holder while a strange high-pitched laughter seeps out of my lungs. I take the knife to my room and begin to saw at my wrists, but the blade is blunt and I am too scared of the pain to make more than a scratch. I hear myself as if from a distance making strangled guttural sounds and I run to the kitchen to get a sharper knife. As I turn from the knife block, Roxanne, my thirty-something housemate appears in a white nightgown looking as pale as a ghost.

"What are you doing?" she demands sharply and I can see she is trembling. Her countenance, full of consternation, judgment, and creepy indignation pierces my drunken stupor like an arrow to the heart. I scream some incoherent words at her, eyes blazing. I feel miles away and realize I have let go of control over my body or mind. The *something* that boiled up as I wrote ten minutes ago in my room has taken command. It gurgles, growls, and bellows, warning her to stay back. Roxanne picks up the phone, mesmerized by the "thing" panting like a dog in her kitchen. It cackles as I am transfixed by horror, seeing as if from another corner of the room, pinned back by an unseen yet undeniably powerful force. She calls Lana four hours ahead of our time zone and wakes her up in the early hours of a weekend morning to listen to the guttural grunting noises I am making in the background.

"Do you hear what your daughter is doing? She has lost her sanity and I don't blame her, Lana, I blame you. You need to get on a plane pronto and get here *now*!" she screams hysterically.

Next, she picks up the telephone and calls Yeshua.

In utter desperation, the horrified Roxanne hastily thrusts the phone toward the spitting cackling beast I have become. Then she shouts hysterically over the carnal growls continuously being emitted from my lips. She swears at him insisting he, as my psychiatrist, should come straightaway. He calmly tells her to call the police and get an ambulance, and then hangs up the phone and goes back to bed. I see and hear all this from far away. Roxanne stares at the disconnected phone in disbelief. No one is there for me in this moment but her. She is weak and incapable. The beast lurches toward her.

"Put that knife down!" she screams, raising her hands in defense.

Somehow, from my vantage far away I am able to force my hand to drop the knife. It clatters to the floor as my body writhes, giving in to the monumental pressure built up inside. I fall at her feet and contort wildly on the floor beneath the heavy four-legged wooden chopping block in the tiny kitchen with linoleum tiles, and then unbidden one hand shoots out, snatches hold of a table leg and lifts the heavy table overhead.

I am distinctly aware of the strength of this looming shadow that has control over my being and my body. The landlords, our next-door neighbors, hear the commotion from the big house next door. They hear sounds that make them believe someone is being murdered and race to the cottage and crash through the front door. Big boned and strong as ogres, they pull the table from my hands and with much heavy breathing, grunting and groaning they finally manage to pin me down. I register they are hurting and bruising me, but I am numb and detached from the pain at the same time. One has to sit on my upper body while the other kneels on my legs. They can barely hold me as I jerk and bite, spit and scream.

Lights and sirens fill the air. Help is on its way and an ambulance, two medics, and the Fire Department arrive on scene with the Police. Four of them seize and sedate me, strapping me forcibly to a gurney in the back of a vehicle. Time stands still as everything goes blank. I awaken to white walls and the faint scent of antiseptic the following morning and realize I am in a hospital. I gaze around the room, and my eyes alight upon the comfortingly familiar face of Nafari's stepmother Nan, staring intently at me from a chair in the corner. She rises and comes to my side.

"Oh, my dear Thea. How are you feeling?"

"I could be better."

"Do you remember anything?"

"Yes, a little bit, but I don't know how I got here."

I struggle to rise and wince in pain as I try to move against wrist restraints that tie me down.

"Don't let them see you do that," Nan whispers urgently in my ear. "They haven't noticed your wrists." I look down to see I have cuts there. Did I try to commit suicide?

"Thea, what happened? They want to take you to some psychiatric ward! Just answer the questions normally. Just say that you had a momentary breakdown. We'll take you home. You can stay with us for a while. Your mom is flying in tomorrow. We will handle this, okay?"

I have a moment to nod my head just as a nurse flutters in.

"Is she awake?" She glances sternly at my protector. "Why didn't you call us?"

She turns to ask me all the special questions that let her know if I am sane or not. As I have been warned, I hide my wrists when she undoes the restraints. After signing release forms, I manage to slip out the door with Nan into the bright sunlight. There I am able to reach a semblance of normality as I am taken home to the family that have never left my side throughout my time in Berkeley. This is the easy part.

Meeting with Lana is not an easy task. She is most concerned and holed up with her best friends. The father of the household once lost himself in a moment of drunkenness when he dropped me off after babysitting their daughters and kissed me on the lips, inappropriately thrusting his tongue in my mouth when I was only fifteen. I have avoided the house ever since, not wanting to make a noise. Now, Lana asks why I won't come stay with her. Feeling vulnerable about the issue, I rashly visit here and relay the reason for my refusal to stay. Reactively, she runs upstairs to confront the man and his wife in their bedroom. I moan inwardly. When will I learn to keep my mouth shut to the truth?

Lana returns to me only to chide me for telling falsehoods. I reach out and slap her across the cheek. The Shadow Being has not left me. It awakens and roars inside its fragile makeshift cage. I run out the door before more damage is done and flee into the hills where I spend the night hidden in the trees. My options are closing in. I am adrift in my own mind, my own world, homeless, and alone. Eventually, my age mates are the ones I run to. My friends Ethan, Dan and Riva, betray my whereabouts to my mother. Lana knows she has lost control of me. What can she do? This time away could cost her job. She must settle me quickly and get back to work.

Fortunately, I find myself in another home up in the hills with the family of my good friend Jeremy at school. He hears my plea for help and comes to my rescue, asking his parents to take me in. His mother Christine makes space in the mansion, happy to have a daughter to dote on in a household of boys. She reminds me of a mother bear, protective, steady, nurturing, and incredibly intelligent. She and I become the best of friends. She immediately becomes my mentor mother and takes over my care.

A SOUL GUARDIAN

It is time for my exams. I am at a loss, trying to balance my schoolwork and my future with the current unfolding reality of my failure to survive successfully, on my own steam constantly on my mind. One afternoon, I find myself, eyes downcast, leaving the University of Berkeley campus library late, carrying stacks of books in my arms. I feel tears welling up inside while my eyes remain dry. I wander down a campus path, filled with dappled light and birdsong, aware of a brook babbling under the bridge below and squirrels chasing acorn nuts, darting furtively across my vision. I notice a very old man bent over a walking stick in a brown oilskin cloak making his way ever so slowly up the path toward me. A few other students hike past us then it is only we two on the path.

As we move past one another, his hand reaches out and grips my wrist with a force I could never have guessed he might possess. I drop my books and papers scatter everywhere. As I bend to retrieve them, he keeps a hold of my sleeve, and then stoops to help me pick them up. His staff drops, and now it is only I who is holding him up. I apologize and restore his stick to his hand. He nods in appreciation and motions for me to walk up the hill with him arm in arm. We walk slowly in silence, one foot in front of the other. At the top of the path, he smiles at me with sparkling blue eyes that gaze steadily into mine as if he knows me. I pause, surprised that before I had not noticed the amazing light shining from them and turn to ask, "Is there anything more I can do for you, sir?"

He is silent and tight-lipped for long moments and then his eyes narrow ever so keenly as he takes my hand warmly in his two. His palms are warm and dry and I can feel energy flooding through them. The moment seems to stretch into eternity.

"It's all going to be okay, Thea. Everything will be okay."

How does he know my name? I don't remember telling him. How does he know my feelings?

"Is that all? Is there nothing I can do for you?" I ask politely, my mind negating any mystical connection.

The crease of his smile deepens as his eyes blaze into mine: clear as blue topaz in a sparkling mountain stream. It will be okay. He nods curtly, tapping his tweed cap, never uttering another word, as he pats my hand and walks away.

Tears spring to my eyes as he leaves and ambles down the road, never turning to look back. I snap back to my current reality and start to walk away. But thinking to check on him, I turn back around and the man is gone! Gone where, I wonder incredulously? There is nowhere to hide and this man could barely walk!

Suddenly, feelings of elation, hope and joy course though my veins. I rush down the path to pick up the bus and decide to head to Blake's mother's house. She is the only person I know who will listen to and possibly believe in my story. I resolve to have more faith, as what this man says is the truth. At least it is the magic truth I want to believe in for now.

An image of an earth diamond, hidden from view deep beneath the core of this world comes to mind. Right at this moment I hate diamonds. In fact, I think they are shiny overrated baubles that rich people wear to prove they are special or worthy of love. I prefer semi-precious gems thinking their jewel tones are more magnificent than any diamond set in silver or gold.

GRADUATION

Christine lovingly sews the buttons on the back of my white boutique dress, as I get ready for the prom. Single again, having broken off my relationships with both Ethan and Blake earlier in the year, I call on Christian who gladly agrees to be my date on my special night celebrating my passage to adulthood in San Francisco. Christian, of the violet blue eyes shows his continual dedication to care for my happiness no matter the time, the day, the year or the mood. Although we haven't seen one another or communicated for the good part of a year he does not hesitate to say yes to be mine for the two nights I require him. I spend what little savings I have to rent him a tux, fly him up the coast, and pay my part of the limo and the dinner out with Ethan, Dan, and Riva.

Saying goodbye to Christian two days later, I am aware that this friendship, our relationship, is unique. I do not hold onto it, and instead we both allow it to be as it is when it is. I don't dare have it as a long-term relationship, just as one does not drink the richest wines. We kiss fondly goodbye and I turn back to my life with a smile. I have extracted a bit of sunshine back into my soul. I begin to think, nothing can take me back to the dreary night of shadows, hospital, and resignation.

The day of graduation is finally here! The white columned Greek Amphitheatre in Berkeley where Bobby McFerrin the guest celebrity is resplendent in summer sunshine. Bobby's popular new hit, "Don't Worry, Be Happy" rises on the wind to honor our passage from childhood to a future of our making. He delivers an impactful speech on personal empowerment. I stand as one with the choir singing, "Lean On Me" and smile, big and proud as my grandmother has come to grace me with her warm smiling presence all the way from Hawaii, having heard that neither of my parents will be there, but then in a surprising turn of events my father Bard rolls in with his brood and he is all I focus on as I sing down the house with the choir. I am deeply moved that he has made the effort to come, after everything.

There are tense moments behind stage as we queue up in order of the last surnames of the alphabet are called up first. My surname starts with a "W." I have a moment of panic. I look for my name on the roster and cannot find it! I realize suddenly and in rising panic and shame that I had just assumed I would pass. I shiver nervously in the line wondering if I will be embarrassed in front of my peers at my ineptitude. I shift nervously from side to side. My peers encourage me, saying it must have been an oversight.

Every step I take feels like lead as I approach the stage, closer and closer, until I begin to feel lightheaded and my heart pounds wildly in my ears, and still, they do not call my name! Then, just when I think I will have to step out of the line, when the chaos of my mind gets too almost too intense to bear, the filament burns out, thrusting me into full presence. I hear a wise familiar voice within:*"Remember dearest, this is your life in the unknown. Your bridge is built on faith."* Then, far in the distance I hear it.

"Calling, Thea…" I rush ecstatically out onto the stage, punch the air while leaping triumphantly upward, catching the audience and official off guard, and the amphitheater erupts in a great ripple of vibrant applause and laughter. I am so real in this moment that my enthusiasm catches the mood of those in the wings! I feel as if the whole world is clapping. My legs are wobbling as I run up into the stands with my high school diploma to find the shreds of my broken family. Shaking uncontrollably, I sit for a long time watching, as each of my classmates from W through A receives theirs.

My mother Lana is in Botswana when she gets the good news that I have passed. I have barely made it, but it is more than any of us could have hoped for and she breathes a huge sigh of relief. She fulfills her promise to send me a ticket to travel through Europe and to visit her in Africa as my graduation gift. She has arranged with her former Cuban college buddy to take me into his exchange program in Spain for three weeks. I plan to meet up with a girlfriend in Pamplona. Chanti and I will train-travel through France and Italy catching a boat to the great port city of Split, Croatia in Yugoslavia to meet our mutual friend Mara, who is on the private island of Vis where her Serbo-Croat speaking family have a holiday home.

Soul Song: Baroque, Renaissance, and Full

17 years–Traveling Gypsy

"Adventure is worthwhile."

— AESOP

ESPANA

As a US Diplomat's daughter, I am privileged to carry a diplomatic passport. Upon my arrival in Spain, the officials at the airport take one look at my diplomatic passport without a visa and refuse me entry. I am held several hours in "detention" until they can work things out. I wait patiently as the hours roll by, wondering where my destiny lies.

The lead coordinator of the exchange group I am to meet up with outside is Hector, an old friend of Lana from college in Boulder, Colorado, who runs summer programs with his wife Ondine in Spain. Hector is waiting patiently and argues for my release for hours while officials remain firm and refuse us contact. Nonetheless, eventually I am released to enter the country and I walk out with my backpack and guitar to find everyone is gone. This is nothing new to me, as it has happened years ago on my trips through Europe and America from Niger, so I don't panic. Instead, I get by on the little Spanish I have picked up from half-attended classes in high school. Fortunately, I am in possession of an itinerary detailing the route we are planning to take from Madrid to Pamplona, so I hail a taxi driver to transport me to the last known group meeting place at Louis IX hotel. I feel so hot, sticky, and disheveled! The hotel informs me that Hector will be driving the long route back from Seville to fetch me. My clothes are rumpled and the hotel is fancy, so I decide it is better for me to stand outside.

My stomach grumbles hungrily, and I wonder how bad my appearance is as passersby give me the once-over and then quickly avert their eyes. I must look a picture in my bright red tie-dyed t-shirt and faded blue jeans. My thick hair is in that awful stage between short and long, and I compare my ugliness with the long haired Spanish beauties that prowl the sidewalks with high boots, make up and fashionable coats. I feel out of place with my backpack and guitar case strapped to my back. Hector pulls up in a hire car just as a blush creeps up my cheeks.

Happy and tired, I ride shotgun in the front of the little rental car Hector has hired as we drive for nearly an hour to Toledo where his wife Ondine is waiting for us with the rest of the group. They are all sitting outside a quaint bed and breakfast inn when we arrive, eating Spanish pizzas and drinking watered down wine. These are the teens I will be interacting with for the next few weeks. They are a proud bunch and I feel completely out of place. The group are tired of sightseeing, but Hector is eager to visit one of the oldest cathedrals in the area and for us to embrace the cultural tourism of the area. I am exhausted, but there is nowhere to lay my head down, since the hotel is still sorting our rooms, so I soldier on, volunteering to accompany him.

The Cathedral is built into a gigantic rock-face, and as we enter, I am overcome with a powerful peace. I feel a strange sense of ease here and I am amazed at the sense of familiarity that overcomes me. I instinctively know it is no coincidence that I am here. Somehow, I know this place from the tips of my toes to the crown of my skull. There is an organ playing in the huge domed room that arches four stories above our heads. Sounds flow melodiously over my being, reverberating in my body, and I feel somehow sanctified, liberated, and magically cleansed. Once again, I am reminded of the garden of song that I stood in years ago, where my grandfather met me and sent me home.

I stand in the center of this space, looking up, soaking in the peace of this place with Hector at my side. He is pleased to see that I am moved. If he only knew! I can feel my guides dancing and swaying with me at last!

Gently, I wish to honor the Holy Spirit that resides here. I tiptoe softly ahead not daring to add any other sound and noticing everything. Hector's historical chatter weaves in and out of my consciousness all the while. Dates and happenings don't matter to me. Something is happening within. *I am awake to the soul of this place.* My spiritual self is being restored to me. I feel like lying face down upon the ground and staying here all night. Instead, Hector and I get back in the car and motor away to Avila and the quaint hotel. Famished and not having eaten for the past 48-hours, I gorge myself in true Spanish-style with a huge three-course meal and sweet desserts. After supper I am barely able to shower and change, before donning my pajamas and sinking into a big puffy white pillow and a deep, dreamless sleep.

BULLRINGS AND LOVE LAMENTS

The next morning, we are up early for more cathedral hopping, for our group is to witness a bullfight, which, we are told, is a big part of Spanish culture. I am not squeamish like some of the other girls who are having trouble watching. I watch stoically, yet I am aware of my clenched jaw, flared nostrils, and shallow breathing. I want to understand what the Spanish culture "gets" from this colorful passion-driven tradition. We sit rapt, stuck to our chairs as one would in a horror flick, and we watch six bulls die in succession over the next three hours in the hot summer sun. I stomach it, yet quietly decide this will never be something I accept under the name of "culture" or "fun," no matter what excuses the Spaniards make. This is rather cruel, unfair and ugly. I remember reading a book called *Ferdinand* when I was a child that showed the meanness of the sport and humanized the bulls.

We complete the day with a tour of Segovia and the viewing of a once beautiful castle in ruin and finally arrive in Pamplona where we meet our Spanish host families with whom we are paired in the city for the next three weeks. I am the only one of the youth group placed with a family who speaks not a word of English. My Spanish is rusty, but we do our best to communicate at their dinner table. They serve up a meal of fish and salad with potato lentil soup. I know I will be well cared for here.

The family consists of a widowed grandmother, her divorced daughter, and 4-year-old grandson. I cheat a few times and speak French to the daughter who understands a bit of that language. The family takes to me immediately, as if I am one of them, and they comment and wonder at how Spanish I look. They embrace me warmly me in their simple world and are sympathetic, friendly, and kind. The grandmother insists on feeding me all day long and teaching me her recipes. I learn how to cook Spanish omelets with chorizo and potato. In the daytime, I spend a few hours in lectures with a Castellan monk who goes by the name of Gabriel, and I learn more Spanish with the group. Some evenings we are collected by Hector and go out flamenco dancing or visit the monuments of different towns nearby.

We are taken to the Spanish opera house at City Hall and wine and dine with the Mayor of Pamplona for whom I sing a song I wrote at the dinner table. The pastry shops amuse me. It is traditional to order a repast of pastry and coffee at the counter where there are no chairs and we imitate the Spaniards who stand upright and throw paper serviettes and muffin wrappers on the floor with aplomb to be swept up later by the staff on hand.

One day, we take a drive up to Basque country where all the houses are painted like the Basque flag in red, white, and green. Here we visit a nature reserve where I feel my heart open wide as I send internal messages to the trees that are growing in harmony together from all parts of the globe. I could get lost here, communing with nature for hours, but my peers are making such a racket, that I am distracted. I feel an overwhelming sadness engulf me as I allow feelings of despair for the earth to awaken in my being. As we leave, I feel a gentle touch upon my cheek, and turn to look back, but no one is there. It must be a spirit of nature bidding me a secret farewell.

Next, we stop at a secondary school celebrating its 100th anniversary. They own two small museums and a small church. The museum of wildlife is full of strange stuffed animal specimens. Some have two legs and two heads and the museum holds gruesome human remains and fetuses in jars! This taps into a deep, macabre, and forbidden curiosity within us all and I feel something dark awaken inside me. I shiver as I take a walk alone wishing to be somewhere else. Eventually, we are headed home to our families and I am happy to sit watching the news with mine and eating a TV dinner in their tiny apartment lounge.

We are in Pamplona for the running of the bulls' festival and carry wine skins full of cheap sweet watered-down wine around on our hips. We continue to fill these up for no charge at various bars and cafés along the street. Everyone is dressed in white and wearing blood red sashes. Fireworks bang and blast open the night sky and doves and pigeons fly in pandemonium to and fro along the tiled clay rooftops.

In the final week with my Spanish family, I become ill, causing me to burn and shake for days... I have been through too much in the past two years. My Spanish family is very worried. They remove the little boy from our shared room and leave me be. Suddenly, I awaken from a fevered sleep to see a shadow squatting in the corner of the room. It has been waking me for two nights in a row. I recognize this entity as the one who had taken over my body only a few months ago in the dead of the night when I had tried to kill myself. It appears smaller and more predatory now. It seems to be smiling at me from the corner. I don't dare ask what it wants. Instead, I clutch at the talisman Bard gave me from the Native American guide years before. It is silver, with two protective hands and a corn and husk in the center. I bid this shadow to leave me be, but it sits tight in the corner and observes my every move. Every time I awake it is there. I want to scream at it, but that would call too much attention and my Spanish family will think I have lost my mind. Perhaps I have. I wonder why this shadow has chosen me.

When my fever reaches a peak, I am taken to a local hospital where I am given an injection and cocktails of antibiotics. I sleep at last and begin to recover rapidly. Once well again, the daughter takes me out with her friends and we walk in the park with her little one, and her married friends and the whole family takes me down to the river. We have a picnic and make a day out of it with neighboring families splashing in the river, laughing, and calling out to one another along the banks.

Adios! I bid my friends and the Spanish family farewell. I am to meet my American friend Chanti at the train station. I bless the room I have stayed in, praying for grace to be upon this small family unit before I take my leave. For a whole three nights the shadow has left me alone. I inwardly request it not to disturb this sweet group of people. My Spanish sponsor family has been a little boat of love in the oceans of mania plaguing my existence since the Niger days. They have received some money for housing me and this will go toward the little boy's future education, but do they know that they have given me more than I can describe to them in our short farewell…a sense of homecoming?

Seeing Chanti again is like breathing fresh air. Her sunny temperament is all familiarity and sisterhood. She is the ultimate blonde bohemian beauty. She takes me arm-in-arm to meet her family friends of Basque descent, where I am left to stay for a few nights before starting our planned journey with Eurail passes on the trains and buses across Europe. Chanti holes up in a hotel with her mother in Pamplona and sometimes visits us during the day and evenings. At first it seems like an odd and selfish arrangement by the two of them.

These Basques speak a bit of English and we sing and play our guitars and write songs late into the night. It is a family of young men who are both extremely gorgeous but look very different from one another. I guess they are half-brothers or cousins. We stay up all night at bars and cafés getting tipsy, eating sweets, having funny conversations about sex, playing board games, and dancing. San Fermin has started, the weeklong festival of the running of the bulls, made famous by Hemmingway in the late twenties. The atmosphere is festive and summery. I fall head over heels for the taller of the two boys in the home–Inaki. He is a Basque through and through, lean and tall with dark hair, a beautiful smile, and poetic eyes. Inaki takes me to his grandmother's place to watch the running of the bulls from her balcony, which is a rare privilege many in the city covet. He and his friends run with the scrambling bulls down the street slipping and sliding on the cobbles in a fearful outrage.

All I see, with my heart in my mouth, is Iñaki. He has captured my heart with his sensitive soul. We flirt casually with one another, but I feel incredibly shy in his presence, even though I am no stranger to relationships. Finally, there is no time left to steal a kiss. The night before I leave, he gifts me with a poem he tells me is just for me:

Quiero dar un cambio en mi vida
I want to make a change in my life

Y volar hacia ti
And fly to you

A prender el arte de amar
To learn the art of loving

Con las alas desplegadas
With wings unfurled

Y volar hacia ti en un sueno
And fly to you in a dream

Del que despierte llorando por ver,
From which I wake up in tears to see,

Por ver, que tu estas a mi lado
To see, that you are by my side

Y tener, tener ese punto hacia el que volar
And to have, to have this vantage to which I always fly

Y traer, traerte un pedazo de mi ancho batir, y lograr
And to bring, to bring you a piece of my widest soaring, and gain,

Lograr que volemos a ras de mi mar
Gain for us so that we fly level along the surface of my sea

A ras de tu mar
Skimming, level to yours

A ras de aquel mar con el que nunca deje de sonar...
Level along the surface of that sea that never stops me from dreaming...

Y volar
...And fly.

He hands me this beautiful heartfelt lament as I leave to begin another adventure with Chanti. I see a boy with a beautiful smile and sparkling eyes. I treasure the sharing of his heart that opens in response to the beat of my own. Though we never share a kiss our souls are entwined for that moment in time. Such is the way of love and how she freely weaves through the hearts of the world.

VENTURING THROUGH EUROPE

Over the next three weeks, Chanti and I travel on Eurail passes with guitars and backpacks slung heavily across our backs crossing through Spain, France, and Italy in record time. The trains are cramped, grimy and sweaty crammed with other young tourists from Europe, America, and Canada. As there are no places to shower, and we can't afford hotels, we sleep on the trains and do our best to stay clean using drops of water from washroom sinks and at the Mediterranean seaside towns we visit briefly along the way. We comb the beaches searching for public restrooms and dive in and out of the sea and the beach showers, taking turns to watch one another's packs and guitars. Chanti is agitated by my lack of spontaneity as I search for travel agents to extend my ticket to Botswana that I carry in a corded purse around my neck. I feel most comfortable to do this here where I speak French.

"Come on, Thea, let's live a little!" Chanti crows happily as she grabs my arm impatiently when I disembark the train in Paris, Nice. We can do your ticket later, come on, it'll be alright. I *promise* you," she pleads. There is a U2 benefit concert happening in the hills this night. We jump for joy at our good fortune and something to do. I sigh inwardly and drop my plans to get to the travel agent. I'm also eager to meet people and have some fun. *Live a little!* The ticket change will have to wait. In the blessedly hot Mediterranean sun, we search for the concert and use the lazy daylight hours to find an almost empty bus to take us uphill, only to discover it has been postponed, so we hike back down and climb onto another bus that takes us close to the train tracks where the last train is waiting to travel to Venice. I can't seem to shake the anxiety of having lost the opportunity to handle my ticket change. This now forces us to get to Yugoslavia faster than either of us would like, spending only a night or two in Italy.

Feeling hot and grimy, we arrive in Rome on the weekend and are disappointed that the Vatican is closed for repairs, however the Pantheon is open and we gain entrance and marvel at the single light source of the domed temple. Afterward Tariq, our foreign exchange friend from Berkeley High, meets us in a plaza nearby. Italian is his mother tongue and he takes us to the best cafés and gelaterias in town where we wolf down copious amounts of the famous Italian pizza and way too many ice creams.

Chanti continues unnerving me with her forays into areas of risk and danger. I never realized until this journey that we are such opposites. I am serious and alert, looking out for the signs of lecherous men, while she is flirtatious, excessively free, and spontaneous, and her concept of money is completely different to mine. She is happy to give everything away, knowing she can replace it easily with her mother's money. Conversely, I am intimately aware of Lana's struggle to rebuild her life after divorcing Searle, and I do not want her to blame me for adding more difficulties to her life. Every penny counts.

There are limits though to the hardship I am prepared to endure, and still count this as a vacation. I insist on getting us a decent hotel room with a bath once we arrive near the seaport town of Ankara on the coast of Italy and prepare to take the ten-hour journey by ferry from Pescara, Italy to Split, Yugoslavia. The shower and bed boost our moods.

Chanti ruefully apologizes for doubting my "big-picture understanding" and I apologize for being so "rigid and irritable." Feeling clean and restored, we enjoy the boat ride to Split, a coastal Yugoslavian port to the east across the Adriatic Sea. At the docks we are struck by the amount of human feces and other garbage pollution floating in the bay. We are herded off the ferry and immediately crushed by a multitude of white townspeople on the landing offering us room and board. We must hold onto our bags tight and keep an eye out for the pickpockets running in and out of the crowd.

In the hustle and bustle, a little wrinkled white lady urgently beckons, and approaches from the sidelines. She speaks to us in broken English and encourages us to come with her. We follow as she walks us briskly down the winding cobblestone streets and takes us up a flight of worn stone stairs to a tiny little room with clean white sheets and a lovely view of the harbor. We find ourselves in the most beautiful part of town and luckily after some serious haggling we find it fits our budget!

The bright sunlit room will be our hideaway for the next couple of days. As soon as we pay our deposit, the stout Croatian landlady bustles away, clearly happy with the deal she has struck with two young women from America. There is no breakfast included. We unpack our bags and head downtown to get acquainted with our surroundings and find a phone to call our friend Mara who is vacationing on the island of Vis, not an hour or two off port. We desperately want to visit her there, but she needs permission from the authorities. The island is off limits to tourists and has been reserved for people of Serbo-Croatian descent to live or holiday away from the buzz of tourist that plagues their shores. We decide to risk it anyway and begin making plans of how we can sneak onto the island at night, but when Mara comes to see us the next day, she cautions us against trying anything silly.

Soon enough we run into other problems. Chanti wants to extend her stay and I am running out of money. Chanti has to rely on Mara and me until her mother can wire her more cash. We are living on bread, cheese, and fruits that we sometimes have to beg for in the marketplace. Then, passing through a local travel agent who speaks English, I discover there is no direct train to Athens and I will need to catch a train to the nearest international airport in the heart of Belgrade in order to travel from Yugoslavia to Athens, Greece where I must soon catch the plane to Botswana. The agent informs me it will take several hours overnight by train to get from Split to the heart of Yugoslavia and its capital city Beograd. I cannot change my ticket as Lana has bought me a special and there are only five days until I must board. Chanti will be left behind, but I cannot wait another second and I must leave in an hour. "Go ahead and book my train ticket," I instruct the travel agent. My Eurail pass doesn't cover this extra cost nor my airfare to Greece. This booking will take almost all my cash. I return to Chanti and Mara to tell them the bad news.

"I don't get it, Thea. I mean how can you just leave me here stranded?" Chanti demands angrily.

"I have no choice," I plead for understanding. "You at least have a mother who can send you money, but I have exhausted all options. Just stay with Mara or take a train to Spain where your mother is." The mood is charged. Chanti sends me daggers with her eyes and turns to Mara for support.

"This is what I told you would happen when I wanted to check my tickets in France, but you wouldn't let me," I finally snap defensively.

She turns away in disgust.

"If you'd only listened to me, we wouldn't be in this trouble," I say to her back. She is pouting and looking seaward.

Mara comes to the rescue.

"Thea is right, Chanti. There's really nothing she can do. Everything will be fine. You will come with me, and we'll see what we can do to get your mom to wire more money. Until then, I'll ask my gran to put you up. Please guys, let's all be friends and get Thea to the train station." Chanti shrugs and shakes her head, refusing to look at me, but gives in at last, finally seeing there are no better solutions. She knows I have commitments to fulfill and that I truly want to see my mother's new home in Africa. Unshed tears sparkle in her big blue eyes and she refuses to look at us. Finally, Mara claps her hands to bring us back to reality. "Now, we must go or Thea will miss the train."

We all wave goodbye at the edge of the tracks.

I feel slightly afraid, not knowing how I will get to the airport once in Belgrade, but I know by now that if I panic I will be lost. I have learned that I am happiest with a plan. Uncertainty breeds anxiety, and anxiety brings me to the edge of my ability to cope emotionally. I walk onto the train without looking back, heading to my next destination alone.

NIGHT MANEUVERS

Once on the train, I find myself squashed between two swarthy men, one of whom insists on slumping his head on my shoulder, drooling and snoring all night long, as we endure the long stuffy trip to the Yugoslavian capitol Belgrade, or Beograd as the locals call it. The train is poorly serviced and the journey is stiflingly hot. We flash in and out of long dark tunnels and there are no lights save for the glowing moon outside. The trip is scheduled to take twelve hours. I am scared to leave my seat to go to the toilet as the train is packed with hot sweaty bodies, some of whom are standing, and I fear someone may steal my seat or my possessions. I don't feel like befriending or talking to the greasy Yugoslav man next to me, but I realize I need to befriend him or die of a ruptured bladder!

I ask him to teach me his language to pass the time. He is more than happy to get acquainted. I learn only a few words. When we disembark at the last stop at 3 a.m. he asks me where I am headed. I do not know where to go or what to do, so I wander the streets with this unkempt man as he leads me down dark dingy alleyways to a surprisingly decent hotel several blocks away from the train station. Upon arrival at 03:30, the hotel receptionist refuses to give me a room until 07:00. I cannot get rid of this man who imposes himself on my company, insisting on sitting with me until dawn. He gestures that he will not be happy until he sees me to my room. I feel trapped and increasingly uneasy in his company. It is clear he thinks he will be joining me. Fidgeting in my chair, I wait until he dozes off and then hurry to inform the female receptionist that I am not with this man and find my peace at last. The hotel security runs him off.

Sleeping the day away, I awake frequently to indulge in several hot showers, luxuriating in the warm running water and washing some of my clothes. I am not interested in more adventure, and looking from the hotel room balcony, I see a grey dark city under a haze of pollution. I have no desire to explore it. In the evening, the hotel management calls a taxicab to take me to the airport where I meet some fellow Americans: New Yorkers on their way to Istanbul. They are horrified to hear how I have been traveling alone and invite me to eat a meal that they generously pay for. They think I am a college graduate, a common misperception these days.

Arriving in Greece, outside the airport terminal, I am approached by a handsome taxi driver in his mid-twenties. He calls himself Nico. We chat amiably in the car on the way to a hotel near the airport and when he learns I am a lone traveler he invites me to his father's restaurant for drinks and traditional Greek meze—the small hot, and cold savory dishes the locals live for here. Nico's father is happy to have me at the restaurant, and I feel safe laughing in their relaxed company. They ask if I know that my name means "Goddess" in the Greek language and gesture emphatically with their hands, creating the shape of a voluptuous goddess in the air. Nico comments with sideways glances that "Thea" in Greek also means "beautiful girl" and I catch him winking at his friend when he thinks I'm not looking.

During the day, fearing to get lost, or waste more of my precious funds, I decide not to explore Athens. Instead, I stay in the hotel. I wash my hair and clothes, and lie on a hard hotel towel on the white tiled balcony to gather rays of sun on my skin, meditate, journal, and listen to music on my Walkman. Unfortunately, jumbo jets fly incessantly overhead affording me no real peace. In the evening after work, Nico passes by to take me out again. On my final night, he insists on being the one to drive me to the airport. As we drive, I notice we are taking a different route, and as he pulls off the main highway and into a warehouse dock, I finally speak up. "Where are we going, Nico and what are you doing?"

Instead of giving me a straight answer, Nico purses his lips and puts his hand on my thigh, patting my leg firmly and gesturing me to be quiet. I watch his jaw clench and jut forward. Suddenly, I am on red alert. I need to catch my flight to Africa. What is he planning? I scan the area ready to take action.

Slowly, he pulls the car into the darkest part of the shipyard. My eyes scan every crevice for any other soul, but I see no one else in this place. My mind is whirling on overdrive and my heart taps hard against my breast.

"Come on, Nico," I huff in exasperation, "I need to get to the airport. There's little time, so why are we here?"

No one, not even a stray dog is in sight. He switches the ignition off without answering me and reaches over, ripping open my blouse and groping at my breasts. He bites my neck and presses his lips savagely on mine while reaching down my shirt with his hand to pinch one nipple painfully. I squirm in my seat trying to undo my seat belt as he begins to undo his zip and twists his stocky well-built body over the gear set, bearing his full weight on top of me in the passenger seat. After the initial shock of my breast being twisted in his fingers, I manage to undo my seatbelt and leap into action, fighting to push him off of me so he hits his head against the rooftop of the car. I shout loudly for him to stop, but he keeps coming for me, and rips at my pants and grunts lustily in my ear, "I want you, forever, Thea."

"YOU, CAN'T HAVE ME!" I kick off from the floorboards of the car and use my free hand to reach out grappling with the passenger door, but he is faster than I and he grabs the handle before I can push it open.

I scratch at him wildly like a feral cat. "STOP IT!"

"NO, NO, and Noooo!"

My fury propels me sideways out of the car door and he clambers very fast out the other side. Insanely, my mind turns to my bags trapped in the trunk of the car. I glance wildly around the empty shipyard for some piece of metal I might use to defend myself. Then suddenly, I catch a glimpse of my Shadow looming up behind him. This time, though, it doesn't show me its face, I only see its fury. A roaring sound fills my ears. HE SHALL NOT HAVE YOU, my Shadow growls, ready for my command to be unleashed.

"Nico, you do not want do this. You will really regret it," I warn him.

I muster the words in a commanding tone and shove him forcibly away. He stumbles backward nearly falling over his own heels and twists his ankle. I can see the shock and horror as he sees the shadow in me loom above him now. There is a moment of concerned consideration on both our parts. As he judges his chances, the shadow has control and leaps. It is inside of me helping me now. I feel my eyes blaze wide and I know I am not alone. The Shadow and I will fight this man to the death if we must... and we will win.

Nico starts forward to fight me, then shakes his head to himself and looks away. His shoulders slump and his arms slacken to either side as he mumbles angrily, "Okay, okay, come on, and get in, Thea, Goddess of the Night. I promise I won't do anymore to you." I hesitate, panting and then get warily back into the car. I need to catch my plane. I cannot be left alone here in this dark dock at night.

We drive in stony silence to the airport. I angrily cross my arms over my breasts so I can stop shaking, shocked that my new friend would betray me so. How could I be so naïve? I was aware of his flirtations, but I never would have believed it could escalate to this. Once at the airport, he follows me everywhere trying to help me with my bags and guitar case. I refuse him at every turn and refuse to pay him money.

Unfortunately, the flight is delayed for several hours and he won't leave me alone. Though I ignore him, Nico paces ominously on the edges of the milling crowd who are also stranded until the next flight takes off. His persistence annoys me and I feel a growl forming within. I shove it back down and find an official who helps me to run the idiot off. My Shadow has left me, slipping back to the depths of my unconscious. I am on my own again. As I board my flight, I hold back a wave of nausea. It was a close call.

Soul Song: Committed, Invigorating, and Clean

17-18 years–Pula!

"...A people without a past are a people without a soul."

— SIR SERETSE KHAMA

THE MOTHERLAND

On the plane to Nairobi, I sit comfortably next to a man from Sudan. We chat during the flight and he tells me he hasn't been home in many years. He seems somewhat apprehensive about returning. Civil wars have been ongoing in his country and now there is a lull in fighting.

"Sudan has changed a lot since I've been home. My brother has been telling me so." He shifts to look out of the window and I sense him wondering what it will be like.

"Are you afraid to go back home?" I ask curiously.

"Not really," he replies, smiling to himself, "only, what they will say as I haven't been to see them in so long."

"How long have you been away?" I ask, curious.

"Ten years."

"Back to our Mamas." I smile up at him.

"The Motherland," he winks and pats my hand.

I nod, wondering. Ten years is more than half my life. It puts things into perspective. He is a good person and he has been living in a world far different to his African homeland. I, too, am a good person and have been living a life apart from family for what feels like an age, yet it has only been months of my own short life. My uncertainty is on an inner landscape while his is concerning the outer landscape of life. We shake hands, wishing each other luck.

When our plane lands in Nairobi, I feel my heart flip and a sense of homecoming floods my senses as I observe all types of Africans coming and going in the airport. The sense of fear I felt in Europe releases its grip on my system. Somehow, here in Africa, I feel secure, embraced, and grounded. I write in my journal:

"This the Africa that calls to me. Africa, who whispers 'come to me, come Thea, come live and work in my soil. I am older than the oldest trees, I am ancient as time, I am vast, powerful, and my arms are warm..."'

BOTSWANA SOIL

The first day I arrive in Botswana is the first day I have seen my mother for several long months...since the time when my shadow broke its chains and the craze of the night took me. Having returned to a sense of belonging, I fall into a deep sleep in the arms of Africa that first night home. My surroundings are strange yet familiar. Being with my emancipated mother who is now only a year divorced, and looking about at some of the belongings she has shipped across continents brings me internally to a place of safety and homecoming. Her garden and home are filled with plants and sunlight that wink and smile at me contentedly. Peace at last! Smelling Lana's eclectic cooking wafting throughout the home, and watching our familiar old cats lick their furry coats in the sunshine, I consider that this must be what stability feels like. I reach for a sense of familiarity or comparison, but it is like trying to catch an elusive butterfly so I give up trying and just enjoy the moments.

Lana has nestled herself into a modest concrete three-bedroomed house built by the Botswana Housing Corporation on a large corner lot. She has used the USAID government furniture with her own pieces of airfreighted art and Botswana bought weaves and baskets to look as if it belongs in a magazine! Lana dresses up smartly for work each morning and instructs her hired domestic staff to care for the home in her absence. Rathedi (pronounced Ra-tay-dee) is a Tswana-speaking local boy, and KT is an indigenous Kalanga woman hailing from the northern parts of the country. In her spare time, Lana trains Rathedi to garden and KT to read English. Lana's heart is healing and she journals daily, filling her house with music, socializing with colleagues, and works hard to rebuild her mental and emotional wellness. Working for the United States Agency for International Development (USAID) as a Human Resources Development Officer is a challenge and a powerful position. It is a big step up for my mother from being an Associate Peace Corps Director in Niger. Botswana is considered a comfort country whereas Niger was a hardship post, so she intimates to me that she feels fortunate to have landed here.

Just like Niger, Botswana is dry and arid, but unlike poverty-stricken Niger, it boasts a thriving economy built on diamonds and a stable democratic governance since gaining independence in 1966. Neighboring countries are Angola and Zambia to the north; apartheid-ruled South Africa to the South, Zimbabwe on its north-eastern border, and Namibia to the west. Most of the country's small landlocked population exist in towns and settlements situated from north to south along the eastern corridor where there is a railway traveling from South Africa to Zimbabwe. The vast Kalahari Desert, home to the indigenous San bush tribes, makes up the majority of land area of the country with a scarcity of water and infrastructure to the southwest.

Most of the people own their own cattle posts or ranches where herd boys and grandparents eke out a meager living raising cattle, goats, sheep and chickens as well as farming crops of maize, sorghum and various roots and vegetables that have seasonal growth seasons. Though Botswana is poor with overgrazed soil and lacking in rain and irrigation planning, it is rich in diamonds, beef, wildlife, coal, salt, and soda ash, copper, nickel deposits, and it has a strong currency. Therefore, it is beginning to attract foreign prospectors and investors from South Africa and other nations who see opportunity and growth potential in both partnerships with its democratic government and/or a stake in the booming private sector. There are approximately 26 languages spoken in Botswana, but many can be grouped together with the national language Setswana, being understood and spoken by the majority of people, and English being the official language used in most of the schools. This seems to contribute to the overall peace and stability in the region and makes communication and understanding fluid and easy between all peoples.

Left to my own devices during the time my mother is at work, I begin to explore the capital city Gaborone by foot. There are only a few main roads that are tarred and it is more like a sprawling dusty town than a bustling African capital. A few donkey carts roll down the roads and stray cattle wander forlornly about looking for water and the tastiest blades of grass. The livestock are not crowding the traffic as I recall the camels, goats, and chickens did while roaming the hot sandy streets of Niamey. There are no open sewers hereto stink up the roads either. In contrast to life in Niger, Botswana doesn't seem to have many beggars.

Real poverty, I am told, beleaguers mainly the rural areas where the Botswana Democratic Party government is challenged to provide basic necessities such as access to clean running tapwater, education facilities and clinics, and enough shelter to its marginalized citizens. Still, the country has managed via subsidized foreign aid programs to have more than most third world countries twenty-two years out of Independence. As there is no civil unrest and the country is at peace in the region, The Botswana Defence Force soldiers are deployed in roadblock service patrols along the border roads and in front of the University of Botswana to help the understaffed police force to keep the peace and ensure citizens are safe from thieves and drug trafficking. Everything looks fairly new, including the pale graded dirt roads that pass between clinics, schools, huts, and medium cost homes.

I spend my days hanging out with some of my new English-speaking friends, part of an eclectic mix of backgrounds and nationalities: Americans, Swedes, Canadians, Norwegians, Koreans, Brits, South Africans, and a small handful of Batswana youth my age most of whom have grown up in the city. Few have cars, but once I get my bearings and learn to drive on the other side of the road, Lana allows me to use her car during the day. I begin my quest for some job experience and find it volunteering for Mr. David Slater the founder of Maitisong: a theatre production company running summer camps at Maru-a-Pula the main private high school in the capital. Soon, I am gifted a short internship helping to file reports and other business in at the Maru-a-Pula highschool reception where I am incredulous that some people have paid for their unborn children to be placed at the school all the way up through the year 2000! Little do I know now that my own unborn children will be students here one day.

The Main Mall is a wide dusty street flanked by office buildings and shops in the center of town where cars are not permitted to drive. Everyone hits the pavement on payday as the mall explodes with locals and a scattering of expatriates. Market stalls are abuzz with music and buyers and sellers of mophane-worm snacks and roast mealies (corncobs), papatas (fried breads), biltong (dried meats). Freshwater bream (fish), hang in trees, along side leather crafts, heavy woven blankets displaying traditional patterns, and beautiful Botswana baskets threaded using the tall riverine grasses from the North sometimes died in different hues of purple, pink, black or green.

Mophane is a tree indigenous to Botswana. It is from this tree the famous Mophane-worms, a kind of caterpillar, are treasure-hunted and harvested during the hot rainy season between November and January. The worms, roasted, fried or stewed are popped greedily into many mouths. Some people are cooking the caterpillars outside in the Main Mall on small gas burners while others sell ready-made dried packets of the worms like chips for the intrepid traveler. The Botswana Book Centre, on the corner of the square at the center of the mall, becomes my favorite haunt and I spend most of my hard-earned pocket money here buying books to help me learn the language.

Men move about comfortably in British or American-style fashion or tailored African prints and Safari shirts. The clothing color and texture, in comparison to the bold bright West African styles that I am used to, seems soft, muted, even understated. Here, people are full bodied, humble, and have a wry sense of humor. Comfort and peace are clear tenets of Botswana society and they laugh more readily than other Africans I have met on the continent.

Botswana's people are far more tolerant than their continental compatriots on issues of race and gender, having had much less conflict with colonialism, warfare or bad governance. Pickpockets are rare, eyes shine with intelligence, and voices are melodic. There is a genuine flavor of refreshing naivety and a collective acceptance of a simpler life here. Polite greetings ring out between friends in open spaces and one hears the clapping of hands in greeting. Though I do not experience any direct challenge for my being a foreigner in expression or posture, strict guidelines of etiquette abound, there is a definite look upon eye contact that reveals a proud shrewd scrutiny of character. Trust is something that is gained through one's actions and integrity. Botswana is a largely Christian society, as white missionaries and various churches have converted the African people in this part of the world 100 plus years ago to the religion.

Botswana's skies, pale blue and sunny by day, deepen to an azure star-filled indigo at night, especially during the winter months. Just under a million and a half other residents and me, witness the constellation Scorpio rise high in domed sky on the cold desert evenings.

ROWAN

What could complete this lovely picture but a close friend or lover? Love comes to visit me in the form of a truly beautiful human being, a ruddy-haired youth called Rowan. He is pale of skin with a faint smattering of freckles scattered across an open yet determined face, all planes and angles except for a medium-sized, round upturned nose, and ample lips that give away his keen sense of humor. His violet-grey blue eyes and lean muscular build dominate my thoughts. We find ourselves bound to one another day and night and can't get enough of each other's company. He tenderly initiates me into the lore of the land, enfolding me graciously into his passion for adventure, and more importantly, the language of fun that has been so long lacking in my world. He is very interested in construction and martial arts where he specializes in Judo, and he has earned a brown belt for his bravery and discipline in competition. We frequent the dojo together where I, too, learn a few moves from his teacher.

Rowan treats me like gold, and up until now I have never experienced such fresh simplicity of ethics in a young man who displays genuine qualities of respect, honor and devotion, touching me deeply – a boy standing for me and standing for love. I know other girls covet my luck, yet I am simply overjoyed in the moments we share and don't put much thought to it.

We while away our free time constructing things in his father's back garden, hanging out having good clean fun: watching movies, playing darts, table tennis, dancing and eating, and drinking beers with his mixed set of friends. The two of us enter a recycling can project together and spend hours building a massive lion out of tin cans that wins us money at the annual local trade fair. I buy myself a microphone to record my music from the money we win.

For six months I am lulled happily into a dream-like state of contentment. I am in great health, attending aerobic and yoga classes weekly, running and swimming, walking and dancing, loving and exploring what it feels like to be seventeen and carefree. The innocence that was long lost to me is returning to me bit by bit. Through these new experiences my heart begins to open and heal. I feel gratitude daily. Only the smallest irritation with Lana's comments on my late-night outings with Rowan distracts my peace. Who is she to dictate my life since I have long taken it into my own hands?

Rowan takes me to visit his family in Johannesburg where his older sister is soon to begin her college education. His extended family has a big property in Bryanston, South Africa in what was previously known as a wealthy white-owned part of the city where Rowan's ancestors had once kept a dairy farm. I find myself easily ushered in by his family, and Rowan keeps me close to him at all times.

TSHEKEDI

One evening Rowan and I head out to a local nightclub in Gaborone called Nightshift to meet up with our friends and enjoy a night on the town. As I pull into the carpark in my mother's canary yellow Toyota station wagon, I notice a slick silver blue Opel Commodore rolling slowly around the lot. I am most impressed by the digital dash with illumined lights glowing into the driver's handsome face. Rowan points at the car and exclaims excitedly, "Oh, Thea, let me introduce you. That's our former President's son. His father was the first president of our country! His Canadian girlfriend has just left to go back to Canada and he looks so lost. Let me out, I need to catch up with him." He kisses me lightly on the lips, jumps out of the car before me, and runs over to tap on the glass of the idling Opel Commodore. The handsome driver stops the sedan and climbs out, flashing a cool white smile from under a thick black-trimmed mustache, and thrusts his long white-sleeved arm out toward Rowan.

He is tall with creamy brown skin, and a decidedly pronounced receding hairline filled out either side with a soft mass of dark, tightly bound curls. I recall that his parentage is a blend of British middle class and Batswana royalty. I watch the two men clap hands and arms then enter into a gregarious conversation, almost mesmerized by one another, before I can even switch off the engine to join them.

I approach quietly to greet this smartly dressed gentleman with an AF radio and keys strapped to his waist, and the strangest thing occurs. I receive an unbidden vision! My eyes fixate above the tall man's head and I see a banner of rippling ribbon appear in mid-air above him. Calligraphic lettering appears in stardust across the banner that read, "*You shall make this man happy one day.*" Then, as quickly as the words appear before my incredulous gaze, they disappear into thin air! I quickly dismiss this inexplicable message and stumble forward as I wait to be introduced. The two men are having so much fun, and I am barely noticed.

Finally, I touch Rowan's arm and he suddenly remembers I am there. "Oh dear, I'm afraid I've been so rude. This is my girlfriend, Thea. Thea, this is Tshekedi Khama."

The man reaches out a lean brown hand and engulfs my small one in his own as he looks me up and down and grins politely, "Nice to meet you. You can call me TK."

We share a few pleasantries and I feel my warm-eyed smile fade slightly as he turns back to Rowan and the two men carry on their conversation as if I am not even there. I think to myself, this Tshekedi is a bit rude, and Rowan too for that matter, as they continue to ignore me obviously enraptured by their own conversation. Finally, Rowan has the presence of mind to invite "TK" to join us in the club with our friends, but the tall man laughs and declines the offer, telling us he doesn't drink and he has no date, so we agree to meet for tea another time. I am still reeling from my vision. What does this mean? I inwardly shrug it off and put it down to my imagination playing tricks with me.

A couple of months later, we meet up with Tshekedi, who is now dating another Canadian girl, a cousin to Rowan's best friend. The strong-boned flaxen-haired Gwen is also strong-minded and close to my age so we form a kinship almost immediately. The four of us begin having meals together, sometimes as often as twice a week, sampling restaurants newly opened in the capital city Gaborone. I notice Tshekedi always pays for Gwen while Rowan and I split our bill.

There is not a lot of entertainment happening in the dusty capital so one creates one's own amusement. The conversations become deeper and I look forward to the stimulating discussions that are born out of our evening get-togethers. It's the far-left liberal girls vs. the more conservative-minded African men. Despite our friendly debates, TK and I feel we can talk to one another for hours. He is 29 and I am 18, but it is as if there is no age gap. Our partners look on and laugh at us in amazement when they run out of words and we keep talking.

Soul Song: Foreboding and Imminent Exposure

18 years—The Shadow Tamer

"How can I be substantial if I do not cast a shadow?
I must have a dark side also if I am to be whole."

— C. G. JUNG

PROVOCATION

All appears warm and sunny during this happy time of my life, where I have few cares and I feel the calmest and most balanced I have ever been. Yet, as bright as the light in my life, the shadows are quietly pooling their energies, planning a coup in the background. Lana and I are generously invited to spend the hot Christmas and New Year holidays with Rowan's family in a tiny cottage on a farm Rowan's father owns in Plettenburg Bay. The farmstead can't fit us all, so I agree to camp in a tent on the lawn with Rowan's youngest sister, Annabelle.

Annabelle and I talk and giggle all night long. Where I tend toward dark thoughts about my past, she brings light, humor, and compassion into the present. Whenever I feel uncomfortable or out of place in their South African family culture or tradition, she always finds a way to reach out and include me. Having lost their mother early in life, and weathered the storm of their loss through unity, love, and prayer, Annabelle and Rowan share a unique bond, as do their other two siblings. The family looks after one another and it is a humbling experience for me to witness at a time when I feel adrift

It is December and hot balmy winds blast the Cape Peninsula coastline. The woods are close by the cabin and Rowan and I make haste for the sheltering trees day and night as lovers do. Still, although I feel happiness in his arms, there is a strange sensation of foreboding creeping over me. I listen to stories of the hired help from years gone by as we explore distant trails on the property, and I begin to feel as if I have been in this land before. I visualize a life living as a white woman half a century ago along this coastline where I picture myself not being nice to the black folk. I fall into the guilt and torment of this unbidden dream and begin having thoughts about it on a regular basis. The dream seems like a possibility of a past life. I begin to worry that I might have been complicit somehow in hurting others based on the color of their skin.

I dare not relay these thoughts to Rowan or his family for fear they will think I have gone crazy, and maybe I am. The pressure inside me is mounting. I can feel it tremble behind my eyes. Lana agitates me as she spends more time and money with Rowan's two sisters than me, buying them gifts in boutique shops in town and spoiling them over long lunches without me. They have been lacking a feminine touch in their lives and Lana fits the bill. They seem to love her quirkiness, even as I am irritated by it, and my ego whispers quietly, "she isn't what you think she is." I am determined to keep punishing her for her neglect and by ignoring her as much as I can.

On New Year's Eve the pressure comes to a head when Rowan's uncle becomes inebriated. We are enjoying a happy celebration when Lana starts tugging on my sleeve and pestering me to tell Rowan that one of his family members keeps groping for the buttons on her blouse. I am embarrassed and shocked and don't know what to do. She seems to be taunting the man by standing next to him instead of staying far away. In exasperation at her refusal to join me, I jump into the van, telling Rowan to grab her and his immediate family so we can leave.

Rowan is doing the rounds to say goodbye to the guests when Lana releases a shrill whoop from across the lawn. I gasp as I see her frantically batting at an inebriated man who is now chasing after her with his hands groping down the front of her shirt. Rowan leaps to her rescue as my heeled foot involuntarily kicks out through the front windshield of his father's car, shattering the glass. I am horrified at the accident and the adults' behavior. Rowan's eldest sister chides me angrily from the back of the van.

"Thea! What were you thinking? Are you crazy?"

She has never been enamored with overt displays of raw emotion and now she sees the perfect opportunity to voice her displeasure at mine. Rowan's other siblings notice the ruckus and pile into the car. I am shocked to see that I have caused such damage to the vehicle and I don't know what to do or say to make it better. My internal temperature spikes like wildfire, as Rowan's family focuses on me breaking the windscreen and not on the issue at hand: their relation's bad behavior.

I find myself shouting incoherently, and suddenly, I leap from the front passenger seat running barefoot into the street along the rows of houses through the suburban neighborhoods of Knysna. Rowan races out after me. I feel myself removed and realize that my infamous shadow beast is back, claiming my body for its own macabre purpose. Rowan runs alongside me, begging me to stop and not having a clue what is coming next. I cannot speak to him, but my shadow whirls to face him without fear. The beast is seething in me. I know it must look terrifying as it spits at him, saying ugly words that I, as Thea, would never utter. I see his eyes widen in surprise. Disappointed and alone, I turn to run, but he grasps my wrist, pulling me toward him and enfolds me in a strong yet tender embrace of love. "I love you, Thea. Please know that nothing will ever take that away."

In the face of this, he burns away all the darkness in a heartbeat and my soul returns, as shadow and beast melt into the stars. I am back, and slump limply against his chest. When I have stopped crying, we walk back to his family and he paves the way for my dignity to be restored. Everyone is silent as we head to our respective beds. I am determined to tame this shadow being that seems to want to control my life. When will my internal light finally be seen?

STEPPING INTO ADULTHOOD

In January 1988, the time has come for difficult decisions to be made. Rowan is applying to the University of Witwatersrand in Johannesburg South

Africa, which is expected of him by his family, and he has also been looking forward to a new life away from the small pioneer-like town of Gaborone. He chooses to become a building engineer. As much as he values my love, he also values his education. I understand this, of course. But I feel as if I want to spend the rest of my life with him.

What are my options? I could follow the love of my life and apply to the university, but my own fear of failure stops me from trying. What do I know about studying at that level? I haven't even a clue what I want to study! No one is able to advise me, and I am unaware that career counselors even exist. I am embarrassed and worried about being aimless while life moves on for my peers here and abroad.

Apartheid is still rife in South Africa. I have never felt comfortable in an environment where people are blatantly sorted and categorized by any particular system, and my soul tells me South Africa is not where I am meant to be right now. My inner voice doesn't just tell me, it screams a definite "NO." As much as I wish to join him, my soul tells me I cannot follow Rowan.

I am very sad, but I must find something to do and I find it difficult to let go without hardening my heart.

A friend of my mother's in Berkeley sends us a prospectus from a massage and bodywork institute in Oakland, California. I read up on it and am intrigued. I don't need a 4.0 grade point average or anything other than a high school diploma to register. This could be the perfect profession for me! I speak to my mother who is supportive yet dubious. She still wants me to work towards identifying a degree program, but agrees to help me fund my return to California and the course. She still has limited resources to assist me, and my father Bard is out of the picture since I have now turned 18 and his responsibility to send my child support has ended.

I am reluctant to go back to what was once something of a nightmare reality living alone in California only months before. Nevertheless, I feel I must and am grateful to have had this small respite in Botswana that has boosted my confidence and self-worth. I have gained some valuable work experience, rallied my strength, and cleared my head.

We kiss each other goodbye, and with full hearts we make our choices. We are mature enough to know we each have a path to take, and his is surer than mine. We agree to stay faithful and try a long-distance relationship.

Back in the Bay, I thrive in the massage school's informal anatomy classes and the two-way nature of massage therapy. I discover that giving is as healing as receiving. I have made the right choice about something at last! In fact, I become addicted to the idea of using massage for healing emotional blockages in the body. The teachers at the school make sense as they describe the emotional wounds that humans sustain through various trauma and the relationship this has to a person's physical body.

It is a different sort of life and more comfortable than I am used to, being a student all day long, and living off the allowance my mother sends. I don't have to look for work immediately and I am staying with my former piano teacher, an Italian American, Tess, and her wonderful husband Byron who works full time as a city planner, and in his spare time plays with the best classical philharmonic musicians. Listening to Tess and Byron playing the piano, viola, and violin together in the evening lights up my mood. In this home I am free to come and go as I please and I am lavished with fresh gourmet meals, organic salads, and love. Tess brings home exotic cheeses from her job at The Cheese Board –a Berkeley cooperative cheese deli she has spent years working in to supplement her piano teaching income.

Adelina, who had gotten me into the rowing crew with her at Berkeley High School, offers me one of her mother's apartments to rent and share. I am overjoyed, as it is just down the road. She is Hispanic like me, but not adopted, so she speaks the language fluently. Her Bolivian father is not generally on the scene and her Caucasian mother and stepfather live in an apartment two doors over from us with her younger brother in the complex her mother owns and manages.

Adelina has recently gotten involved with Levi, a Jewish-American boy who is trying his hand as small-time drug peddler. She has started a new modeling career and become bulimic, binge eating and purging regularly before her stomach can fully digest. I feel guilty as she surprises me and Levi with her newfound exquisite culinary talents, producing fancy gourmet meals by candlelight in our flat, only to excuse herself, hiding, unresponsive, in the bathroom for what seems like hours as I bang on the toilet door. Whenever the two lovers come home, late in the evening, I cringe, listening to raised voices and things slamming in her bedroom. I am paralyzed in fear of the old domestic violence from my not-so-distant past, and I experience a maternal urge to come to her rescue.

Nonetheless, I dissuade myself from getting involved, as I have never been invited to do so. I feel dismayed by my own weakness and lonely for Rowan whose photos I tape to the walls of my room reminding me of our love and the happy sunny days I shared with him in Botswana.

My dreams of living in harmony with Adelina are squashed by this new reality. She becomes snappy and irritable around me and is rarely ever home. This is not fun at all. I work hard, scrubbing the kitchen day and night, clearing their dirty dishes while the dirty energy builds up in every corner of the upstairs flat. Adelina and Levi show no appreciation for my efforts to create a happy space. More than this, things start disappearing from my room: an expensive topaz ring Lana gifted me at graduation that was acquired in Brazil, an equally valuable Moroccan leather jacket my mother bought for me in Istanbul, and other clothing items I find Adelina "borrows" from my closet without permission.

One cloudy day after an argument erupts between the three of us over a moldy rug that Levi has been storing in our dining room, I decide, to hell with being nice! I pace the floor impatiently, huffing to myself, "I'm the only person paying the bills here, and for what? To be treated like something from the gutter?" I resist such a notion with all my might and haul the heavy moldy carpet out the front door and throw it over the edge of the double story building where it crashes into the bushes below. Grabbing my keys from the kitchen counter I leave to attend class at the massage college, feeling a smug measure of satisfaction at having cleared the space. I return in the late afternoon to find the apartment has been vandalized! Writing is scrawled all over the walls and the refrigerator using my lipstick. Thea sucks. Thea is a bitch, whore, and loser!

I call Tess and her husband picks up the phone. "That's unbelievable!" he exclaims horrified. "Thea, honey, I'm concerned for your safety. Hang tight. I'll be there in a few minutes and call the police if anyone comes." When he sees the destruction, he helps me move immediately. Together, we pack my things in his pickup and lock them safely in his garage. "I think you should find another place to stay. Your friends know you may be here and I don't want trouble. Their behavior is bordering on psychotic."

I flee to certain sanctuary with my mother's friend in the hills. Eva again takes me in. She is always glad to have my company and is willing to rent me her spare room for very little. I feel at home here, but I want to find work quickly and another place to stay because she is a loner who values her privacy. Fortunately, I have done this before under worse circumstances, but I am embarrassed to be in this situation again.

Rowan and I still write to one another daily and he is always on my mind. I miss him so much it hurts, and we have agreed to remain true to our vow not to be romantic with anyone else. His schooling is progressing well and he has won first prize in a sailing regatta and a safari for two to Pamuzinda Safari Lodge in Zimbabwe that he says will expire if not taken within a year. I realize I will need to secure a job quickly to save up enough to visit Botswana so we can make the trip to Pamuzinda together.

At last, I find a decent job as a production assistant in a tiny family-run jewelry factory, creating the perfect color tones of Fimo clay for the creative artist-owners, gluing on the metal backings to their modern designs of earrings, pins, and pendants, as well as filing and filling catalog orders. I am able to factor in a lot of over time, as this job does not require much physical energy. At the same time, I secure a place to live a few blocks away in a quaint area of Berkeley closer to my childhood home.

A single man inhabits the house in his early thirties, and he is renting from a lady called Misha who works as a court reporter in Santa Fe, New Mexico. Misha returns to paint her house and to our mutual surprise we share a similar story of abandonment and rejection as adoptees, thus establishing an immediate bond. Misha treats me like a little sister. Family members who are not family are becoming an intricate web of support. Slowly but surely, I begin to establish this world as my garden and heart connections as my home.

The job at the jewelry factory becomes tedious as I work my fingers to the bone and spend long hours feeling underappreciated for my efforts. Our bosses are nice enough and they try to establish bonds with some of us by eating lunch with us at the bagel factory up the road and walk with us there and back. As it turns out, in a freak twist of fate, one of the bosses is Nafari's uncle. The other factory worker who sits with me in the cloistered studio daily doing the same job as me, is the ex-girlfriend of another of Nafari's uncles on his mother's side.

Susanne has studied homeopathy but is currently not practicing and hails from England. Susanne and I chat for hours as we work and become bosom buddies, whiling away the long hours with our bodies suffering under the lack of natural light. We are fascinated by each other's stories.

Soon, I am able to buy my ticket to Botswana to visit Lana and have an adventure with Rowan. I am so excited to see him again and re-cultivate the love that still burns in my heart; but when Rowan arrives and we pack up to go on our long journey north, things are not as I have imagined. Rowan is hard to reach, distant, and closed. I make attempts to ask him what is wrong but he shrugs me off casually. We spend hours not speaking on the dirt road to Kasane and the Chobe National Park, and a chasm of disconnection yawns between us. I study the chiseled lines of his beautiful face. He seems sad and is not open to my prying.

The lack of communication triggers my deepest fear: abandonment. I become defensive and angry to compensate for my worry. Has he been seeing someone else? Perhaps his older sister has advised him to end our long-distance relationship? I believe deep down she doesn't favor me. He is back to drinking and smoking again, which he had given up while with me before. I feel further from him now that we are in the same space than when we were halfway around the globe. I have been focused on healthy living, and though I am not a teetotaler, I prefer a relationship that is clear of substances, especially cigarettes which I despise.

We pitch our tent in the late afternoon in Kasane. We agree it is best to be away from the rest of the tourists and the ablutions for privacy so we choose a flattened patch of land at the far end of the campsite near the river. It is a domed three-pronged tent for six so we put our bags and supplies in one section, and leave the other parts open, facing the ablutions and river's edge while we sleep in the third compartment.

As we settle for the first night of camping, we feel a vibration on the sand below our sleeping bags. We both stop talking and listen. We discern it is a herd of elephant making their way through the bush toward us and they sound close. We bolt upright and haggle with one another about what to do. Should we leap out of the tent and run for the concrete ablutions or stay put and hope for the best? Although my instinct tells me to run, I prefer to either fight or freeze in the face of danger. I don't want to risk an elephant charging us. Rowan desperately wants to sprint out of the tent. When we hear their breathing and the parting of grasses near our heads it is too late.

The reeds erupt with low stomach rumbles and loud huffing noises all around our tent. We hear splashing and wading in the river only 20 meters away. One dark shape blots out the stars overhead that once peeked through the open netting of our tent. Rowan gestures me to move silently to the other side of the tent and we hear a warning growl of the matriarch above... Abruptly, torchlights flicker on outside and the shadow of her body becomes visible through the thin canvas. Some South African tourists are awake, shining torches our way. I begin a silent internal prayer to myself, and soundlessly transmit another telepathic plea to this elephant that no harm should befall us. I am helpless on my knees, humbled and apologetic. We were so selfish to place our tent here. I hope the lights switch off, as I am afraid it will anger the wild elephant standing right above us. Placing my hand on Rowan's bare back I feel sweat soaking his body. He reaches up to unzip the tent cautiously, and then whispers urgently in my ear, "Thea, can you run?"

I look at him as if he is crazy, but see he is dead serious. I tap him and shake my head no, refusing vehemently. The moments stretch tensely between us. He knows if he goes he will put me in danger.

A tourist calls out to us to ask if we are okay.

Rowan and I cringe in horror. We both wish they would be silent. The torch flashes. Rowan puts up a hand and somehow gestures them to shut off the light. We hear another camper tell them to stop it and the lights wink out throwing us into darkness once more. I can hear the breath of the matriarch standing guard overhead. I sense with all my being that she is not pleased. I beg Rowan to keep still and to forget running and after what feels like hours we hear them leave. She hovers above, never going to the water's edge until the last of the herd leaves. Then, she too, moves out, whacking our tent where we had once been sleeping with one final slap of her trunk that would have seen us injured, if not dead, had we still been there.

Finally, I allow Rowan to unzip the tent. He is relieved but angry with me for not following him to the ablutions. We settle back down, but I cannot sleep. I feel as if I have locked minds with the elephant and I keep vigil all night giving gratitude for my life. In the morning, when we break camp, we find big feline tracks have circled our tent in the night. Perhaps it is a leopard or a lioness. We are not familiar with bush lore so we cannot tell, however from now on we decide to sleep near other campers and forgo our own privacy.

OUT MY COMFORT ZONE

After the trip to the Chobe National Park and Pamuzinda, I must return to America and to my job. I am saddened to leave Rowan again and I wonder how we will keep our relationship intact. Once I return to my routine, the long hours, lack of sunlight, and boredom set in and I clash with my boss over systems in the office. I argue that the production line could be faster if he would only allow us to help him file papers, and he is miffed that I organized his documents without his permission. It is time to move on, so I resign. I decide that I love working with the human body, so now that I have graduated massage school I have some confidence to try college. I would like to go into the healing profession and so clueless of options I gravitate to the idea of becoming a doctor one day, but my grade point average will not allow me to make the leap to pre-med, so I set about finding a community college by the sea in Santa Cruz, California where I can study the prerequisites necessary to enter a recognized university.

I discuss my choice with my mother who is ready to finance me, and my colleagues at work who help me hatch a plan. They are also bored of the venue for their work. They agree to rent a place with me there and commute the 90 minutes to and from work weekly. Reba, a brunette with shoulder-length tresses and big doe eyes is one of the female design workers who, though appearing meek and mild, is bold enough to ask if she can move south with me and commute twice a week with her work. The company sanctions this idea almost immediately, since they are in need of more table space. The other factory worker and my close friend Susanne travels a lot and returns to her home in England frequently on other business, so I have the house to myself much of the time.

I love living by the sea. I am determined to study day and night, but find myself highly distracted. I take long walks by the ocean, I meet new friends, but feel the familiar loneliness sink into my bones. Rowan hardly telephones or writes anymore and I miss him terribly. I amuse myself with glances at an older boy in my speech class who I learn plays in a popular reggae band locally.

I try to keep active by riding my bike or listening to music. Once I call Rowan in South Africa and he seems almost angry I have made contact. He tells me when I come to see him in December we won't be able to spend much time together as he will be doing construction work for a Greek girl's father who we both know. I have heard stories of the glances he gave her at parties and I know his heart is wandering. As the days pass, I lose hope of ever retrieving our love and decide to break off our long-distance relationship before I get hurt.

This is becoming a pattern of mine in all my relationships. I get in deep and then break away if I sense the intensity slipping. Rowan and I have lasted longer than any other relationship I have experienced. My pen continues to write, breaking off our relationship. My heart disagrees. My fingers take down the pictures of us from my bedroom wall, and mournfully I pack away his sweet gifts and bundle his love letters into a box that I stuff to the back of my closet. My heart does double back flips and I run out to the sea. Later, I will discover letters of care he wrote before I made this decision. Outpourings of his soul, true and like our friendship of old, but I cannot marry that with his clipped tone and words on the phone. I have to make the choice before I am more hurt.

I call up Tshekedi's girlfriend to tell her the news, and am surprised to learn that TK is supposed to travel to visit her in Canada soon. I am so excited to reconnect to my beloved days in Botswana through them. "Why don't you two come and visit me? I have plenty of room and we can all hang out on the beach and the Santa Cruz Boardwalk!"

"Yeah, okay. Sorry about Rowan, but that sounds great. I'll let you know what TK says when he arrives."

I realize I need a job, as the money my mother sends me is not enough to sustain going out for lunch or buying the clothes I need and want. Unfortunately, with so many students in the area, there are few part-time jobs available. I scan the newspapers, finding little or nothing that I am qualified for. Then I discover there is decent money available for artist models. I am dubious. Is it safe to go and model nude at an artist's home?

I suddenly have a brainwave as I remember sketching nude models that posed in class at my art college in Oakland that I attended one summer between semesters in high school. It all seemed so professional and natural. There was nothing pornographic or distasteful about it. All the great painters of the Renaissance had nude models as subjects. They must get paid something. Perhaps the junior college I attend has openings for models in its art classes? I look on the board outside the college reception and find they do!

I admit it is out of my comfort zone, but I am proud of my body and I need the money. I swallow my pride and offer myself for the position. They accept me, but tell me they require different models for different classes so it will not be a steady job. I take it on anyway.

The artists are all seated in a semi-circle with their easels and pencils out when I walk in. I am instructed to undress and don a satin robe that the art instructor hands me behind a Japanese Shoji screen. The instructor sets up the lamps and a platform in the center of the room. It is time to walk out and drop the robe. My heart beats hard in my chest as I imagine the poses I would personally want to draw, the lines, waves and curves and how the light falls best on a body. I step onto the podium, avoiding the gaze of the class.

The instructor positions my form creatively for the first pose. I am given an instruction to pose anew every 20 seconds. I must be innovative. I draw on memories of sculptures in the art museums of Greece and Washington, DC. It feels so unnatural. I feel stiff and wish I had been given more instruction by the professor of the type of look he wanted. I pose like a statue and pose again every 20 seconds for over forty minutes as the students scratch on their papers. I notice students I know here from my public speaking class and English Lit. I feel a blush begin to develop on my cheeks and shove it down determinedly. My face and body must not become red. I am committed to continue. At the end, barefoot and dressed in the robe, I am allowed to view the student's sketches. They all have such different depictions of the same pose! I am proud to be a part of their renderings, a part of me immortalized in the art.

After gathering my confidence, I decide to brave a trip to Carmel on the weekend to pose for some female artists at their home studio. This is a completely different experience. I am stuck in one pose that they choose for me to hold for three hours without moving, holding a bowl in my hands and sitting lotus-style on a podium. They feed me warm soup afterward, pay me a tiny fee, less than a hundred dollars, and send me packing, a two-hour drive north without a tip. I decide the pay isn't good enough and quit this type of work.

The experience has left me with mixed feelings. I have always been comfortable with my body. I have lived a liberal life with parents who were comfortable with nudity. My high school friends and I, both boys and girls, bathed together without touching in communal hot springs or saunas and I have watched African women dance topless across the desert sand. My clients have undressed before me to be massaged with hot oil. However, displaying my body for amateur painters for money feels odd. The mere fact that I haven't told my mother what I am doing tells me all I need to know, so I quit after two more stints...

Soul Song: Roaring, Strong Contralto

18-19 years–A Nudge from The Mother

"Whatever happens to your body,
your soul will survive untouched."

— J.K. ROWLING

THE MOVING EARTH

The day is October 17 1989, a hot windless scorcher. Dizzy from another tidal wave dream, I awake from an afternoon doze surrounded by study books and scowl at the sound of a dog barking incessantly down the road. I have been having lots of dreams of tsunamis where I am caught in between giant tidal waves, and must watch others be pummeled into the sand while I remain safe at the crest. The dreams feel real and are hard to shake.

I can hear my housemate Reba calling out from the other room, asking if I want any of the herbal tea she is about to prepare. Susanne is in England again, so it is just the two of us in the house. "Sure, I'll have some tea," I shout beyond the bedroom door then swing my feet lazily off the Japanese futon mattress and pad into the open dining area and lounge.

Reba offers me tea in an oversized mug and we chat amiably as she sits back down to continue making her Fimo clay jewelry order. After drinking the tea, I return both our mugs to the sink, wash a few dishes, then head for my bedroom again, intent on completing the last homework assignment.

I am stopped between the hall and my room.

A sonic rumble rolls toward us from the West. It builds rapidly into a loud roar and the ground begins rocking hectically back and forth beneath my feet. I glance out the front door where I see telephone poles swaying and turn to shout a warning for Reba who is rising in alarm from her jewelry making station.

"Oh, my word, what shall we do, Thea?"

"I don't know, just don't go into the street. There are live wires out there!" I scream over the roaring clamor.

"Let's get under the doorframe, NOW!" I grab hold of the front door as the ground swells under my feet, throwing me off balance.

It takes Reba mere seconds to heed my call and she is there, holding onto the doorframe as I grab her waist with one arm and the doorframe with my other hand, helpless as flower pots crash off our shared bookshelf and the large windowpane in the lounge begins to buckle and bend. We pray it doesn't break. We look out onto the street and see my heavy Volvo station wagon leaping and bouncing inches off the tarmac that is now rolling in large waves in our direction. Holding on for dear life, we watch as a neighborhood cat is propelled in an upward trajectory, yowling midair as it falls in a bundle of fur into an open storm drain down the street.

Fifteen murderous seconds pass before all is quiet and the sounds of sirens ignite the air. Reba and I run to help the cat out of the drain then try the telephone, but the lines are jammed. We are both shaking and in shock and run around to check the house for damage. There is little visible damage to our home, save a few cracks in the plaster walls, but there is a large crack in the center of the street and other homes are damaged nearby. It is getting dark now but we are too scared to move, when suddenly the power goes out.

Reba owns a small radio that runs on battery power and we tune into the news on every station hearing wilder stories by the minute. We hear that the famous Bay Bridge in San Francisco has collapsed and cars have fallen through. Forty or more cars are trapped beneath an overpass and there is massive damage further north.

The earthquake has originated a few miles away and we are less than ten miles from the epicenter and should prepare for giant aftershocks. Reporters sensationalize the event saying an even bigger quake could still hit us and no one can predict when. County officials are closing the highways and gas lines have been damaged, hence fires have broken out in our town so they have turned the city power grid off until further notice. We are advised to fill up cars on petrol and diesel, which may run out if trucks can't get in.

The night passes in fear as we experience more tremors. I manage to get through to some loved ones and discover everyone I know is okay, but not everyone they know is. It sounds like we are in a warzone. The following day, stories pour in on the news about downtown disasters. Helicopters fly noisily overhead, and the President declares a state of emergency and deploys some of the National Guard to the worst-case scenarios along the coast to search for bodies trapped in the rubble. People are asked to stay at home. Police have arrested some workers at a famous coffee house downtown who refuse to stop a search for a colleague in the rubble and who are considered to be causing a safety hazard as they continue to search at their own risk all night in the dark.

The next day, I head to the supermarket for supplies and find two long queues of people lining up outside. I ask why we can't go inside to the food market and people in line say it is the same everywhere; there is damage to every building in the vicinity so the owners won't take the risk of endangering customers. As we chat, I realize our neighborhood took less of a hit than most. Other's homes have been pulled off their foundations, and some homes have been split in two! I realize how fortunate we are. Though never heard from and unseen, God's guardians and angels are still with me.

"What are they doing up there?" I ask, pointing to the front of the queue. A dark-haired man with a checked green and grey flannel shirt and hands tucked in his pocket replies, "Oh yeah. You're allowed to buy either a fifty-dollar bag or a hundred-dollar bag and what you get is what you get. How much money do you have on you?" Fortunately, I have enough as I was at an automated teller machine several days before and have not spent the cash. I know Reba will pay me half the money so I go for the hundred-dollar grocery bag. I am grateful to receive a torch, batteries, matches, candles, bread, pasta, sauce, soup, a bag of apples, nuts, and some canned food and salad makings. It is enough to see us through for a week or so.

When I return home, Reba has left a note to say that she has gone indefinitely to stay with her boyfriend and tells me she has left Susanne's cat behind. The poor animal looks traumatized and squats, fat and grey, in its cage in Susanne's bedroom, scaring the heck out of me with its wide glassy stare. It has grown up most of its life caged in a pet store and is more comfortable inside that cat box cage than out. It hovers in the back, neurotic and untouchable. The cat seems to be having trouble breathing. I am scared to change its water bowl or feed it, as I am worried it may bite or scratch me. Nevertheless, my work cleaning out cat's cages for a pet shop in high school helps me to get the job done.

Another problem arises when the water is switched off by the city due to damaged pipes and possible contamination citywide. When it is turned back on, I discover my shower drainage and toilet are blocked. I call a plumber to investigate and as he unblocks the pipes, sticky sewage sprays up like a fountain all over the floor, walls, and bathtub. I try to clean it but it takes the better part of a day to get the worst of it off the tiles and I am forced to use the toilet and sinks in the park across the street. The tremors keep coming, mostly at night, and school is closed for three weeks, as the entire library needs cataloging since the earthquake caused all the shelves to fall over... I consider that I am cut-off and trapped with the responsibility for the house squarely on my shoulders. All my friends and roommates are far and most have fled to other parts of the state. How is it that I keep finding myself abandoned and in such situations?

I decide to call on my father, Bard, who now lives in the Southern part of the state of California that was untouched by the quake in San Diego. It is my fervent hope he will take me in for a few days until my town returns to normal. The thought never crosses my mind that perhaps he might have taken the initiative to call me to make sure I am okay...

"Hi, Dad."

"Hey Thea, how are ya?"

"Well, I've survived the quake."

"Oh yeah? That's good. It was a big one."

"Yes, and they aren't sure if a bigger one is coming or not. Almost one hundred people have lost their lives. I'm really having a hard time here. The roads are closed to go north and my roommates have left me and I'm really scared. The aftershocks keep coming...Dad, there's a crack in my ceiling and it keeps getting bigger with each shock. I was thinking of traveling to San Diego with my Korean friend, Lin. Her parents live there too and so we thought of traveling together since she doesn't have a car. Can I stay with you?"

There is a long pause.

"Dad, are you there?"

After some time, he says, "You know Thea, you'll be right in the middle of my family."

"Oh, okay. Never mind then. Forget I asked. I must go. Bye."

I slam the phone down and giant sobs rack my body. How can he do this? I am stunned. I cannot believe my ears. I am angry, too. I think of Rowan's family in Botswana. They would never leave one another in such a situation. Am I not a part of Bard's family?

I sense I am not ready to hear the answer. My heart sinks to the bottom of my belly and I cry myself to sleep as my wounded inner child cries out painfully.

"You are a rejected, undeserving, unloved, poor, and pathetic victim." The words I once heard in vitro. I must be worthless, I think gloomily to myself. Everything I have seen so far has showed me I am. I am uncared for and as good as trash to my father, expendable, not good enough!

In the days that follow, I pack up and drive to San Diego anyway, carrying three other girls who are desperate to get away in my car. Lin and I go to her parent's home, but as soon as we arrive, my car breaks down and her father's mechanics say they cannot fix it. I know little about cars and so I gift it to Lin's father who says he can use the parts and he pays me eighty dollars for it. At last my body and mind break down from the mental and emotional strain and I become extremely ill with a high fever. Lin's parents nurse me in bed day and night. When I am well, Lin's father loans Lin his car and we drive back to Santa Cruz.

It is time to take care of business. I have decided to leave Santa Cruz. I drop out of college, get Suzanne's permission to put her grey cat down, pack up the house, hand my keys to the landlady, and hire a U-Haul truck to move back to Berkeley where Misha happily houses me. Then, I place a beggar's call to my mother. She has recently moved to a much larger house opposite the Botswana National Stadium and she seems sympathetic and willing to bring me home.

Soul Song:
Romantic Strings Quartet

18-20 years: Courtship

"Slow and steady wins the race."

— AESOP

REFLECTIONS

Standing still and barefoot upon the supportive motherland once again, I observe my client's breath reverently as he breathes life on the table before me. The gentle yet firm healing touch of my warm hands combined with the therapeutic natural oil mixed specially by my new boss melts the cords of tension that bind his ability to function effortlessly. I breathe in and out too and am aware of more than just this room. To be here, using my gifts and my certification in this small wooden Hansel and Gretel style hut with herbs and oils hanging from the walls is beyond my wildest imaginings of serenity in the aftermath of the hectic move back to Botswana from California.

As I gaze out upon the green fern-cloaked garden outside the window, my mother and her community in Gaborone have received me warmly and generously, and through her personal network of friends and acquaintances I have landed a job working for a French healer, helping her plethora of expat clients who come seeking massage, healing, and natural facials.

Happy as I am, it is bittersweet to be back in Botswana without Rowan's presence in my life and ghosts of our relationship haunt me everywhere. The small town has emptied of the young people I knew so I decide to look up Tshekedi and phone his twin brother Anthony's home on more than one occasion, always getting the answering machine with his jovial recording: "Howd'ya do-ah, see you've met my, ah… faithful… answering machine. Well, we're all out now, TK, Tony and Margaret, but if you leave your message after the tone, we'll call you back…" I leave several messages to call me but he doesn't.

Lana introduces me to all the young folk in town she knows. Some are U.S. Marines, others young entrepreneurs, and a scattering of local artists, painters, and pianists. I take up babysitting in the evenings. Celebrating my nineteenth birthday at Gaborone's only truly exclusive fish restaurant, Reflections at the Oasis Motel, a lonely white building along the dusty Tlokweng border post road to South Africa, is a treat. My mother takes me out with Rowan's father and another friend. Reflections restaurant is a single room that can hold about 18 guests at a time and is covered wall to ceiling in mirrors. We dress up in fancy clothing and jewelry to go out.

Before long, I hear that Rowan is back in town to visit. To my delight, he calls me up to invite me to have dinner with him and his brother at their father's house, which they have to themselves while he is away on business. It will be the first time we have seen one another in months. My heart flutters wildly in my chest. All the feelings of the love we once shared begin stirring within and I try to remind myself how he was so distant the last time I saw him.

I arrive to find I am not the only guest. Awkwardly, Rowan's suspicious ex-girlfriend is also present for supper. I am determined not to show any surprise that she is in our midst. I inwardly groan. His younger brother casts sheepish glances my way, apologizing wordlessly for his brother's behavior. None of Rowan's antics impress me in the slightest.

After dinner, we retire to the sitting room where he and his ex-girlfriend offer to make us some tea in the kitchen and disappear for well over forty minutes, leaving the brother to entertain me. When they finally return, I stand up to leave. I have had enough rudeness for one night. I say thank you and bid everyone goodnight.

Rowan knows me all too well. This could be the end of a lifelong friendship. He leaps across the room to grab me and exclaims that I should wait as he has something for me. He stumbles off only to return with a funny little clay creature sporting a tag that says, "I am a stargazer. You should always keep a stargazer by you to remind you of your dreams…" He insists on walking me to the door and then my car.

The following day Tshekedi calls. He apologizes for me not being able to reach him and explains he has been away on a business trip to Hong Kong. He asks me out to see him over dinner. This begins a series of dates almost every night and lots of time spent together on the weekends. I am enthralled by his wit, charm, and vision. He is a great listener and talks about interesting things. We are never starved for conversation. I am not, however, picking up any signals that he wants more than friendship or companionship. I am not even sure what I want myself.

When he drops me off, I think he will kiss me, but he is ever the gentleman, never intruding on my space. He doesn't seem to have a love interest on the horizon. I see Rowan once more and then end it in a messy way. Romantically, I feel like I am now just a stopgap, being used for his pleasure until he discards me once again for his foreign life back at the Wits University in Gauteng.

I date Tshekedi for over a month, waiting outside Lana's for him to pick me up every evening. Everyone else bores me. I go hiking with "TK" as he keeps reminding me is his preferred name and we take his dogs with us.

I am introduced to his older brother, Lieutenant General Seretse Khama Ian Khama, an astute decorated Commander of the Botswana Defence Force and the Paramount chief of the Bamangwato tribe one night at the President Hotel on the Main Mall. TK and Anthony are there. Anthony's girlfriend Margaret is present together with an old friend of the Khamas from the Machel family in Mozambique. My mother lends me her best jewelry for the occasion. As a conservationist, she admires his work forming anti-poaching units and deploying them to the far reaches of the Botswana bush and has briefed me on this history. The Commander leans forward as soon as we meet to begin a 20-question grill. Fortunately, I like questions!

Still, no kisses from Tshekedi. I am yet to meet his mother.

After returning from a short business trip, he decides to test my interest, and stops calling or taking me out. I assume he is busy with his life, so I too get busy with massage clients, reading, art and social life. I miss his company in the evenings, but imagine he needs his space. I am not his girlfriend and am under no illusions of any claim to knowing his whereabouts. When he eventually breaks down and stops by on his motorbike I am not home so he drops a note for me at the door. I call after a week of not seeing or hearing from him. His tone is clipped and sullen on the other end.

"Hmm, so I see you've learned how to use a phone."

This is the first clue I ever receive that perhaps he thinks our relationship is more than a friendship.

SCENE 36

Soul Song: Tremulous, Traditional, and Lilting

19 years–First Kiss

"You feel that there is an avalanche coming when you meet the right person."

— SHAKIRA

SWAZILAND

TK offers me a trip to see a long-lost Canadian love interest of his elder brother, who is visiting her parents in Swaziland. It is his final ploy to get me on my own and lure me away from my mother. On the way down, he checks my date of birth in my passport and nearly passes out, not realizing I am so much younger than he. The car ride is fairly quiet and I introduce him to the sounds of James Blunt and Enya's Orinoco Flow on my cassette. He thinks the alternative music I listen to is odd but he is willing to overlook anything to be with me. Slowly, we are falling into a kind of natural easy partnership.

Still slim, and sporting my new nineties-inspired long layered haircut, lean brown legs, and dark eyebrows, I feel attractive and ready for a new love. I consider what it would be like to make love to a real man, someone much older than me, well-spoken, well-traveled, and worldly like this young chief in his fancy car, with full mustached lips, and a cheeky smile. He is treating me like a princess, generously refusing for me to pay any bills and taking me places. I love the fact that he is clean cut, well-mannered, and he doesn't smoke or drink. He wears expensive cologne and is never a bore, always ready with a story or joke to tell. He knows a lot about politics, but he never overwhelms me or makes me feel that my views go unheard, and he takes great pleasure in showing me his old haunts, eagerly bringing me into the world of his adolescence.

One day in Swaziland, he lets me drive his car to a market on the side of the road so I can look at the curios there: the beads, baskets, blankets, and carvings that I am so taken with. "Choose whatever you like and we'll buy it later," he tells me, happy to sit at the hotel watching the news.

I happily disappear into my own world for what seems like two hours. I wander about, talking to the friendly vendors, making eye contact and connections as they tell me their stories and try to barter with me. In exchange for their good-natured banter, I eventually pick out a set of crafted pottery cups and bowls for a friend's upcoming wedding gift, and a mid-sized rose wool woven rug that I know I can't do without. I have fun picking and find lots of ceramic handmade beads for my mother to add to her collection. I pile up my goods and return with Tshekedi who chooses some earrings and a necklace for me, insisting I take something for myself. That night we visit his friend and eat with her parents. There, I politely excuse myself early from the table and play with their pets. I feel somewhat left out of their conversations, which are all about the "good old days" of their shared past.

We return to the hotel and shower separately in the shared bathroom. Now dressed in my nightwear, I hop into the double bed next to his and we turn out the lights. Tension and silence fill the room. We are each thinking thoughts of the other. How will this relationship evolve?

At last, he breaks the tense silence.

"Are you awake?"

"Yes."

"Would you like a massage?"

"Really?"

"Mhm."

"Yes, of course I would. That would be wonderful."

I take off my top in the dark, truly unafraid to show my body and he straddles my hips, letting his long sensitive fingers feel and prod the small-knotted muscles of my back. This lasts for several minutes before he decides to go get some cream that he lathers on my skin and then starts again. I show appreciation with gentle sighs as he finds all the spots that need work.

The massage ends abruptly and he kisses my back and jumps into his bed, leaving me wanting for more. I am too shy to initiate anything else, but what more does he want? I had my top off, for goodness sake, and I am pretty sure he wants me. What a frustrating man!

THE FIRST KISS

The next day we hike all over Swaziland and I make myself available at every turn for a kiss. I am now sure I want to date this handsome man. The kiss never comes but sometimes I think I see him thinking about it. He seems embroiled in reliving his past. He even tells me stories of past relationships here. At last he shows me his old stomping grounds at Waterford, the boarding school he attended in adolescence. He shares the trauma of being bullied in the forest, the laughter and antics of his twin brother Tony, and all the pranks they got up to at the boarding house, plus stories about his friends and family. He tells me about returning to university later for animal husbandry thinking he would help his father with cattle on his cattle farm perhaps.

As we walk and talk, I notice the land is spectacularly beautiful, green, and hilly with man-planted pine forests and cold-water mountain streams that wind and gurgle past big grey boulders. After walking around the old school grounds, which are still closed for the Christmas holidays, he asks if I want to hike up the last hill... "T" Hill.

I decline with uncommon indecision as we stand in the trees just off the trail. My bladder is full to bursting and I can't see where I will relieve myself in privacy. I can tell he really wants to hike up there. I would love to as well, but I am too embarrassed to tell him of my predicament. I look up as some tourists walk past us down the path, and at this moment he takes me off guard, taking my chin in his hand and planting his mouth awkwardly on my lips. I return his kiss in surprise and when it is over I feel shy and relieved the tension is gone, but I do not know what to say. He senses this and firmly takes my hand in his to lead me toward the car. "Are you sure you don't want to go up the hill?"

"Well," I admit, "I do need the loo."

"Oh!" he laughs, "Why didn't you tell me? I'm sure we can find one open." But everything is locked, so we rush to the hotel.

That evening we try perfecting our kisses once more and our bodies move into rhythm at last.

Soul Song: Rich, Full Melody

18-19years–Cultural Differences

*"Preservation of one's own culture does not require
contempt or disrespect for other's cultures."*

— CESAR CHAVEZ

MATOPOS

Having cemented our relationship and bonded physically, Tshekedi
and I return to life in Gaborone and we are now inseparable.
Rowan and our peers are amazed at how quickly TK and I have
formed a bond, not knowing of the months of dinner dates we have had when
they were all busy shunning me. After one tense movie night at a mutual
friend's home, it is clear most of them do not approve of our union. Our
time in the capital is brief as TK is keen to cart me away again, and he
hatches a plan to call in a favor to borrow a friend's showroom Landrover
and succeeds in getting me to come away with him on the long hot trip to
Matobo National Park in the southern part of Zimbabwe near Bulawayo.

The journey to Bulawayo takes us about ten hours so we start early in the
morning. The road is well kept but only one lane runs close to the railway
line. It is only tarred to Francistown and from there we travel on a long dirt
highway seeing only an occasional car coming the other way and giraffe
grazing and walking across the road ahead. I have traveled this road once

before with Rowan in my mother's yellow Toyota Cressida station wagon, but this is different being driven in a brand-new Landrover pick-up by the new man of my dreams. The skies are a gorgeous blue color with big billowing white clouds overhead, and we see no signs of civilization for miles. I find it incredibly romantic.

TK's plan is to end up in Shakawe in the northwestern tip of Botswana at the start of the Okavango Delta. The Okavango is a one-of-a-kind inland delta exceptional to this area and the world for its special ecological structure. Tshekedi's family is taking a leisurely boating holiday staying at a fishing camp retreat here that they rent during holidays dubbed Wenela. Shakawe is a little pastoral fishing village where a few tour operators have rented land to run fishing camps, lodges and houseboats along the deep blue water lilied channels of the hippo and crocodile infested tributaries of the Okavango river that snake their way through ten-foot tall reeds filled with exotic birdlife, crocs, and hippos.

Our first stop after Bulawayo in Zimbabwe is Matopos, a collection of solid granite hills in the park, and home to the tomb of the infamous British imperialist Cecil John Rhodes, founder of Rhodesia, which used to encompass present day Zambia and Zimbabwe prior to their complicated independences from colonial rule. Knowing my love of nature and spiritual inclination, by now TK is keen to show me the hills as they have spiritual significance to the indigenous peoples of the area.

We begin a long trek up to the top of the Malindidzimu hill in relative silence. Looking around, I feel the mystery of the hills and strange landscape vibrate all around me. Not another person is in sight and there is a slight breeze ruffling my hair. Only a few woodland birds chirrup softly in the trees and the sound of our heavy breathing breaks the stony silence. Huge granite boulders in the shapes of heads and faces line the ascent. I feel as if the rocks are waiting, watching, and somehow even judging our intrusion.

WENELA

We pull in noisily to the entrance of Wenela, hot, tanned and dusty after the drive across the border post from Zimbabwe. TK drums his fingers on the steering wheel, eager to introduce me to his mother, former First Lady Ruth Khama, whose deeds for the country, orphans, the disadvantaged, Red Cross and women precede her. She was a wife to the first President and Botswana's founding father, Sir Seretse Khama, prior to his untimely passing in 1980. Seretse was the royal paramount chief and proud heir of the Bamangwato tribe, the largest tribe in the country, and had met TK's mother Ruth in England while studying law there in the 40s. After learning of their love affair and union, there had been dismay by Seretse's uncle Tshekedi in Bechuanaland (the name of Botswana prior to its independence in 1966.)

Bechuanaland, then a British protectorate, worried that should Seretse marry out of the tribe, a British white woman at that, the neighboring apartheid regime might not take kindly to the marriage. Sure enough, when the white-run South African National Party found out about the impending marriage, they warned the British they would stop selling their much-coveted uranium supplies to them, who were, at the time, at war and busy assisting the Americans with a nuclear bomb building project. They would need all the uranium they could get. When they failed to stop the marriage between Ruth and Seretse, the Brits conspired to exile the couple for a period of six years after returning to Bechuanaland.

Ruth and Seretse, however, surmounted the odds against them and became famous for their resolute resistance to the notion of colour having any bearing on a person's potential as a human being. In the 60s they led Botswana out of colonialism and built a proud nation with democratic principles at its heart. Seretse was knighted during his tenure in office, and his wife became a Lady. Those close to her have alerted me that I am not to call her Ruth, as she prefers to be addressed as Lady Khama, Lady K, or "Mother." I try on Lady Khama, but it seems so formal, so I stick with Lady K, as I feel I only have one mother, Lana, who I now call "Mom."

Unbeknown to me, our escapade to Zimbabwe is somehow unknown to the others and they have been unable to reach us as we are out of radio signal. We are a day late in arriving at the Wenela camp and TK has not informed them we are on the way, so naturally they are perturbed and concerned when we arrive. It is, therefore, not all smiles when we turn up at Wenela unannounced at lunchtime. I am given a shrewd and icy stare from Lady Khama when I hop out, in dusty shorts and a casual top from the vehicle, and am given a perfunctory handshake. Tshekedi sends me off sheepishly to the kitchen where I am immediately shooed away by Margaret and Lady Khama alike who smirk and snicker to themselves. I feel unwanted and undesirable in their company. The rest of the family takes their matriarch's lead and I feel their unpleasant glances in my direction as I walk the grounds. No one explains the intense hostility toward me.

Instead of explaining their moodiness, TK hands me over to the hyenas, so to speak. Time at the table is not spent talking about the country as I had expected, but complaining about other leaders abroad, debating the international news, and a rigorous discussion and gossip ensues about people they all know and criticize fiercely. The holiday turns into an opportunity to trash liberal thinkers and Americans at every turn until eventually I refuse to dine with them, feeling hurt, as I catch their sly glances toward me every so often, trying to gauge if their provocative talk has touched me, and how deeply.

As no one asks my opinion, I think it best to keep my mouth shut and show a poker face. I have learned table manners and to be polite in company yet inwardly I am seething and full of my own opinions. By the second day, I cannot hide my emotion and refuse to come out of the room until TK's older brother Ian, the Commander of the Botswana Defence Force, is sent to talk me out of my self-imposed prison, where I have stuck my head in a book in the thatched room Tshekedi and I both share.

In the afternoons, the three brothers go off together and I am left with Margaret, with whom I find nothing in common and difficult to talk to. We sun in silence by the poolside or read quietly alone not talking to one another much in the shade of the big river trees. Lady Khama plays host to old colonial friends in the area for tea or retires to her room or the kitchen, always keeping her fair skin out of the sunshine. Apparently, it is not for her to make us welcome, but it is expected for us to come to her. At night, Ian organizes us into teams for games of charades, or relay races and anything else he dreams up for his own entertainment. He rarely plays but loves watching us make fools of ourselves, commenting snidely from the sidelines.

The grounds of Wenela are stunningly beautiful and I amuse myself by practicing gymnastics on the shady green lawns that roll down to the swollen river channel below. Tall reeds grow high on the other side, barring any view of the swamps beyond. We travel the winding waterways downstream to the Okavango panhandle on a double decker boat to seethe red sandy cliffs that rise majestically out of the reflective steel blue water below. The cliffs are peppered with the dark burrows of the flamboyantly feathered rose-colored carmine bee-eaters with turquoise heads that turn quickly from left to right. Sitting on the boat watching nature patiently take away the sting of rejection that I feel ever present in my life, I find my true north, my ever-abundant home, and lean back into the arms of my newfound lover. Tshekedi kisses the top of my head warmly and I feel my heart quiet.

At last, after what seems like an age, we drive onto the dusty highway and return home. After the unhappy trip to Wenela, TK and I are shaken by his family's rejection of me, but still committed to our love. He spends much of his time with me at Lana's home and even most nights. Lana has long given up interfering with my personal life.

SEPARATE AND UNITED

Whenever I am at Tshekedi's place, Anthony and Margaret give the cold shoulder and I discover that Margaret is very particular about the use of her pots and pans. She sees the kitchen as her domain as she is the only cook between the three housemates. One morning, I make the mistake of scratching one of her pots, and though I apologize profusely, and TK and I run to buy a new one, it is not good enough. She is furious and tells TK to inform me that I must stay out. Thereafter, few words are spoken between us and I tend to hide in TK's bedroom if we are visiting. I feel like an imposter in the house and am even fearful of encountering them in the passage to the bathroom.

One evening, while dropping me home, TK broaches the subject that his twin and the girlfriend are unhappy because I failed to bid them hello once when I arrived at the house and it is customary in Botswana to greet even those you are familiar with. I am not used to this. When sharing homes in America, housemates and partners were always much less formal. I think they are just trying to find yet something else to criticize me for. I ask him if they just use custom when it suits them for they might have just told me outright and be done with it. Now it seems like an excuse for their bad behavior.

The next time the conversation comes up, I am told that his older brother has spoken about possibly investigating me to see if I am linked to a spy organization. I am outraged and indignant.

"Whaaaat?"

"Well, he has to be careful. He's the Commander of the Botswana Defence Force and answerable to the President."

"I feel sick, TK. Are you telling me you have nothing to do with this? Why would he care about me? You know me well. I've told you my entire life story. Is this how you people welcome girls into your family?"

"It isn't everyone. It's just that your mother works for the US Government. Please don't tell anyone. I wasn't supposed to tell you."

"How would you respond if I said my government or a member of my family were investigating you? In fact, they'd have more reason to investigate you than me. Why not investigate every mixed relationship between a foreigner and a citizen of your country then? I'm tired of hearing your excuses for your family."

I pull my skirts up and fumble to get out of his car, slamming the door behind me and calling for the guard to open my mother's gate.

Two months pass, and despite our troubles, TK is still committed to being with me. To prove it, he presents me with a car of my own. It is a very good second-hand gold Opel Rekord with a stick shift. The interior is pristine and the engine sound. I show my delight by screaming and dancing around the car and hugging and kissing him all over. He is very pleased with himself. My mother looks on in amazement as it is presented.

Soon after this extravagant gift, I lie comfortably in his arms watching the early morning light play with the dust particles blowing lightly through the open window, and he leans over to ask me to marry him. His eyes search mine hopefully and I have visions of what we could be to one another. I see myself standing on a podium in long white gowns administering to a huge crowd of people. My heart beats hard against my chest...a poignant vision of a future me.

I kiss him impulsively and tell him yes, yes, of course, I will marry him, but later get cold feet and say that what I meant was in principle yes, but his life is not in order. He doesn't have a home for us to be in and neither of us is financially stable at the moment. I am only 19. We must see what it is like to live together, to be together. He agrees that emotion has overpowered him and without speaking about it we both start on a mutual mission of empowerment. I want to empower him by having him move out into an apartment with me, and he wants to help me to start my own spa business.

I decide I will travel to America to finish massage school. I want to have a different skill that no one else in the market has and then I can get a work permit to practice. I start planning the trip and write to my friend Misha whose home I rented in Berkeley before Santa Cruz. She says she is more than happy to host me and my old room is ready and waiting for my return.

I bid farewell to TK and go off to study Shiatsu, Twe-Na, and Acupressure techniques in Oakland California.

IN MY DEFENSE

I arrive back to California and pick up with friends I have left behind. My best friends from high school feel jilted by my absence. My ex-lover and best friend Ethan tells me that he feels abandoned by my lack of communication. He has been battling cancer and he feels I should have come to be at his side. Another love crush from high school days weighs heavily on my heartstrings asking me to come home. Ethan, Riva and Dan can't understand my lifestyle or the way I am treated by Tshekedi's family. They are concerned I am falling victim to simple survival and something that is not good for me.

TK is in the business of selling defense equipment amongst other commodities to the Botswana Government. They question how I can be the pacifist they know and still be with someone who is so conflicted with my core principles and in this business? Pangs of guilt plague me to my core. How can selling any kind of arms be good? I argue that he is ethical about what he buys and sells, from whom he buys and to whom he sells, and that there is a rigorous democratic system in place to avoid corruption, so although his brother is the army general, he has to jump through even more hurdles than others to prove his sales are legitimately good for the taxpayer and the country. I tell them of some of the other dealers I have met who have no scruples and I beg them to see it is better him than them. He also sells lifesaving equipment and other goods to other government departments and the police that we need for safety and protection.

My friends remain dubious. Deep down, so am I. It is far from the liberal left-wing democratic upbringing I have had in Berkeley that says by not selling and buying arms we are saving the planet, and says we are somehow more intelligent that those who do. But is this the truth? Are we any better, or are we hiding behind that rhetoric? When it comes to national pride and protection wouldn't we expect to be protected by our armies? In reality would we allow ourselves to be overruled by a nation who didn't care about our right to live or be free? What about the corrupt arms dealers I have come to know about while traveling with Tshekedi? Is it not better to promote ethical dealers in the world? My friends say there is no such thing. Then what is the man I know and love involved in? My head spins with these questions until I question no more.

The fact I love this man who I share my life with becomes paramount. All thoughts of right and wrong flee from me when I remember this. I love the way he reasons; his mind is that of a business magnate, his spontaneity is refreshing, his spirit is all-encompassing, his ideas engaging, his love of the finer things in life is comforting, and we share a love of travel. I wish they could meet him.

SCENE 38

Soul Song: Valiant, Dramatic, and Timed

20 years–Building Blocks

"There's a point, around the age of twenty, when you have to decide whether to be like everyone else the rest of your life, or make a virtue of your peculiarities."

— URSULA K. LE GUIN

RITE OF PASSAGE

A new gym complex has been built in the village and we are offered employment there on a volunteer basis to help get it off the ground and sell lifetime memberships. There is a space there for a small beauty salon and massage center and TK encourages me to set up my own business there. Our mutual friend is a manager there and will pull strings to get me the space. I am not so sure. I don't think I have the funds to set up. He offers to front the money and buy the necessary equipment. All I need to do is look for a beautician and recruit a receptionist, and I need more training.

I have signed up for the Anatriptic Arts Conference and Fair for body workers, massage therapists, and people in the spa industry held in San Francisco, California where I wish to go and study Russian Sports Massage, buy equipment on discount, and work on my logo for the business. Misha says I can come stay as her guest for three weeks and Yeshua, my mentor psychiatrist who gave me pro bono sessions during my last year of high school is waiting for me to meet a friend of his who is also an adoptee. Yeshua introduces me to Janine who is of Dutch-Kenyan lineage and in her late thirties. She is an exquisitely beautiful divorcee with a son in a boarding school in Southern California and she is eager to share her story and wants me to help her find her African father, who turns out to be a known political figure in the Kenyan Cabinet.

Janine has managed to find her biological mother through a private investigator and this piques my interest. I am also starting the search for my birth mother and have been through the libraries and the counties coming up with dead-ends every time. She shares that a private investigator helped her find her original birth certificate and through that avenue she was able to track her mother down. I wonder if I can do the same and take the number of the private investigator shoving it into my wallet where it may stay until I come of age, safe and sound. Janine encourages me not to wait, but if I can, to see the lady soon as investigations of this nature take awhile, and as I will soon be 21, I can at get a head-start.

I call immediately and go to see the woman. She shares that she will begin the search, but normally the only way in is to literally bribe officials to open the sealed files as state records are held out of bounds for adoptees unless the biological parent has requested to be contacted. Mine has not. I promise Janine to start helping her to connect with her father, which proves much more difficult than imagined, as ministers in Kenya are not as easily accessible as ministers in Botswana and this is a highly sensitive subject.

Upon my return home, Tshekedi and I move into a tiny two-bedroom apartment together and set about decorating and making our home. We are both at the peak of our fitness and share a love of aerobics, weight training, and are the first to set up a spa in the new Health and Recreation Center building that has taken the small town of Gaborone by storm. It is a gigantic entertainment facility complete with a water park, water slide, bowling alley, squash and tennis courts, huge indoor-outdoor restaurant, hairdressing salon, boutique shops, and kid's crèche. I have a captive market for my massage business here and do all I can to rake in the business. Eventually, at capacity and taking in sometimes ten clients a day, I end up needing a break and getting physiotherapy for the tendons in my hands. All this new income enables me to help TK pay rent on the small apartment.

I am now the proud, if untried, business owner and massage therapist for The Integral Bodycare Centre where I hire staff and run my own beauty and day spa salon offering a full range of services to the public. I work long hours and train in the evenings. I watch the landlords and managers make big mistakes in service delivery inside the gym facility and I am outspoken, which embarrasses TK. In addition, his mother despises our relationship and tries to keep me out of public events as his date.

I am so stressed by my relationship with TK and his family that I begin to lose a lot of weight. When I step on the scale I weigh a mere 58kgs and I am under-weight for my body size by at least eight kilos. Not only do I contend with sour vibes from his mother, but his twin brother and bride as well. Women are vying for Tshekedi's attention like a pack of jackals circling and waiting for any opening. The trouble is, his ego is flattered by all the attention, and he gives them all the openings they need. We fight like cats and dogs in our little flat and sometimes I end up getting hurt physically.

I turn 21, coming of age at last, and TK and Lana host a huge African dance party where I insist the guests put on ethnic clothing and dance the night away. I am dazzled at the combined efforts of my mother and my boyfriend and gaze around the hired restaurant hall at the supportive crowd I have somehow managed to acquire as friends, all from various backgrounds, faiths, and ethnicities. Looking around I feel truly loved.

TK's biggest private gift is his promise to help me find my biological family that has been lost to me for the past twenty-one years. He assures me he will be the one to help me finance this journey. I have finally reached the age where I can begin legally to open the dusty records.

Soul Song: A Lilting Hymn
21 years: Full Circle

"There are a thousand ways to kneel and kiss the ground;
there are a thousand ways to go home again."

— RUMI

A SCURVY REUNION

It all begins with a call from the private investigator telling me she has spoken with my maternal grandfather named Pedro. My birthmother Marla has just been to see her father to share the secret her mother took to the grave, and he has kicked her out of his home upon this knowledge, telling her he never wishes to see her again. It is enough that she has brought disrepute to him by giving birth to another girl after me with a black man whom she claims has raped her. Now Pedro is shocked to the core to learn that there is now a young woman (me—a part of his extended family)out there who is lost to him.

"I would have raised her myself!" he yells angrily slamming the door in Marla's face, with the intent to shut her out of his life for good, and he turns back inside to sob ferociously in the arms of his new wife, Dot. The pain of learning this secret is excruciating.

Pedro never looked for his twin brother once he had discovered in his early 70s that they had been separated. His parents had wanted to give him a chance at a better life in America, unable to take two children with them, while his twin brother was left to another fate, growing up with relatives in abject poverty in Mexico City. He would never want to face that man, and now this? His daughters and their mother have been a curse and brought him nothing but despair and embarrassment.

After his first wife's death, he learned that Marla and her sister Donna are smalltime drug dealers, eking out an unhappy existence since falling into the practice late in high school while he was out making a living for them all in South America. Today they not only deal but are also adult junkies waiting for their luck to run out while hustling to keep the habit going. Only on rare occasions have they phoned him to bail them or their kids out financially, and he always caves in due to a soft spot for his defenseless grandkids. Marla and Donna blame him for never being there emotionally and forcing their mother into staying as his wife until her dying day. During his absence in the war, his first wife had fallen in love with another man and upon his return he could not let her go to him, keeping her under the Catholic tradition of legal marriage vows and refusing to divorce her. He had run the suitor off and kept his wife his own until her dying day.

In more recent years, Pedro has moved houses twice and changed his number numerous times, but his girls always find him one way or another. He is well-off due to his years of hard work in the contract flooring industry and he is now retired with a new woman to grace his life. He prays to enjoy his last years without all the drama and hurt from his brood. His youngest child Bobby, the only son given to him by his first wife, lost his life in a terrible car accident that wasn't his fault, on his way to receiving his college degree many years before and it nearly broke Pedro. This shook his faith and now he is not so sure there is a God though he pretends there is just to keep up appearances.

This latest news from Marla has threatened his heart, and his wife Dot tells him to sit down in his lazy boy chair in front of the TV as he swears out loud for a long ten minutes, unable to hear how loud he is due to his hearing aid being turned on low. Dot rushes to fix him a meal and bring him a cup of her good old-fashioned cocoa mix. He is breathing hard when she returns to the lounge and sees he is near collapse.

"Calm down dear, here you go. Let's talk about it."

It is winter in California and they sit down together undermatching blankets to talk about what they have just learned. Dot, no stranger to a broken family life herself advises him to cool down and let it go.

"At least we can hope the baby got a better life, honey." She comforts him.

A day later, the phone rings as Pedro is getting ready to go and play his weekly game of golf with his buddies up the road, so Dot picks up the phone. After listening to the caller for the first two minutes she turns whiter than her own hair. "Pedro, honey," she calls to him as he gets to the front door. "Please wait a moment, will ya? I think you want to get on the other end of this phone and hear what this lady has to say…"

That night I receive a call at 3am while staying at Lana's house where I am currently staying apart from Tshekedi for a night or two. I rush down the dark hall, in my bathrobe, as I am closer to the phone than Lana, who will be in a deep slumber at this time of the morning.

"Hello?"

"Yes, I'm calling for uh, Thea."

"Mhm, this is she. Who's this?"

"Thea, it's your grandfather Abe speaking. I'm Marla's daddy."

"Whaaat? I'm sorry, oh my God, I mean, oh my goodness! Hi, Grandpa!"

We talk for an hour or more, filling each other in on our lives and crying tears of joy. Pedro shares the state my mother Marla is in as a drug addict and dealer and tells me the news that my older brother is in prison. He advises me not to make contact with them, but how can I not? I have been waiting my whole life to hear Marla's voice. I beg him to give me her number and I call her the following day.

Marla's voice breaks into deep wracking sobs as soon as she knows she is talking to her long-lost child. She relates the happenings of my birth and I feel the gunshot and the beating as if it were yesterday. I feel sick to my stomach, recalling the memory of the hollow sensations in my bones. My body twitches uncontrollably as I listen to the details and recapitulate them within my brain. "I'm here now, Momma," I tell her. "All will be well. I'm okay. I haven't had an easy life, but I'm learning to have a better one now."

Lana hovers nervously down the hall sipping herbal tea and trying to remain neutral. I have no idea what is going on in her head. This is my time and I need her to be supportive, but she keeps pacing and looking at me with intense concern.

"You don't know these people, Sweetie. Don't you think you should visit them with a friend?"

"Maybe you're right," I reply non-committedly.

But in my heart of hearts I know this is something I must do alone. Within weeks I am on a plane.

My friend Misha puts me up in her home as always. Having lived in foster care herself for many years, she understands the depth of my urgency and puts up no resistance when it comes to my comings and goings. I hire an Avis car and head to my grandfather first. I find my way using new GPS technology installed on the dash and note it is only about forty minutes away from my home-base, in downtown Berkeley.

As soon as I knock, Pedro opens the door wide and engulfs me in his arms. To my surprise, he is giant of a man with wavy white hair and he looks a lot like Lana's late father whom I had met in spirit 10 years back.Pedro pulls back to look at me and then he and his wife Dot usher me in and begin to tell me tales of my natural family's history. He has made me a big scrapbook of photos and we open his memory trunk. I see he has a medal there from World War II. He shows me the family photographs and I see myself in the faces of my mother, her brother and cousins especially, but not so much my mother's sister Donna. My half-sister and half-brother don't look too much like me, but he shows me a picture of their father, instructing me to take the photos with me that are most important to me.

I ask him if he has a picture of my father and he pauses, clearly thinking about it, but then denies it.

"That guy disappeared years ago, and good riddance in my opinion. He did try to help your mother with your brother and sister, but she can really mess things up, your mother Marla, yes she can."

As he is talking, I see photos of one or two men who could be my natural father Jose, and stow these pictures away, even though he says they are just friends of Marla's. I slip them into my jacket pocket just in case.

As the day wears on, my grandfather invites me to spend the night. I am feeling less and less comfortable in his presence and I cannot pinpoint why. I suppose I am emotionally drained and feel suffocated in the home. I feel as if Pedro wants to possess me and keep me from my mother. I don't appreciate his racist comments about my younger sister Desiree and his excuses why he denies her as a family member. Travel weary and jet-lagged I struggle to keep my eyes open. I decide that I need to return to Michele's house and a sense of normality.

Immediately, after supper Pedro is called to a Neighborhood Watch meeting and says he will be back soon. As soon as he leaves, his wife Dot quickly runs to get my coat. She tells me if I want to leave, I must leave now when he isn't here or he simply will not let me go. This greatly unnerves me! I do as she urges and hurry outside to my rental car. I thank her and say I will be in touch later. She wishes me well on my way as I speed off into the night.

THE MEETING

The next day, I make the long drive up North to Sacramento. Marla insists on meeting me at a petrol station in the middle of nowhere and says she will show me the way from there. I try to keep to the speed limit, but find myself continuously edging way above. All these years of guessing, wondering, and wishing are about to come to an end. *What will she think of me? Will we look alike? How will it be to meet my older and younger sisters? Am I dressed up too much? Will she look like the pictures my grandfather showed me, green-eyed, voluptuous, and long brown hair?*

I arrive at the petrol station on time and park. I'm glad I brought some perfume in my bag because my nerves have made me perspire. I need to relieve my bladder; however, I'm scared I will miss her if she comes. I look around and no one fitting Marla's description or car is here. I move into the gas station convenience store and fix my make-up, put on deodorant, and spray on the perfume. When I look into the mirror, I see a glow all around me and don't look as bad as I imagined I'd looked in the car.

I stand in the shop and take time cooling off to look at magazines. A young African American salesman approaches softly and strikes up a conversation with me, and after a few introductions he hands me his card. I can't say I'm interested in the slightest, yet I humor him since he seems friendly enough and I need to talk to someone. I shyly find myself telling him what I am here for. He is amazed and wishes me well but he ominously warns me this place is a pick-up place for drug dealers.

A beaten-up car suddenly pulls up and parks. A sinking feeling follows as I watch two short squat women get out of the car and look around. I can see their butt cracks peeking out above old jeans that are falling down below their waists. One of them has short grey hair and is missing teeth and she looks to be in her late sixties. The other has glasses on and wavy salt and pepper hair, puffy hands, and she sees me and grabs the short older lady by the shoulder. I walk toward her. Something pulls me magnetically forward. Our eyes meet and lock through the glasses she wears. Once I am near, she reaches out to grab me and enfolds me in her arms. My heart is beating hard. I smell the stench of chemicals; cigarettes, alcohol and stale sweat pouring out of her pores. I nearly gag and find myself wanting to run the other way.

"My baby, oh my baby girl." Marla weeps effusively into my shoulder. Her knees buckle as she pulls away to see me better. Then she turns shakily to her friend.

"Brandi, I can't take it. Really, you gotta get us home."

"Hi Brandi, I'm Thea." I turn to the grey-haired lady and reach out my hand. She doesn't take it. Instead, she hoists her falling jeans ineffectively up onto non-existent hips and scowls at me. She is about 5 feet 4-inches in height and as 'butch' as they come. Rather unfriendly, she looks capable of packing a mean punch. She grabs my biological mother's hand in hers and I wonder, is this Marla's lover?

"Are you okay honey, we can leave this joint and go…?" Brandi says.

"No that's alright, it's her," Marla replies faintly.

Brandi squints into the afternoon sun and protectively scans the area with her piercing blue eyes. Abruptly she notices something and asks me pointedly, "Who's that black dude over there staring at ya, girl? Do you know him?"

"I just met him. He's a salesman; you don't need to bother with him."

"Humph. Let's get in the car, ladies. I don't like standing around here where there may be cops around. Thea, you get in and come with us."

Marla is already backing inside as tears are rolling unbidden out from under her glasses. She acts fragile. As she reaches up shakily to take her glasses off, her black top falls back to reveal multiple needle bruises up and down her forearms and on the tops of her puffy hands. Her green eyes look faded and dull and the pallor of her olive skin is a sickly bone color under a wavy mop of salt and pepper hair. I work out that she is only 45 but she looks closer to 60. I notice a sheen of perspiration beading up on the faint downy black hairs that frame her upper lip.

"Um. No thanks," I tell them both firmly. "I need to take my car. I can't leave it here. If anything happens to it, I'd be in trouble since it's a rental car."

Brandi is settling herself and Marla in the sedan. The scowl hasn't left her face.

"Alright, Miss Fancy pants. Suit yourself," she says sarcastically, "but you'd better keep up. How's your driving skills? Follow us closely. It's kind of complicated to get to my place, and that's where we're a-goin' from here."

I hurry to my car, nodding at the salesman who tips his cap toward me a bit too sadly as I get behind the wheel. I feel deflated, disappointed, and a little wary to follow these two old hags. That is your mother. Couldn't she have tried to look good for your arrival? A voice from nowhere starts chattering internally. I suppress the voice and drive out.

I wish to the high heavens that it wasn't her, that there was some mistake, but sadly, I recognize her scent from when I was a baby. It simultaneously nauseates and repels me. She is a mess. She is my mess. More than anything, I am shocked at how much I want to run away. My grandfather was right. But I won't give up that easily. I need to meet my siblings and hear their stories.

We arrive at Brandi's house in the projects area of town. I have taken careful stock of where I am and how to return to the highway, because I have no intention of staying here tonight.

The house is filthy and full of old plates, smelly socks, unpaid bills, and coffee mugs with cigarette butts in them. I am glad I am wearing blue jeans. Brandi begins interrogating me and doesn't leave me alone with Marla once. The hours pass slowly until finally my two sisters come in. My younger half-sister of mixed race, Desiree, is dressed way better than anyone else thus far. Apparently, she doesn't live here, but she is being fostered by Brandi's aged parents up in the suburbs.

"She's the spoiled one," my older sister Kirstin smirks wryly.

Running up and down, frantically looking for a pack of smokes, my older sister seems high on something. I estimate she at least seven months pregnant. Kirstin is long-limbed and rangy, with thin mousy brown hair sticking to broad manly shoulder, and a pointy broken nose, blue eyes, pale skin, and a mouth full of overlapping teeth. She probably takes after her father, I think to myself. I can find no similarity between us save for perhaps a hint of the Gomez jawline of my mother's side of the family. According to

Brandi and Marla, all of Kirstin's six children before have been taken away by the State since she ran off and neglected them in various scenarios. They swear this one will be different because suddenly they are feeling broody and plan on helping raise the little one if it gets to that.

"Come," Kirstin gestures to me when there is a lull in our conversation. "Wanna get a snack or something? I need to go buy some smokes. You don't want to hang around these old bags too long, do ya?" I follow her out the door, eager for fresh air more than anything else. My head is spinning. The place I find myself in is dark, ugly and I feel it sapping my mood. My head is reeling with information about my mother's dark past and mine by default. I don't want to offend anyone here and get kicked out before I have learned more.

Kirstin drives an old Ford low rider and we sit and chat in the small town's rush hour traffic on the way to the store. She tells me our brother is incarcerated in the state penitentiary at Folsom prison and lost one eye when he fell down some stairs when they were kids and impaled his face on a broken bottle our ma had left lying at the bottom. He apparently just got a new glass eye so he no longer wears a patch.

"Yeah. You're lucky. We didn't have it so good." Her face twitches and she scrubs it with one hand.

"Hey, you know what? I don't know who the father of this babe inside me is," she confesses ruefully. "I got two guys fighting over it. We'll have to get a paternity test I guess, haahaha."

Wow. She must have been hurt so badly. I think to myself. I am quiet, contemplating.

She is devoid of emotion and sports a carefree laisse-faire attitude toward everything.

"Do you remember my father?" I ask her, hopeful for some information.

"Yeah. He was a pretty good guy to us. He looked after your older brother Lonnie and me for a while. But his business with Mom is their own; I'd rather not get into it. We haven't seen him in years. Last I heard, he was in San Jose."

Wow. San Jose is where Searle's family live.

I am amused at the proximity of where we all live in relation to each other. This reminds me of the popular urban myth popularized recently around the world: "six degrees of separation" that presupposes we are all linked to all life by a mere six degrees.

My little sister Desiree, who at fourteen is already taller than me, offers to keep me out of the dreary drug house when Kirstin and I return with junk food and snacks. Desiree is still an adolescent and I offer to take her to Africa with me to get her away from this drug dealing lifestyle if she so chooses. She says she will think hard about it. She knows if she stays here her life could go the way of our half-siblings, Lonnie and Kirstin. Back at the house, my mother and I have a moment alone in the kitchen at last. Marla pours out her heart to me. Apparently, I have my father's eyes. *Damn. I always wanted green eyes like hers.* I tell her that in the adoption report the officials have swapped her looks for Jose's, either erroneously out of incompetence or deliberately to shake me off the trail, if ever I started a search that way. The genes we seem to share show up plainly from the nose down to the jawline. We all have the same cheeks and jawline.

Before long, it gets dark, and I am determined to return to the familiar surrounds of my friend's house in Berkeley. I promise to return to visit. But my mother's keeper, Brandi, isn't having it. She wants me to stay. They have had a few police stop by to check on their activity while I am there. They relay how they had a break-in two nights ago and were held against the wall by the thieves, but prevailed and fought their way out of the mess. I am feeling the bedbugs crawling on me already. I am determined to take my leave before dark. I feel their smothering possessiveness the same as how I felt while meeting my grandfather.

My inner voice calls to me in a silent warning.

Thea, they have no hold on your life. This was given away when you were placed in your adopted family's home. There is danger here.

I stand up from the couch and announce that I need to go to the toilet to clear my head. The bathroom is pretty, pristine, paper white, and there are big fluffy matching towels folded neatly on the open shelves. Something leads me to focus on these towels and I follow a weird impulse to peer between them. Under the third towel I find a metal meat cleaver with dried blood and what looks like pieces of blonde hair attached. *Now I am freaked out for sure!* It is time to go. As I walk through the dingy lounge, I shout over my shoulder that I need to move my car off the street due to the parking laws. Once I get to the car, I put the key in the ignition and I call them out of the house.

"I really have to go. It was good to see you all. I just remembered I promised to feed the dog at my friend's house in Berkeley that I'm looking after and I have to get back there. I'll come visit again after I've been to see Lonnie at the prison. It was a great day. BYE!" I wave and blow kisses.

Brandi runs out of the house and starts shaking her head meanly.

"Oh no you don't...Hey, you can't just come here and then leave your mother like that!"

A vein is bulging in her neck.

Marla steps out onto the pavement. "It's okay, honey, but how will you find your way out?"

"Oh, it'll be okay, I'll find the way, I always do," I tell her self-assuredly.

Soul Song: Ordained, Orchestral, and Composed Older: Mother Africa

"Simple in actions and thoughts, you return to the source of being. Patient with both friends and enemies, you accord with the way things are. Compassionate toward yourself, you reconcile all beings in the world."

— LAO TZU, TAO TE CHING

THE JOURNEY ON

My brother Lonnie and I write to one another, and long to see each other past the grey prison walls in which we both live: mine inside my head, trapped in the past, his in reality from the penitentiary where he is doing time. He claims to have taken the rap for his wife who shot and killed a perp at a party where things definitely spun out of control. His wife is in prison while their baby lives with her parents. She has divorced my brother Lonnie and married another man whom she met while incarcerated. This is the life he lives. He managed to get his own sentence reduced, came clean, and now lives in anxious anticipation behind the bars at Folson, a prison notorious for holding murderers, rapist and the evil of the world. Finally, he is released from jail on good behaviour and his sentence is reduced further.

On a return visit to our mother while pregnant with my daughter, she tricks me into coming with her on a dangerous drug deal to a creepy work-shop by the railway tracks where I am lucky to escape with my life. This act of leading me into her dungeon tells me how removed she is from care. That is the last time I choose to see her.

My younger sister Desiree attacks and robs me in a kind of manic hysteria when I finally manage to get her away with me alone. Later, she is imprisoned and pregnant by her 16th birthday, which she spends between the cold stark walls of a prison cell. The last I hear from our family, she gives birth there and I don't know how that child has been raised or with whom. Lonnie and I have a battle of words that I take personally and in the blink of an eye our relationship ends. He has done the unthinkable and allowed another inmate to have the phone details of our grandfather Pedro. I am trying to protect Pedro who is getting older and cannot afford to move house again. He is very upset that Lonnie has given away his details to a criminal. It backfires on me and my brother disowns me, furious that I would try to insert myself into his business.

As I am come to terms with my fate and the reality of my birth family, so too am I fighting much subtler battles with the Khamas. Tshekedi and I have moved into an apartment together and share the rent. He has helped me to start my own massage and beauty business and I am working long hours there at a local health and recreation center. But all is not gold and roses. Our life together is strained. I have never been fully accepted by his immediate family, I am different: my ideas, my outlook on life, and my culture. The tribe are more accepting and so too are members of the extended family on Seretse's side whom I seem to meet on my own.

I discover the hard way that in Botswana culture, even if a woman is living with a man, there is an unwritten rule that he is free game for other ladies, but the woman is not. Women continuously throw themselves at my boyfriend without another thought to how it will affect me. His family seem to support anyone who is remotely different to me. This causes us to have major arguments that I never win. I fear for my mental, emotional and physical wellbeing. My mother has moved to her next post in Namibia and my support system is virtually nonexistent.

I make a hard decision in October 1992. I say goodbye to my one true love and I pack my bags, bound for America. TK is stunned to come home one day and find the movers already there. I gift him the spa business, or curse him with getting rid of it. He begs me to let him take me on holiday, first to Cape Town and then Namibia. As I turn 22, I leave the continent with a new outlook: we will not break it off completely, we will see if we can withstand staying apart. If in eight months we are no closer to an agreement for him to move closer, or to marriage, then we will break it off.

One soul in the Heavens has another plan for us…

On July 19 1993, I give birth to a strapping baby boy: Kaedi Sekgoma Khama in Windhoek, Namibia. Two months later, I return to start a journey fraught with twists and turns in Botswana as a kept mother. This life does not suit my personality and I revolt, causing drama and struggle in our relations. Motherhood comes naturally for me above all else, though happiness still eludes me. I feel disempowered, unappreciated, unseen, unheard and generally way out of my comfort zone. I distract myself with my art, journalling, female friendships and playdates for my son. Nevertheless, twenty-three months pass and on a Friday on June 16th, 1995, I give birth to a bright baby girl: Tahlia Naledi Khama. She is the only girl grandchild born to Lady K. and our relationship improves thereafter. My circle of friends widens and slowly I am absorbed into the community.

Several years pass before my life as a Khama begins and I am adopted by the Bamangwato tribe and elders. Incidentally, around the same time, I disown my birth family and Bard disowns me. Lana and I begin an estranged relationship and so I lose all personal connection to my own family members and a friend must walk me to the altar. Just over four thousand people attend the wedding ceremony at the Kgotla, the tribal meeting grounds in Serowe where I am made to feel more welcomed than anywhere else I have ever been on this earth. I am initiated by the women and dance to the beat of an ancient code, feeling the rocky earth rise up to meet the pulse of life throbbing in my bones. The tribal elders and the tribe dance in one of the largest gatherings Bangwato have witnessed since Sir Seretse Khama's passing.

Over the years, I discover rejection is a funny thing. The idea of separation is a flaw of the human condition and a construct of our conditioned mind. How we feel it is dependent on how we perceive it. I walk through the fire of rejection and separation over and over with my heart on my sleeve. My marriage to TK will be my second journey into the forge. It will polish and cut me until the final product is worn. Six years into my marriage, I am reunited with Lana and we bury the past definitively. Today we are close once more and the wounds are only pale scars left as faint reminders. My life has taught me to let go of expectation, to love unconditionally, and to shine brighter than the sun. My destiny is to bring us home to our truest selves. I accept the calling. I know how it is I must be. Nature is working with me. I am a breath of heaven with the strength of stone. I now know how the game is played and I stand beyond the edge of the board, looking down as an archetypal mother, changing the course of my children's DNA forever – come to think of it – their children after them.

In the end, when I had nowhere to go but within, I achieved closure with my past and began to build my present and future trajectory. It has been a steep mountain to summit and a story for another time. In the process of having my ego squelched I became a mentor, a mother, a queen and humanitarian with the quest to see harmonious relations thrive between peoples, plants and animals. I am here, rooted to the raw red earth, as my journey, like the weaver birds that keep building new nests in the palms outside my home, begins again and again. Mother Africa nods sagely, in a gentle sign of appreciation. Her lips curve upward and without words she dances with me and others beneath tall acacia trees, encouraging us all to soar higher on wings of jubilation.

My heart skips a beat as I consider where I have come from to where I am now, experiencing the many risings and fallings of my life and what is yet to come. I continue to forgive those who would blight my light.

The Light smiles from within now. It embraces me wholly. I am her and she is me, together we will build worlds within worlds until Theia emerges in full illumined glory again and again.

About the Author

Thea Khama is a California-born mixed heritage goddess living in Botswana with her husband, several dogs and cats and sometimes, her two grown children: Kaedi Sekgoma and Tahlia Naledi Khama. She loves to cycle, gym, swim, dance, cook, read, write and spend time alone and with friends in nature. She works as a Professional Consciousness Coach and runs psycho-social support groups in her spare time. Privately, she is a regular meditator and prayer warrior and her network of friends extends around the globe.

CPSIA information can be obtained
at www.ICGtesting.com
Printed in the USA
LVHW051127171120
671905LV00005B/78